Wake Up and Smell the Coffee -

Southwest Edition

Laura Zahn

Down to Earth Publications
St. Paul, Minnesota

Other books by Laura Zahn:

"WAKE UP & SMELL THE COFFEE - Pacific Northwest Edition"
"WAKE UP & SMELL THE COFFEE - Upper Midwest Edition"
"Room at the Inn/Minnesota - Guide to Minnesota's Historic B&Bs, Hotels and Country Inns"
"Room at the Inn/Wisconsin - Guide to Wisconsin's Historic B&Bs and Country Inns"
"Room at the Inn/Galena Area - Guide to Historic B&Bs and Inns Close to Galena and Dubuque"
"Ride Guide to the Historic Alaska Railroad," with Anita Williams

To Jim

who makes Down to Earth Publications work
by being the volunteer driver, luggage handler, map reader,
bookkeeper, scanner, map maker,
computer teacher, computer-table adjuster,
shelf maker, closet mover, drawer fixer, heavy box lifter,
advisor, supporter, partner,
food tester, dish washer,
babysitter and
upper-when-downer.
Not necessarily in that order.

Published by **Down to Earth Publications**
1032 W. Montana
St. Paul, Minnesota 55117

Distributed to the book trade by **Voyageur Press**
123 North Second Street
Stillwater, Minnesota 55082
1-800-888-9653 or **612-430-2210**

ISBN 0-939301-92-X

Library of Congress Cataloging in Publication Data

Zahn, Laura C., 1957-
Wake Up and Smell the Coffee - Southwest Edition.

Includes index.

1. Breakfasts 2. Cookery 3. Bed and Breakfast Accommodations - Southwest - Directories

TX 733.Z3

Dewey System - Ideas and Recipes for Breakfast and Brunch - 641.52

Cover Illustration by Lynn Fellman, Golden Valley, Minnesota

Maps by Jim Miller, St. Paul, Minnesota

Many thanks to
Kristina Ford, Ann Burckhardt, Kathy O'Neill, Mary Zahn,
the Voyageur Press staff and sales reps,
Lynn Fellman, Leslie Dimond,
Peggy Taylor, Nancy & Roger Danley, Loretta Schmidt, Betsy & George Delforge,
Paul and Mary Ellen Kelley, Marjorie Martin, Petie Bartram, Lea Pace and Vince Mollan,
Louise Stewart, Karen and Frank Battese, Barry Gardner, Sharry Buckner
and my handsome husband, Jim Miller.

Special thanks to the innkeepers
for sharing their best recipes and artwork,
for their cooking hints and ideas,
for their contacts and willingness to "spread the word"
and for their enthusiasm and encouragement.

I also thank them for the privilege
of being the "middleperson" in communicating their favorite recipes
to many hungry cooks and readers.

Introduction

✒ Boy, there really is something about "Southern hospitality."

Perhaps it's in the drawl, the way "How are you?" sounds when spoken slowly and with that lilt that makes it sound like the inquirer honestly cares about the answer, and is going to stand still and listen to it. Or perhaps it's a slower pace, or the *illusion* of a slower pace, that makes a visitor slow down and relax, drinking it all in.

Of course, innkeepers are professionals when it comes to hospitality. If they can't make a stranger feel like family, they won't be in the Bed & Breakfast business long. And that's true for innkeepers from all over, whether they were native Southerners or not.

And professional innkeepers know that one of the things that helps a guest feel right at home is offering homemade food. It doesn't have to be fancy fare. In fact, the term that's used for old-fashioned down-home cookin' these days is "comfort food." A plate of cookies served warm from the oven can do more to make a visitor feel at ease than all the gourmet food in Paris.

B&B guests are twice as lucky. They often are welcomed with a beverage or snack when they check in in the afternoon, or they may be invited to share hors d'oeuvres with other guests and the innkeepers before the guests head out for dinner. In the morning, they are treated to a homemade breakfast that folks just don't bother very often to cook for themselves these days.

"Wake Up & Smell the Coffee." You can do it in these B&Bs. Innkeepers whose inns are featured on these pages are those who have traditional B&Bs. The kitchen is in the same house as the guestrooms (though there might also be a separate guest house available, for instance). That means that the smell of German Cinnamon Rolls or Orange Walnut Bread or Finnish Pear Pancakes or Fresh Apple Muffins baking -- along with fresh coffee brewing -- can waft up the stairs and drift under the door to awaken slumbering guests. A number of these innkeepers note that "no alarm clock is needed here." The aroma of breakfast cooking does the trick.

The other requirement was that the recipe be "from-scratch." Guests can throw together some refrigerated dough coffeecake just as quickly as an innkeeper can. (Besides, some recipes with soup or cake mixes or other pre-packaged ingredients can be downright weird.) Careful readers will find occasional use of frozen bread dough or buttermilk baking mix, but that's about it. Those ingredients were seen as time-savers without being too artificial. These recipes are designed to use real food for real people. Spelling out all the ingredients also makes it easier for those with dietary restrictions to make modifications.

Other than those requirements -- that guests really can lie in bed and smell breakfast cooking, and that recipes be "from-scratch"-- there's not any other characteristic that can be shared.

The size of the B&Bs ranges from one guestroom to a dozen. The inns are Queen Anne Victorians, adobe, contemporary "ranch" style homes, farmhouses, even a 51-foot luxury yacht. They range from a 250-year-old estate once owned by Spanish settlers to brand new homes built specifically as B&Bs. The historic homes may have been built by a hardware store owner, a pioneer liquor distributor, a "suffragist," a prominent local politician, Native American families, or as summer homes for wealthy families. Breakfast might be served to the guestroom, in the formal dining room, by the pool, or outside with a view. The innkeepers who now own and/or operate them include former school teachers and administrators, exotic finch breeders, an interior designer, antique dealers, caterers, landscape architects, an antique auto collector, an obstetrical nurse, a retired aeronautical engineer and a soap opera star.

Their recipes are as varied as they are. Many are old family recipes, handed down for generations. Many are creative recipes devised by innovative cooks. Many are new twists on old favorites.

Just because all the recipes are "from scratch" does not mean they are difficult or time-consuming to prepare. Hurry Up Cake, an easy coffeecake, makes that clear in its title. Some, like Apple Butter, can simmer all day, or yeast breads can take hours to rise and rise again. But many are simple -- like Date Bars á la Bernice, Hot Crab Dip, Creamy Fruit Dip or Baked Deviled Eggs. Many others — several French toast and fruit recipes, for starters -- can be prepared the night before and finished in the morning, or Pumpkin Cream Cheese Roll-Up, which can be made well-ahead of time and frozen. One of the beauties of this recipe collection is the inclusion of many time-saving recipes, since innkeepers may *look* like they have all day to prepare this leisurely meal, but they are busy people, too.

More and more scientific evidence indicates that breakfast, just like Mom said, is the most important meal of the day. It seems to provide energy that lasts all day, and it may help determine metabolism and how the body handles stress or what it will crave for the rest of the day.

Of course, no one is going to be inspired to rise early and cook their heart out every morning of the week just because of these recipes. But on weekends, more individuals and families are taking time to eat breakfast, and this collection can provide enough new ideas and variety for more than a year's worth of breakfasts/brunches. Plenty of the entrees, including egg casseroles, quiches, pancakes and waffles, make perfect fare for evening meals.

Then, while preparing a Southwest cookbook, there was the inevitable, "Whoa, *hot* food for breakfast?" Sure, there are recipes in here with a "bite," but that's pretty much limited to the egg dishes. The muffins, coffeecakes, fruits, pancakes, French toast, waffles, desserts, holiday favorites and snacks are typical of good cooking that can be found all across the U.S.

So get cooking! Just don't forget to try not only the recipes, but the B&Bs, too. Even people who say, "I'm not a breakfast eater" can be swayed here. (It's different when someone else has prepared it, served it and cleans up after it.) Go and be pampered. Then come home and smear up this cookbook with the kitchen "batter spatters" that prove it is well-used and well-liked.

Contents

Breads

Preserves, Butters, Spreads & Sauces

Fruits

Entrees

Eggs:

French Toast:

Pancakes:

Waffles:

Other:

Things You Should Know

● Before beginning, please read the entire recipe to find out how hot to preheat the oven, what size pan(s) to grease, or how many hours or days ahead of time the recipe must be started.

● Baking and cooking temperatures are listed in degrees Fahrenheit.

● Remember to preheat the oven to the temperature listed in the recipe before baking.

● Assume that white (granulated) sugar is called for in these recipes when the ingredient listed is "sugar." Powdered (confectioner's) or brown sugar are listed as such. All-purpose white or unbleached flour is listed simply as "flour."

● Brown sugar is "packed" into the measuring cup, not loose, unless otherwise specified.

● Use of oatmeal in these recipes means uncooked oatmeal (the terms "oats" or "rolled oats" weren't used, instead of "oatmeal," because they may mean different things to different people). Usually either "quick-cooking" or "old-fashioned" oatmeal can be used.

● For yeast breads or for preserves and recipes which involve canning, read the package instructions on yeast or pectin thoroughly. You may wish to consult an all-purpose cookbook with detailed instructions for these processes.

● Recipes have been listed in chapters according to the way in which innkeepers serve them. For instance, you will find some fruit dishes in chapters other than "Fruits," and dishes that could be suitable as "Dessert for Breakfast" are included in other chapters because the innkeepers serve them as snacks, holiday fare or even entrees. The table of contents, therefore, also serves as an index so you can double-check other chapters at a glance.

● While the format of the recipes has been standardized, the directions remain in the words of the innkeepers as much as possible.

● Innkeepers had the opportunity to double-check and re-test their recipes before printing. Not all recipes were tested by the author, despite the "tester's comments" on many recipes. Some recipes were tested but no comment was made simply because none was necessary. Testing was done in a non-commercial home kitchen. "From-scratch" recipes were solicited. Recipes which were tested and turned out really awful or which were submitted but contained a number of pre-packaged ingredients were rejected.

● Most innkeepers encouraged experimentation with their recipes, such as substituting or adding ingredients for personal preferences or health reasons. Many of these recipes, they said, were devised through their experimentation with a basic recipe.

● Before eating the food being prepared, cooks are urged to make sure any dishes using egg yolks or egg whites are heated to at least 160 degrees Fahrenheit, which is necessary to kill salmonella virus that may be present in raw eggs, or to use pasteurized eggs, which may be purchased in small cartons in the dairy sections of some grocery stores.

Texas B&B Map Key:

1. The Historical Hudspeth House, Canyon
2. Yacht-O-Fun (on Lake Texoma), Richardson
3. Davanna House, Jefferson
4. The McKay House, Jefferson
5. Roseville Manor, Jefferson
6. Rowell House, Jefferson
7. Stillwater Inn, Jefferson
8. Rosevine Inn B&B, Tyler
9. Red Rooster Square, Edom/Ben Wheeler
10. Wild Briar Inn, Edom/Ben Wheeler
11. Durant Star Inn, Sunnyvale
12. The Bonnynook B&B Inn, Waxahachie
13. Tarlton House, Hillsboro
14. The Oxford House, Stephenville
15. Ash-Bowers-Jarrett House, Palestine
16. The White Horse Inn, Galveston
17. Small Inn, Bacliff
18. Durham House B&B, Houston
19. Raumonda, Columbus
20. The Brenham House, Brenham
21. Long Point Inn, Burton
22. The Pfeiffer House, Bastrop
23. Carrington's Bluff B&B, Austin
24. The McCallum House, Austin
25. The Wild Flower Inn, Austin
26. Das College Haus, Fredericksburg
27. The Delforge Place, Fredericksburg
28. Magnolia House, Fredericksburg
29. Antik Haus Inn, New Braunfels
30. White House B&B, New Braunfels
31. Crystal River Inn, San Marcos
32. The Norton-Brackenridge House, San Antonio
33. Swan and Railway B&B Inn, LaCoste
34. Casa de Leona, Uvalde

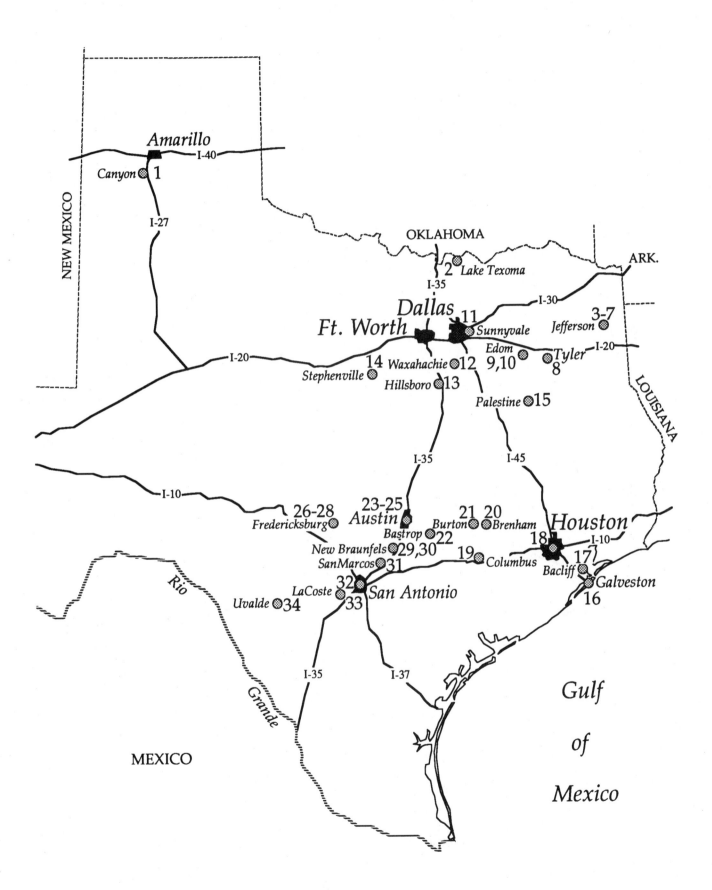

New Mexico

Amarillo
I-40
Canyon ⊙ 1
I-27

Oklahoma

I-35
2 ⊙ Lake Texoma

ARK.

I-30

Dallas 11
Ft. Worth ⊙ Sunnyvale
3-7
Jefferson ⊙

Edom ⊙
I-20
Stephenville ⊙ 14   Waxahachie ⊙ 12   9,10   Tyler 8 ⊙   I-20
Hillsboro ⊙ 13

LOUISIANA

Palestine ⊙ 15

I-35

I-45

I-10

26-28
Fredericksburg ⊙   23-25
Austin ⊙   21 20
Burton ⊙ ⊙ Brenham   Houston
18
Bastrop ⊙ 22   I-10

New Braunfels ⊙ 29,30   19
SanMarcos ⊙ 31   Columbus ⊙   17
Bacliff ⊙   Galveston
16

LaCoste   32 ⊙   San Antonio
Uvalde ⊙ 34   33

Rio

MEXICO

I-35   I-37

Grande

Gulf

of

Mexico

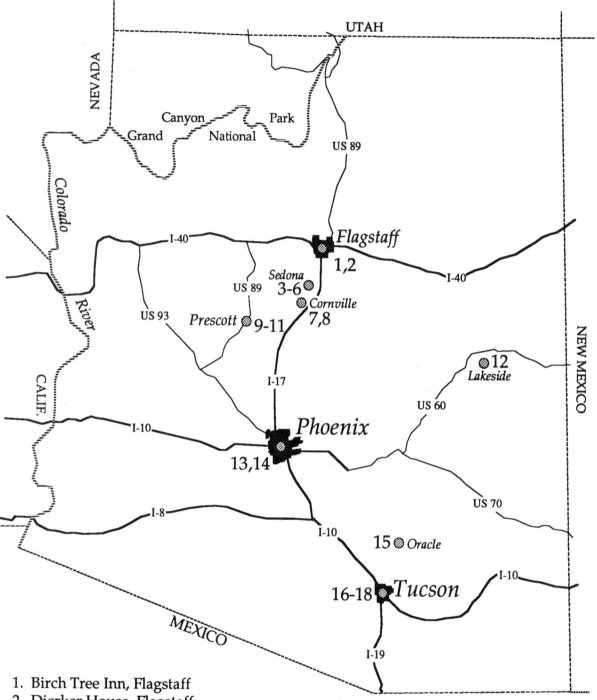

1. Birch Tree Inn, Flagstaff
2. Dierker House, Flagstaff
3. A Touch of Sedona, Sedona
4. Graham's B&B Inn, Sedona
5. B&B at Saddle Rock Ranch, Sedona
6. Sipapu Lodge, Sedona
7. Country Elegance B&B, Cornville
8. Pumpkinshell Ranch, Cornville
9. Lynx Creek Farm, Prescott
10. The Marks House, Prescott
11. The Victorian Inn of Prescott, Prescott
12. Bartram's White Mountain B&B, Lakeside
13. Maricopa Manor, Phoenix
14. Westways Resort Inn, Phoenix
15. Villa Cardinale, Oracle
16. The Brimstone Butterfly, Tucson
17. Copper Bell B&B, Tucson
18. Peppertrees B&B Inn, Tucson

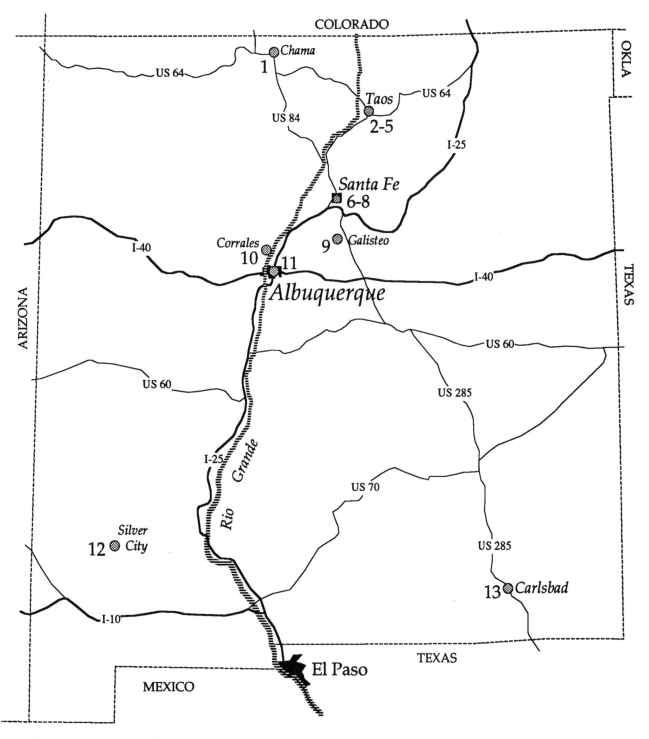

1. The Jones House, Chama
2. La Posada de Taos, Taos
3. Orinda, Taos
4. Salsa del Salto B&B, Taos (El Prado)
5. Whistling Waters B&B, Taos (Ranchos de Taos)
6. Adobe Abode, Santa Fe
7. Alexander's Inn, Santa Fe
8. Grant Corner Inn, Santa Fe
9. The Galisteo Inn, Galisteo
10. La Mimosa B&B, Corralles
11. Casita Chamisa, Albuquerque
12. Bear Mountain Guest Ranch, Silver City
13. La Casa Muneca, Carlsbad

Why start the morning with the same old (boring) glass of orange juice? B&Bs break all the rules for the morning eye-opener. Many B&Bs serve a variety of unusual juices or fresh-grind the coffee beans or stir a little almond-flavored liqueur into the morning coffee. Read on to see how some innkeepers add variety, as well as nourishment. A variety of frappés and "smoothies" make the best use of fruit and juice combinations. Fresh Texas peaches go into a refreshing peach soup. Irish coffee greets guests at St. Patrick's Day in Cornville, Ariz. Ice cold pineapple rum punch is served by the pool on a steamy afternoon by Galveston Bay. Hot Spiced Peach Punch instead of hot cider warms up guests aprés ski in Flagstaff.

Beverages

Almond Tea

Ingredients:

    3 tablespoons instant tea
    2 cups cold water
    1-1/2 cups sugar
    2 cups hot water
    1 12-ounce can regular lemonade concentrate, frozen
    2 quarts water
    3 teaspoons almond extract
    3 teaspoons vanilla extract

- Mix instant tea and cold water.
- In a separate bowl, mix sugar and hot water.
- In a separate jug or kettle, mix lemonade, 2 quarts water and almond and vanilla extracts.
- Pour tea into sugar mixture. Pour that mixture into lemonade mixture. Stir and chill thoroughly.

Makes 15-20 servings

from **The Oxford House**
563 North Graham Street
Stephenville, TX 76401
817-965-6885

"The trick to this recipe is mixing the ingredients in their order," said Innkeeper Paula Oxford. She has been making it to serve at Oxford House wedding receptions, bridal and baby showers and holiday buffets, as well as church functions. "It has always been a major topic when served and most everyone wants to know the ingredients."

The ingredients for success at this four-guestroom bed-and-breakfast inn are a carefully-maintained 1898 Victorian mansion, years of restoration by Paula and Bill Oxford, and plenty of Texas hospitality, including a hearty breakfast. Many Stephenville-area residents enjoy the mansion-turned-inn for catered events such as holiday parties and luncheons, since the large dining room can accommodate up to 50 guests.

Paula and Bill took on restoration of the home in 1985. Judge W.J. Oxford, the home's builder, was Bill's grandfather. Restoration included releveling the house, rewiring and replumbing, painting, wallpapering, rebuilding the porches, refinishing the hardwood floors and laying vintage reproduction carpeting. Letters, pictures, hats and gloves were stored during the process.

Other Oxford House recipes:
Schnecken (German Cinnamon Rolls), page 77
Raspberry Bars, page 190

Cranberry Smoothie Fruit Drink

Ingredients:

    4 cups cranberry juice
    1 cup peach, strawberry, vanilla or plain yogurt
    1-1/2 cups mixed fruit (oranges, bananas, apples, pineapple, berries, et al.)
    1 cup ice, chopped

Also:

    Nutmeg

➤ If chopped ice is not available, take a tray of ice cubes, crush in a heavy-duty blender or put in a heavy plastic bag and smash with a rolling pin.

➤ Place all ingredients in a blender. Blend on "high" for 30 seconds.

➤ Serve in a clear pitcher or wine goblets, sprinkled with ground nutmeg.

Makes 6 one-cup servings

from **The Galisteo Inn**
Off Highway 41
HC 75, Box 4
Galisteo, NM 87540
505-982-1506

"This is a very elegant drink to serve for breakfast in place of plain juice," said Innkeeper Joanna Kaufman. "Although I like it best with just banana, it is good with almost any fruit and it is a great way to use up leftover fruit."

Joanna and Wayne Aarniokoski own this eight-acre estate, which includes the 250-year-old hacienda, once owned by one of the region's Spanish settlers who ranched here. Set under huge cottonwoods and made of adobe, the inn is a fine example of New Mexican territorial architecture.

Inside, guests find 12 guest rooms, each with a Southwestern feel. Natural woodwork sets off adobe walls. Some guest rooms have corner fireplaces, some have sitting areas, some view the pasture and lawn, others view the courtyard. Each is named after a regional tree. Outside, guests can stretch out in lounge chairs on the lawn, work out in the 50-foot heated lap pool that's open in the summers, or take a bike or horseback ride. They can also explore the rest of Galisteo, located 23 miles southeast of Santa Fe, founded as a Spanish colonial outpost in 1614. Today, it's home to an active arts community that embraces Spanish and Native American traditions.

🏠*Other Galisteo Inn recipes:*
Cranberry Raspberry Muffins, page 47
Galisteo Inn Cornmeal Scones, page 50
Chocolate Chip Banana Nut Bread, page 68
Galisteo Inn Cornmeal Waffles, page 154
Pumpkin Cheesecake, page 174

Fresh Peach Soup

Ingredients:

   6 to 7 large ripe peaches, peeled, pitted and quartered (about 3 pounds peaches)
   1/4 cup sugar
   1 cup plain yogurt
   1/4 cup fresh-squeezed orange juice (usually 1 large orange)
   1/4 cup fresh-squeezed lemon juice (usually 1 large lemon)
   Dash of peach schnapps liqueur, optional

Also:

   Fresh mint leaves
   Fresh peach slices

- In a food processor or blender, puree the peaches with the sugar.
- Add yogurt and blend again.
- Add orange and lemon juices and optional schnapps and blend again.
- Continue blending until the mixture is smooth.
- Pour soup into a bowl, or leave in the blender container, and cover. Refrigerate overnight.
- In the morning, pour into cups. Garnish each with a mint leaf and a peach slice before serving.

Tester's Comments: Easy and refreshing. Wonderful as a summer cocktail, with or without liqueur. Don't even think about using canned peaches, which is why Betsy Delforge put "fresh" in the title.

Makes about 6 cups

from **The Delforge Place**
710 Ettie Street
Fredericksburg, TX 78624
512-997-6212

Betsy Delforge serves her version of this popular Texas Hill Country recipe to guests as the first of a seven-course breakfast that leaves no one hungry and everyone impressed. Betsy's breakfasts are renowned in Fredericksburg, and even guests who aren't able to stay in her four-guestroom inn should try to arrange breakfast there.

The mint garnish is picked in Betsy and George's garden, and guests may be served on the patio there. For the peaches, the Delforges don't have to go much further. Gillespie County is the Texas peach capital, producing perhaps 25 percent of the state's fruit from mid-May through mid-August. Visitors can get a taste of the 15 varieties grown in the county at roadside stands.

Other Delforge Place recipes:
Belgium Torte, page 33
Mushrooms with Eggs, page 127
Cornmeal and Rice Griddle Cakes, page 147
Chocolate Potato Drop Cakes, page 181

Fruit Frappé

Ingredients:

1/2 gallon (2 quarts or 8 cups) orange juice
2 cups melon cubes OR
2 cups fresh peach slices OR
2 to 3 ripe bananas AND
1 cup fresh or canned pineapple
2 large fresh mint leaves
Sparkling water, optional

Also:

Lemon slices
Nutmeg

- Pour half the orange juice into the blender.
- Add all of the fruit and blend.
- Add the rest of the orange juice and mint leaves and blend again.
- If using sparkling water, blend in "a generous splash."
- If mixture needs chilling, refrigerate until cold.
- Pour into chilled glasses. Garnish each with a lemon slice and a dash of nutmeg.

Makes 8-10 servings

from **Sipapu Lodge**
65 Piki Drive
P.O. Box 552
Sedona, AZ 86336
602-282-2833

A pitcher of chilled fruit frappé greets guests in the kitchen and dining area of Sipapu Lodge. As guests arrive for breakfast, they may sip this concoction, sit at a comfortable picnic table and talk with the mother-and-son innkeeping team Lea Pace and Vincent Mollan as breakfast is prepared.

Lea, who taught school in California for several years, returned to her native state in 1988 to run Sipapu Lodge with Vince. Vince had been operating the inn since 1987 on a weekends-only basis, driving to Sedona each week from L.A., an exhausting commute that could not be kept up forever. As full-time Sedona innkeepers, now Vince and Lea occasionally get to explore the Red Rock country, almost in their backyard, which draws guests to their home.

Other Sipapu Lodge recipes:
Spinach Dill Sauce, page 96
Fruit Tacos, page 104
Hot, Spiced Melon, page 108
Southwest Egg and Bean Burritos, page 135
Spaghetti Squash Supreme, page 157

Grant Corner Inn Orange Frappé

Ingredients:

4 cups orange juice, fresh-squeezed
Juice of 1 lemon (2 to 3 tablespoons)
1 large banana
6 strawberries, fresh or frozen
1/4 cup heavy cream
6 ice cubes

Also:

Fresh mint leaves

- Crush or break up ice cubes if using a non-heavy-duty blender.
- Place all ingredients in the blender. Blend on high speed for 1 minute.
- If frappé is not thoroughly chilled, place blender container in the freezer.
- Serve in frosted, stemmed goblets and garnish with fresh mint leaves.

Tester's Comments: With the fresh-squeezed juice and whipping cream, this nutritious eye-opener tastes really decadent, but isn't. Plan for seconds.

Makes 6 servings

from **Grant Corner Inn**
122 Grant Avenue
Santa Fe, NM 87501
505-983-6678

At the Grant Corner Inn, a frappé of some sort has become a breakfast beverage tradition. The chef is free to create a new blend every day. "The cook only needs to taste as he goes," said Innkeeper Louise Stewart. "The beauty in these drinks is that they usually need no sweetener other than the natural fruits. My one hint is that they be served very, very cold." At the Inn's busy breakfast time, the frappé mixture is prepared ahead and stored in the freezer. Then each guest's drink is individually blended.

Not only is the frappé popular at this 13-room inn, but so is breakfast, open to the public by reservation. The Inn's kitchen enjoys a fine reputation for its homebaked pastries and gourmet entrees, so much so that Louise wrote "The Grant Corner Inn Breakfast & Brunch Cookbook," with 177 pages of recipes. Louise, husband Pat Walter and daughter Bumpy opened the Inn in 1982. They transformed a three-story Colonial home (yes, on the corner of Grant Avenue downtown) into a charming inn with a white picket fence.

Other Grant Corner Inn recipes:
Cheese Danish Coffeecake, page 36
Cathy's Finnish Pear Pancakes, page 146
Plum Cottage Cheese Pancakes, page 149
Cortés Hot Chocolate, page 168
Sour Cream Ambrosia, page 176

Irish Coffee

Ingredients:

    2 jiggers (3 ounces) Irish whiskey
    2 to 4 teaspoons sugar
    2 cups strong, very hot coffee

Also:

    Whipped cream, chilled

- Warm two 8-ounce stemmed glasses or coffee cups.
- Pour in 1 jigger whiskey per cup.
- Stir in 1 to 2 teaspoons sugar per cup.
- Fill cups to within one inch of brims with hot coffee. Stir to dissolve sugar.
- Float chilled whipped cream on top of the coffee, to the brim.
- Do not stir. Sip through the cream.

Makes 2 servings

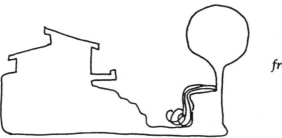

from **Pumpkinshell Ranch**
11005 East Johnson Road
HC 66, Box 2100
Cornville, AZ 86325
602-634-4797

Innkeeper Kay Johnson knows she didn't have to study at Maxim's in Paris to put this recipe together. But it's a delicious brew and she uses her French cooking background in plenty of more complicated creations. Kay enjoys serving theme breakfasts at her contemporary B&B, and Irish coffee is likely to be on the menu around St. Patrick's Day. She'll also knead up some homemade Irish soda bread for B&B guests.

Having Kay cook for you is one of the treats here. Not only has she studied cooking, but she's taught it, too. Her specially-designed commercial kitchen attests to the fact that she takes cooking seriously. Her almost-unheard-of breakfast menu reads better than some restaurants: guests have their choice each morning of biscuits and gravy, two types of quiche, breakfast burritos, hot apple granola, a chili egg "puff" casserole, huevos rancheros and pinto beans, German pancakes with homemade strawberry syrup, two types of pancakes, Eggs Benedict, Eggs Florentine, crepes, breakfast "sandwiches" or old-fashioned bacon and eggs (which some guests actually do choose).

Other Pumpkinshell Ranch recipes:
Aunt Gladys' Buttermilk Biscuits, page 44
Morning Glory Muffins, page 54
Zucchini Muffins, page 62
Hollandaise Sauce, page 90
Irish Soda Bread, page 171

Pineapple Rum Punch

Ingredients:

6 cups pineapple juice
5 cups rum
2 cups sugar
1/2 cup lime juice
2 cups additional pineapple juice for each of three batches of punch

- In a very large bowl, mix 6 cups pineapple juice with rum.
- Mix in sugar and lime juice, stirring to dissolve sugar.
- Pour into three one-quart containers and freeze.
- When ready to serve, place one quart of frosty mixture in a pitcher or punch bowl. Add 2 cups pineapple juice and mix thoroughly. Serve immediately.

Makes 6 servings per batch of punch

from **Small Inn**
4815 West Bayshore Drive
Bacliff, TX 77518
713-339-3489

A frosty glass of this punch might be the perfect accompaniment while chatting by the private swimming pool or while sunning or fishing on the private dock on busy Galveston Bay, all options for guests here.

This Inn is aptly named on two counts: it has but one guestroom, and its owners are Harriet and George Small. But there is nothing small about the hospitality, or the view, or the breakfasts.

Harriet and George's contemporary home faces the bay, where they enjoy a gorgeous view of all the action: sailboats, shrimpers and ocean-going ships. Since 1981, guests have been enjoying it, too. Harriet opened one barrier-free guestroom that year, an early entry into the B&B business. But she and George have traveled all over the world in B&Bs, and she has a catering background, so the B&B combined her talents and interests.

Guests are served up a full breakfast by the pool each morning and plenty of personal attention. Harriet can direct them to the best seafood restaurants along the Bay and the best dancing clubs, as she and George enjoy stepping out for a night of dancing once in awhile.

Other Small Inn recipes:
Sunday Morning Muffins, page 60
Persimmon Bread, page 73
Raisin Pumpkin Bread, page 76

Raspberry Rouser

Ingredients:

1/3 cup pineapple juice, chilled
1 10-ounce package frozen raspberries, thawed
1 8-ounce container raspberry yogurt

Also:

Mint leaves

- In the blender, combine juice, berries and yogurt.
- Blend on medium-low speed for about 30 seconds, or until smooth and thick.
- If desired, pour mixture through a sieve to strain out raspberry seeds.
- Pour into chilled glasses, garnish with mint leaves and serve immediately.

Makes 2 large servings

from **Casa de Leona**
1149 Pearsall Highway
P.O. Box 1829
Uvalde, TX 78802
210-278-8550

This thick raspberry drink is served to Carolyn and Ben Durr's guests before a full breakfast. Guests may have breakfast in the dining room, in the courtyard of this Spanish hacienda, or in the gazebo overlooking the Leona River.

Carolyn and Ben have four guestrooms in their B&B, which they opened in 1987. The hacienda has white plaster walls and red roofs and sits on 1400 feet of river frontage. Carolyn, an artist who works in ceramics, jewelry and oil paintings, suggested turning the estate into a B&B once their children were off to college. She and Ben had stayed in B&Bs on their travels, and it was a business that was compatible with her home-based art studio and gallery. This is the fourth Texas home the Durrs have owned and restored.

The 17-acre estate has several fountains and a porch with a view. "Guests enjoy sitting on the front porch watching the sun go down or the deer go down to the river to drink," said Carolyn. Guests are supposed to make themselves at home -- even raid the icebox, Ben said. Carolyn occasionally caters other meals besides breakfast, and guests may arrange to have her give them a tour of the border towns, Eagle Pass, Texas and Piedras Negras, Mexico. Uvalde is located about 83 miles west of San Antonio and about 40 miles from the Mexican border.

Another Casa de Leona recipe:
Indian Fruit, page 109

Spiced Peach Punch

Ingredients:

1 46-ounce can peach nectar
1 quart (4 cups) orange juice
1/2 cup brown sugar, packed
2 tablespoons lime juice
3 3-inch cinnamon sticks, broken into smaller pieces
1 teaspoon whole cloves

- In a large kettle, mix all ingredients until sugar has dissolved.
- Heat slowly until almost boiling.
- Strain out cinnamon sticks and cloves. Serve in warmed punch cups or mugs.

Makes 8-12 servings

from **Birch Tree Inn**
824 West Birch Avenue
Flagstaff, AZ 86001
602-774-1042

"This is a delightful change from hot cider or wassail as the evenings get cool," said Innkeeper Sandy Znetko. She and Ed and co-innkeepers Donna and Rodger Pettinger may join guests in the living room of this restored home après ski for a cup of this treat. "We all enjoy hosting."

Guests are always intrigued to hear how the Znetkos and the Pettingers, friends for 35 years, bought and restored this home into a five-guestroom inn close to downtown Flagstaff. "Donna and I had a party-planning and catering business in Southern California before moving here to Flagstaff in January of 1989," Sandy said. They had researched the idea of opening a B&B and came upon this house in Flagstaff a year-and-a-half before buying it and moving in.

The Midwest-style farmhouse was built in 1917, but was best known as the home of Mayor Joseph Waldhaus for 40 years. In the 1970s, it was a fraternity house, where 22 guys hung their hats. The two couples and some of their adult children worked on restoration, including adding and renovating bathrooms and redoing the heating system. The entire house was redecorated with heirloom antiques and Donna and Sandy's handmade pillows and crafts.

Other Birch Tree Inn recipes:
Pineapple Stuffed French Toast, page 140
Hoogie Googie Cake, page 186
Saucy Spice Bars, page 191
Hearty Vegetable Soup, page 199
Layered Mexican Dip, page 203

Cinnamon and breakfast go together like, well, like chocolate and nuts. There's enough cinnamon in many of these tantalizing coffeecakes to fill the whole house with a comforting aroma and rouse anyone with half a sweet-tooth straight out of bed. (There's even a coffeecake with coffee in it!) The best thing about coffeecakes may be that it's socially acceptable to eat them for a first or main course rather than holding off until dessert. Two of these recipes showcase Texas' fresh blueberries and peaches, and a number of them use locally-grown pecans. They may taste like you slaved all day, but several recipes are fairly simple and quick to prepare with ingredients often on-hand in your pantry.

Coffeecakes

Applesauce Streusel Coffeecake

Ingredients:

"Master Mix:"
- 4 cups flour
- 2 tablespoons baking powder
- 2 teaspoons salt
- 1/2 cup vegetable shortening

Coffeecake:
- 2 cups "Master Mix"
- 1/4 cup sugar
- 1 teaspoon cinnamon
- 2/3 cup unsweetened applesauce
- 1/4 cup vegetable oil
- 1 teaspoon vanilla extract
- 1 egg, beaten

Streusel topping:
- 1/4 cup "Master Mix"
- 1/4 cup brown sugar
- 2 tablespoons nuts, chopped
- 2 tablespoons butter
- 1/2 teaspoon cinnamon

☞ To make Master Mix: In a large bowl, mix flour, baking powder and salt. Cut in shortening until mixture is crumbly. (Store in a covered container for up to eight weeks).

☞ In a large bowl, combine the 2 cups of Master Mix, sugar and cinnamon.

☞ Stir in applesauce, oil, vanilla and egg.

☞ Pour batter into a greased 9-inch round cake pan.

☞ To make streusel topping, combine Master Mix, brown sugar, nuts, butter and cinnamon, mixing with a fork or pastry cutter until crumbly. Sprinkle over coffeecake batter.

☞ Bake in a preheated oven at 400 degrees for 20 to 25 minutes or until a toothpick inserted in the center comes out clean. Serve warm.

Makes 6 servings

from **Whistling Waters B&B**
Talpa Route, Box 9
Ranchos de Taos, NM 87557
505-758-7798

The handy Master Mix finds its way into Jo Hutson's biscuits and pancakes as well as this coffeecake. She often serves this quick cake to guests staying in her pink adobe home, located on the outskirts of Taos. Jo and Al bought the home in 1986. More than 200 years old, it is one of the area's oldest, having been occupied by a number of families sharing the central courtyard. The layout around the courtyard gives lots of privacy. Nearly all rooms are set off by low or skinny doorways and are up or down a step or two from each other.

Al remodeled the house, one side of which was in ruins, before the Hutsons opened their B&B in 1988 with one guest room (today they have three). He did much of the work himself, including building a pottery studio across the drive for Jo. Jo also is an accomplished watercolor artist. The B&B is decorated in Southwestern art, antiques, quilts and other country touches.

Belgium Torte

Ingredients:

2 cakes baker's yeast (or two packages active dry yeast)
1 tablespoon sugar
4 eggs, beaten
1/2 cup butter, melted
1/2 cup vegetable shortening, melted
1/8 cup plus 1/3 cup warm water (no hotter than 115 degrees)
4 cups flour
1/2 teaspoon salt
6 cups peaches, blackberries, apricots, prunes, applesauce or other canned, drained and mashed fruit or cooked, dried and pureéd fruit

🍴 In a large bowl, sprinkle the yeast with sugar. Add 1/8 cup warm water. Stir to dissolve the yeast and sugar.

🍴 In a separate bowl, beat eggs, melted butter and melted shortening.

🍴 Pour butter mixture into the yeast mixture. Add 1/3 cup warm water. Then stir in flour and salt. Dough will be very buttery.

🍴 Cover with a clean dish towel, place in a warm place free of drafts, and let rise about 40 minutes.

🍴 Punch the dough down, cover, and let rise again, about 30 minutes.

🍴 Divide the dough into four equal parts. Place each quarter in a greased pie plate. With your fingers, press dough across the bottom and 1/2 inch up the sides. Let dough stand for 5 minutes.

🍴 Spoon fruit on top of dough. Then bake in a preheated oven at 375 degrees for 15-17 minutes.

🍴 Remove pans from oven. Cool for several minutes. Cut in pie wedges and serve warm or cold.

Makes 12-16 servings

from **The Delforge Place**
710 Ettie Street
Fredericksburg, TX 78624
512-997-6212

Guests may start Innkeeper Betsy Delforge's gourmet breakfast with this pastry. These four pie plates of danish are served in generous slices, perhaps serving eight guests, along with coffee for an early continental breakfast. Betsy uses local fruit, such as peaches or blackberries, as filling, but "any canned, drained, mashed, fresh or cooked dried fruits" will do. This recipe reflects George's family heritage; he is of Belgian descent. Much of the glass in their 1898 inn comes from his family of Belgian glassblowers.

🏠*Other Delforge Place recipes:*
Fresh Peach Soup, page 24
Mushrooms with Eggs, page 127
Cornmeal and Rice Griddle Cakes, page 147
Chocolate Potato Drop Cakes, page 181

Blueberry Peach Coffeecake

Ingredients:

1-1/4 cups flour
1 cup sugar, divided
1 teaspoon baking powder
1 teaspoon baking soda
1/4 teaspoon salt
3/4 cup margarine, melted
1/2 cup milk
1 egg, beaten
1 teaspoon vanilla
1 teaspoon lemon peel, grated
3 medium ripe peaches, peeled, pitted and thinly sliced (or frozen slices thawed and drained)
2 cups fresh blueberries (or frozen berries thawed and drained)

Topping:
1/2 cup flour
1/4 cup sugar
1/4 teaspoon nutmeg
2 tablespoons margarine, softened
1/2 cup pecans, chopped

- To make Topping: In a small bowl, mix flour, sugar, nutmeg and margarine with a fork until crumbly. Stir in pecans. Set aside.

- In a large bowl, combine the flour, 3/4 cup sugar, baking powder, baking soda and salt.

- Stir in margarine, milk, egg, vanilla and lemon peel.

- Pour into a greased and floured 9-inch springform pan.

- Sprinkle batter with half of topping. Place fruit on top of topping.

- Sprinkle fruit with remaining 1/4 cup sugar. Then sprinkle with remaining topping.

- Bake in a preheated oven at 375 degrees for 45 to 55 minutes or until a toothpick or knife inserted in the center comes out clean.

- Cool 5 minutes. Run knife around inside of springform pan, remove sides and serve.

Makes 6-8 servings

from **Rosevine Inn B&B**
415 South Vine Avenue
Tyler, TX 75702
214-592-2221

"This recipe is served during the summer when the fresh fruit is best and available. Guests sometimes return in the winter and ask for it again, so then we have to use frozen fruit," said Rebecca Powell, innkeeper. While Tyler is "the rose capital of the world," it's also blessed with fresh fruit and is one of the state's major peach-producing regions. Breakfast is served family-style in the dining room of this home, which Rebecca and Bert built and opened as a B&B in 1986. Their inn has four guestrooms, a hot tub and fireplaces.

Other Rosevine Inn B&B recipes:
Blueberry Honey Butter, page 85
Rosevine Breakfast Bake, page 131

Blueberry Pudding

Ingredients:

 1 cup sugar
 1 tablespoon butter
 1 egg
 2 cups flour
 2 teaspoons baking powder
 1 cup milk
 2 cups fresh blueberries
 1 tablespoon sugar
 1 tablespoon flour

Also:

 Milk or cream
 Sugar

- In a mixing bowl, cream 1 cup sugar, butter and egg.
- Sift the 2 cups flour and baking powder together.
- Stir the dry ingredients into the egg mixture alternately with the milk.
- Wash blueberries. Sprinkle with sugar and flour. Stir to coat berries. Fold berries into the batter.
- Pour into a greased and floured 8-inch square pan.
- Bake in a preheated oven at 375 degrees for 40 to 45 minutes or until a toothpick inserted in the center comes out clean.
- Cut into nine squares. Serve warm coffeecake in a bowl with fresh milk or cream poured over, then sugar sprinkled on top.

Makes 9 servings

from **The Bonnynook B&B Inn**
414 West Main Street
Waxahachie, TX 75165
214-938-7207

"In my great-grandmother's day, pudding was a lot different than what we think of today," said Innkeeper Bonnie Franks, who serves this as a coffeecake. Bonnie grew up eating this dish, made with fresh huckleberries, in the Pocono Mountains in Pennsylvania. "Typically, if you weren't down for breakfast by 8 a.m. on a Saturday or Sunday, you could count on not getting any of the pudding." She is more lenient with guests' weekend breakfast times. In addition to this coffeecake, an entree and a fruit dish is served in the formal dining room of this 1880s home, one of more than 225 properties in Waxahachie listed on the National Register of Historic Places.

Other Bonnynook B&B Inn recipes:
Pennsylvania Shoofly Squares, page 40
Morning Surprise Pears or Apples, page 110
Applesauce Pancakes and Syrup, page 143

Cheese Danish Coffeecake

Ingredients:

1 package active dry yeast
1/4 cup warm water (no hotter than 115 degrees)
2 tablespoons sugar
1 egg, beaten
2 to 2-1/4 cups flour
1/2 teaspoon salt
3/4 cup butter

Filling:

12 ounces cream cheese, softened
1/2 cup sugar
1 teaspoon lemon juice

Also:

Powdered sugar

- For the pastry: In a small bowl, mix yeast, warm water and sugar. Let stand about 10 minutes until bubbly. Stir in egg. Set aside.

- In a mixing bowl, sift together flour and salt. Cut in butter until the mixture resembles coarse meal.

- Add yeast mixture and mix well.

- Divide the dough in half. On a lightly floured surface, roll each half into an 8 x 10-inch rectangle.

- For the filling: Beat cream cheese, sugar and lemon juice until smooth.

- Spread half the filling on each rectangle, lengthwise down the middle.

- Fold sides to middle, overlapping flaps a bit. Fold up the ends of rectangles about 1-1/2 inches.

- Lift carefully to greased cookie sheets. Bake in a preheated oven at 375 degrees for 25 minutes, or until golden brown. Remove from the oven and leave coffeecakes on cookie sheets to cool.

- Dust the cooled coffeecakes with powdered sugar and serve.

Tester's Comments: This is a wonderful, buttery-rich yeast pastry that requires no rising time. The cream cheese filling is even better with 1/2 to 3/4 cup raspberry jam beaten in.

Makes 12 servings

from **Grant Corner Inn**
122 Grant Avenue
Santa Fe, NM 87501
505-983-6678

This is one of the homemade pastries that has put this Inn on the hospitality map. Breakfast always includes a basket of muffins, coffeecake or breads, plus a frozen fruit frappé and the guest's choice of two entrees.

Other Grant Corner Inn recipes:
Grant Corner Inn Orange Frappé, page 26
Cathy's Finnish Pear Pancakes, page 146
Plum Cottage Cheese Pancakes, page 149
Cortés Hot Chocolate, page 168
Sour Cream Ambrosia, page 176

Cinnamon Nut Coffeecake

Ingredients:

1 cup butter
2 cups sugar
2 eggs
1 cup sour cream
1 teaspoon vanilla extract
2 cups flour
1 teaspoon baking powder

Filling:
2 teaspoons cinnamon
5 tablespoons brown sugar
3/4 cup pecans, chopped

Also:

Powdered sugar

- In a large bowl, cream sugar and butter. Beat in eggs one at a time.
- In a separate bowl, combine sour cream and vanilla.
- In another bowl, mix flour and baking powder.
- Beat the flour and sour cream mixtures alternately into the butter mixture.
- Pour half the batter into a well-greased Bundt pan.
- For the filling: Mix the cinnamon, brown sugar and pecans. Sprinkle the mixture over the batter.
- Spoon the remaining batter on top of the filling.
- Bake in a preheated oven at 350 degrees for 60 to 65 minutes. "Cake will rise, then fall slightly."
- Cool for at least 10 minutes before removing from the pan. Sift powdered sugar over the top of the warm cake.

Tester's Comments: Grease the Bundt pan very well or this rich coffeecake won't come out in one piece.

Makes 10-12 servings

from **Magnolia House**
101 East Hackberry Street
Fredericksburg, TX 78624
512-997-0306

"At Magnolia House when we are having a traditional Southern breakfast of eggs, bacon and ham, hash browns, gravy, a fruit plate, nut muffins and homemade biscuits, we also like to do something sweet," said Innkeeper Geri Lilley. "My Uncle Alex can't start his day without a sweet and when planning the menu, we always think an Uncle Alex may be with us. This coffeecake smells so good and is a favorite with our guests." Geri, an ex-Houstonian and former rancher, opened six guestrooms in 1991 in the house she restored. The home is set underneath five large magnolias.

Other Magnolia House recipes:
Aunt Tommy's Sausage Quiche, page 118
Apple Brown Betty, page 180

Hurry Up Cake

Ingredients:

1 cup sugar
2 eggs
1 cup sour cream
1-1/2 cups flour
2 teaspoons baking powder
1/2 teaspoon baking soda
1 teaspoon vanilla extract

Topping:
2 tablespoons sugar
1 teaspoon cinnamon

- In a large bowl, cream sugar, eggs and sour cream.
- In a separate bowl, combine the flour, baking powder and baking soda.
- Stir the dry ingredients into the egg mixture.
- Add vanilla and beat well.
- Pour into a greased 8- or 9-inch square pan.
- For topping, mix sugar and cinnamon together. Sprinkle over coffeecake batter.
- Bake in a preheated oven at 350 degrees for 20 minutes or until a toothpick inserted in the center comes out clean.

Tester's Comments: Surprisingly good for lack of butter and spices. Easily varied by adding apples or berries.

Makes 6-8 servings

from **The Jones House**
311 Terrace Avenue
P.O. Box 887
Chama, NM 87520
505-756-2908

"When I got my college apartment in 1961, my grandmother gave me an index card box of recipes she had copied in her lovely handwriting," said Innkeeper Sara Jayne Cole. "She picked out those she thought a student would have time to make." Sara Jayne is still using the recipes, and this one is a quick coffeecake for her B&B guests.

Sara Jayne and Phil Cole found this 1926 house while they were in town when Phil was surveying for the Cumbres and Toltec Scenic Railroad. They bought it specifically to operate as a B&B, moving up from Santa Fe where Sara Jayne had watched the B&B "industry" develop. They completed renovation, added bathrooms and opened four guestrooms in 1988.

Other Jones House recipes:
Blue Corn Waffles, page 151
Carrot Cake, page 196
Picnic Basket Quiche, page 208

Oatmeal Breakfast Cake

Ingredients:

1 cup old-fashioned oatmeal
1-1/4 cups boiling water
1/2 cup unsweetened applesauce
1 cup sugar
1 cup brown sugar, packed
2 egg whites
1 teaspoon vanilla extract
1-1/2 cups flour
2 teaspoons cinnamon
1 teaspoon baking soda
1/4 teaspoon nutmeg

Topping:
1/2 cup brown sugar, packed
3 tablespoons milk
1/3 cup nuts, chopped
3/4 cup coconut

- Combine oatmeal and boiling water. Let stand 20 minutes.

- Generously spray one large Bundt pan with non-stick cooking spray.

- In a large bowl, mix applesauce, sugar, brown sugar, egg whites, vanilla and cooled oats.

- Stir in flour, cinnamon, baking soda and nutmeg. Stir just until blended. Pour batter into pans.

- Bake in a preheated oven at 350 degrees for 30 to 45 minutes or until a knife inserted in the center comes out clean. Let coffeecake stand for 5 minutes, then remove it from pan.

- For Topping: In a small saucepan or microwave-safe bowl, stir together brown sugar, milk, nuts and coconut. Heat and stir until sugar dissolves. Pour hot topping over the coffeecake and serve.

Makes 10-12 servings

from **The McCallum House**
613 West 32nd Street
Austin, TX 78705
512-451-6744

"Be sure not to overbake," advises Innkeeper Nancy Danley. "Try substituting chopped dates for the nuts and coconut to further reduce fat." Nancy tries to stick to low-fat foods as much as possible while serving a full breakfast. "I don't usually tell the guests that this is almost fat-free until they've eaten a piece -- then they're so happy they have some more!"

The family-style breakfast is a leisurely, fun affair in the formal dining room of this 1907 home. Nancy joins guests and the conversation flows as smoothly as the coffee and juice. Breakfast may be served on the built-in buffet and on antique dishes. Even the smallest details, like fresh flowers and a pressed-design in the butter, have not been overlooked.

Other McCallum House recipes:
Lemon-Glazed Oat Muffins, page 52
Mexican Puff, page 125
Migas, page 126

Pennsylvania Shoofly Squares

Ingredients:

    3 cups flour
    1 cup sugar
    1 cup vegetable shortening
    1 teaspoon cinnamon
    1/2 teaspoon cloves
    1 cup molasses
    1 teaspoon baking soda
    1 cup warm water

- In a large bowl, cut together flour, sugar and shortening with a pastry cutter or fork.

- Remove 1 cup of the mixture and set aside for topping.

- To the remainder, stir in cinnamon, cloves and molasses.

- Dissolve baking soda in warm water. Then mix into molasses mixture.

- Pour into a greased 8 x 12-inch or 9 x 13-inch pan. Sprinkle with reserved crumbly topping.

- Bake in a preheated oven at 375 degrees for 25 to 30 minutes or until a toothpick inserted in the center comes out clean. Cut into squares. Serve warm or cold.

Tester's Comments: If you like molasses cookies, you'll love this coffeecake. (Ignore the yucky color of the batter; it bakes up richly dark.) Ingredients are often on hand in the pantry.

Makes 12 servings

from **The Bonnynook B&B Inn**
414 West Main Street
Waxahachie, TX 75165
214-938-7207

"This is a recipe that was my great-grandmother's and is a part of my grandmother's recipe book that we use at the inn," said Innkeeper Bonnie Franks. "We kids were brought up on it." Originally, it was a Pennsylvania Dutch Shoofly Pie, baked in a pie shell, but Bonnie modified the recipe and now serves it as coffeecake.

Bonnie and Vaughn Franks bought this 1880s mansion, built during the cotton boom, to renovate as a four-guestroom inn. "We soon became expert caulkers during the six-year house renovation," she notes. But they never questioned their decision. Bonnie had stayed in many B&Bs, so she knew she "loved the whole concept," she said. "The real surprise has been the nice reception by the public of not only our breakfasts, but our lunches and dinners, as well."

🏠 *Other Bonnynook B&B Inn recipes:*
Blueberry Pudding, page 35
Morning Surprise Pears or Apples, page 110
Applesauce Pancakes and Syrup, page 143

Peppertrees' Coffee Coffeecake

Ingredients:

1/2 cup butter	Topping:
1 cup sugar	1/2 cup brown sugar, packed
2 eggs	1/2 cup flour
1 tablespoon finely ground coffee beans	1 tablespoon finely ground coffee beans
1 teaspoon vanilla extract	1/4 cup butter or margarine
2 cups flour	1/2 cup white chocolate chips
1 teaspoon baking soda	1/2 cup nuts, chopped
1 teaspoon baking powder	
1 cup buttermilk	
1/2 cup white chocolate chips	

- In a large bowl, cream butter and sugar.
- Add eggs one at a time, beating well after each addition. Then stir in coffee and vanilla.
- In a separate bowl, combine the flour, baking soda and baking powder.
- Stir the dry ingredients into the egg mixture alternately with the buttermilk.
- Mix in white chocolate chips.
- Pour into a greased 9 x 13-inch baking pan. Smooth out the top.
- For Topping: With a fork, mix brown sugar, flour, coffee and butter together until it is crumbly.
- Stir in chips and nuts. Sprinkle over batter.
- Bake in a preheated oven at 350 degrees for 45 minutes or until a toothpick inserted in the center comes out clean. Remove from oven and cool 10 minutes before serving.

Tester's Comment: This got rave reviews from mocha-lovers. FYI, white chips used were vanilla milk chips.

Makes 16 servings

from Peppertrees B&B Inn
724 East University Boulevard
Tucson, AZ 85719
602-622-7167

"When I first came to America and was invited for coffee and given coffeecake, I always came away puzzled because the cake that was offered never seemed to taste of coffee," said Innkeeper Marjorie Martin, who hails from England. "I was literally expecting a cake flavored with coffee." This one does the trick. Instant coffee can be used in place of the ground coffee beans, but the flavor will be different, she said. Marjorie has such a large recipe collection of favorites that she's published her own B&B cookbook. Guests in the main house or the guesthouses always come away well-fed.

Other Peppertrees B&B Inn recipes:
Prickly Pear Syrup, page 95
Bananas and Strawberry Cream, page 101
Peppertrees' Scottish Shortbread, page 173

Saddle Rock Ranch Jammie Cake

Ingredients:

1 8-ounce package "light" cream cheese
1/2 cup margarine
1/2 cup sugar
1 cup skim or low-fat milk
2 eggs, beaten
1 tablespoon vanilla extract
2 cups flour
1 teaspoon baking powder
1/2 teaspoon baking soda
1/4 teaspoon salt
1 18-ounce jar low-calorie jam or fruit spread

Topping:
1/2 cup brown sugar, packed
1/2 cup pecans, chopped

- In a large bowl or food processor, combine cream cheese, margarine and sugar.
- Add milk, eggs and vanilla.
- In a separate bowl, combine the flour, baking powder, baking soda and salt.
- Stir the dry ingredients into the egg mixture. If using a food processor, blend about 20 seconds.
- Spray a 9 x 13-inch pan with non-stick cooking spray. Pour two-thirds of the batter into the pan.
- Dab small spoonfuls of the jam or fruit spread over the batter and gently spread it around.
- Spread the remainder of the batter on top of the jam.
- For Topping: Combine brown sugar and pecans. Sprinkle mixture over the top of the batter.
- Bake in a preheated oven at 350 degrees for 40 minutes or until a toothpick inserted in the center comes out clean.

Tester's Comments: Don' t worry if the jam "sinks" to the bottom during baking; call it "Upside Down Jammie Cake." The more spreadable the jam, the better (heat it in the microwave first, if necessary).

Makes 8-12 servings

from **B&B at Saddle Rock Ranch**
255 Rockridge Drive
Sedona, AZ 86336
602-282-7640

Guests at this ranch estate may enjoy Fran and Dan Bruno's Jammie Cake poolside or in the sunny rock-walled breakfast room. The Brunos opened their B&B in the former estate of Barry Goldwater. Once a 6,000-acre homesteaded ranch, in the 1940s and 50s it was used to film western location shots that showed up in movies starring John Wayne, Randolph Scott and Hopalong Cassidy. The Brunos have two guestrooms in the main house and a guest cottage, all of which have outstanding views of scenic Sedona red rocks.

Other B&B at Saddle Rock Ranch recipes:
Grandma's Date Nut Bread, page 69
Peachy Wheat Germ Waffles, page 156

Most innkeepers love muffins because their guests do, and because muffins usually are easy to stir up, yet require only a short 20-minute-or-so baking time. So it's no surprise that many innkeepers wanted to share a favorite muffin recipe. This collection has several healthy recipes, with bran, oats or whole wheat flour, as well as some rich, exotic muffins with sour cream, cashews and coconut, or raspberry jam. Many use locally-grown ingredients, such as apples, peaches, blueberries, blue cornmeal or pecans. A precious few have batter that can be stirred up in advance, then covered and refrigerated until breakfast time rolls around. All of them will add variety to what otherwise might be ordinary "ho-hum" breakfasts.

Muffins, Scones & Biscuits

Aunt Gladys' Buttermilk Biscuits

Ingredients:

  1/3 cup vegetable shortening
  1 cup buttermilk
  1-1/2 cups flour
  2 teaspoons baking powder
  1/2 teaspoon salt
  1/4 teaspoon baking soda

Also:

  Sausage gravy, preserves or honey

- Melt shortening in a 9 x 13-inch pan as the oven preheats.

- Pour buttermilk into a large mixing bowl.

- In a separate bowl, sift together 1 cup of the flour, baking powder, salt and baking soda. Stir into the buttermilk.

- Pour about two-thirds of the melted shortening into the dough and mix.

- Stir in the other 1/2 cup flour to make a very soft dough ("keep it as soft as possible -- it should stick to your fingers").

- Sprinkle flour under and over the dough ball before patting it out. Pat out 1/2 to 3/4-inch thick.

- Cut with a small biscuit cutter or a glass that has been dipped in flour before each cut.

- Place biscuits in the pan, on top of the melted shortening. Turn over each biscuit to grease the top.

- Bake on the top rack in a preheated oven at 475 degrees for 10 to 15 minutes, until the *bottoms* of the biscuits are golden brown.

Makes 12 biscuits

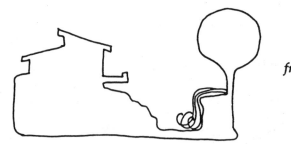

from **Pumpkinshell Ranch**
11005 East Johnson Road
HC 66, Box 2100
Cornville, AZ 86325
602-634-4797

"Aunt Gladys had six children and a husband who loved her biscuits, which she made every morning for 40 years," said Innkeeper Kay Johnson. As a child, Kay was a "city mouse" visiting her "country mice" cousins, and she learned to love those biscuits, too. Aunt Gladys, Kay said, "is a very smart woman. She made a dozen biscuits and if you didn't get out of bed on time for breakfast, there were none left. That happened to me only once." Guests at Kay's two-guestroom B&B can choose to have these biscuits with gravy.

Other Pumpkinshell Ranch recipes:
Irish Coffee, page 27
Morning Glory Muffins, page 54
Zucchini Muffins, page 62
Hollandaise Sauce, page 90
Irish Soda Bread, page 171

Blue Corn Pineapple Muffins

Ingredients:

2 cups buttermilk baking mix, such as Bisquick
1/2 cup blue cornmeal
1/3 cup sugar
Pinch of baking soda
1 egg
1/3 cup vegetable oil
1 20-ounce can crushed pineapple, drained
1/2 teaspoon vanilla extract
1 cup milk

🔰 In a large bowl, combine baking mix, cornmeal, sugar and baking soda.

🔰 In a separate bowl, beat egg lightly. Stir in vegetable oil, pineapple, vanilla and milk.

🔰 Pour pineapple mixture into dry ingredients and stir until well-mixed.

🔰 Fill 12 greased or paper-lined muffin tins three-quarters full. Bake in a preheated oven at 375 degrees for 15 to 20 minutes or until light brown.

Makes 12 muffins

from **Lynx Creek Farm**
Off Highway 69
P.O. Box 4301
Prescott, AZ 86302
602-778-9573

"These muffins are southwestern and fruity but not too sweet," said Innkeeper Greg Temple, who suggests substituting almond extract for vanilla and garnishing each muffin with a dollop of sour cream. Greg came up with this recipe out of necessity. "I had bought a 25-pound bag of organic blue cornmeal from the co-op because that was the smallest amount I could order, so I knew I had to start cooking something with it!"

Cornmeal is not the only thing organic at this busy farm. Greg and Wendy Temple operate a 25-acre organic apple orchard, where Granny Smith, Red Rome and other varieties grow, and guests can pick-their-own. The fruit, vegetable and herb gardens are organic, too. The Temples also raise a number of species of exotic finches and parrots, for which Lynx Creek Farm has earned a reputation among bird breeders. But many guests first hear about this B&B through its cooking school. Each month, a different menu theme is featured, and students prepare feasts such as "a French Countryside dinner" or "an Indonesian Barbeque." Students stay overnight in a guestroom in the main house or two spacious apartments overlooking Lynx Creek. The B&B/farm/school is located about five miles east of Prescott.

Another Lynx Creek Farm recipe:
Potato Quiche Ranchero, page 129

Cashew Coconut Whole Wheat Muffins

Ingredients:

1 cup whole wheat flour
1 cup unbleached flour
2/3 cup brown sugar, packed
1 tablespoon baking powder
1/2 teaspoon salt
1 egg, beaten
1/3 cup vegetable oil
1 cup milk
2/3 cup cashews, chopped
2/3 cup coconut

- In a large bowl, sift together flours, brown sugar, baking powder and salt.
- Stir in the egg, oil and milk just until all ingredients are blended.
- Fold in cashews and coconut.
- Fill 12 paper-lined or greased muffin tins three-quarters full. Bake in preheated oven at 400 degrees for 20 minutes or until a toothpick inserted in the center comes out clean.

Tester's Comments: Cashews are so wonderful, why not in muffins? These are great and they freeze well. Reheat cautiously in the microwave.

Makes 12 muffins

from **The Victorian Inn of Prescott**
246 South Cortez Street
Prescott, AZ 86303
602-778-2642

These muffins are often on the breakfast table when guests from all four guestrooms sit down together in the formal dining room. Innkeeper Tamia Thunstedt, a nurse, enjoys taking care of her B&B guests, including a hearty breakfast featuring homemade muffins, fruit and an entree.

Tamia opened her B&B in 1990 in one of Prescott's finest Victorian homes. Complete with a turret and gingerbread trim, the Queen Anne home was built in 1893 by the district attorney. Previous owners completely restored the two-story home. Tamia, who teaches obstetrical nursing, has made operating the Inn a family business, and she is helped by her parents, sister and daughter, Eve. Located on the corner of Cortez and Carleton streets, the Inn is just one block from the town square, and one more block from antique shops and restaurants. The home is decorated with period wallpaper, antiques and other Victorian touches, many of which are handmade.

🏠 *Other Victorian Inn recipes:*
Linzer Muffins, page 53
Amaretto and Applesauce, page 100

Cranberry Raspberry Muffins

Ingredients:

    1/2 cup butter
    1 cup sugar
    2 eggs
    1 teaspoon almond extract
    Half of a 16-ounce can whole berry cranberry sauce
    2 teaspoons baking powder
    1/4 teaspoon salt
    2 cups flour
    1/2 cup milk
    1-1/2 cups fresh or frozen "dry pack" raspberries

- In a mixing bowl, cream butter and sugar. Mix in eggs, one at a time. Then stir in almond extract.
- Open the cranberry sauce and drain off any juice. Stir half the cranberries into egg mixture.
- In a separate bowl, mix baking powder, salt and flour.
- Add dry ingredients to cranberry mixture alternately with the milk. Mix well.
- Slowly fold raspberries into batter.
- Fill 18 lined or greased muffin tins.
- Bake in a preheated oven at 375 degrees for 20 to 25 minutes or until a toothpick inserted comes out clean.

Makes 18 muffins

from **The Galisteo Inn**
Off Highway 41
HC 75, Box 4
Galisteo, NM 87540
505-982-1506

Innkeeper Joanna Kaufman enjoys these sweet-tart muffins, but she may substitute any berries in season. "It also makes a terrific sweet bread."

Joanna and Wayne Aarniokoski bought this 12-guestroom adobe estate on eight acres after vacationing from California. "We thought someday when we retired we'd do a B&B in northern California," she said. "Fortunately, we didn't wait that long!" Besides enjoying New Mexico and the innkeeping lifestyle, their new business "is too much work to be considered retirement!"

Other Galisteo Inn recipes:
Cranberry Smoothie Fruit Drink, page 23
Galisteo Inn Cornmeal Scones, page 50
Chocolate Chip Banana Nut Bread, page 68
Galisteo Inn Cornmeal Waffles, page 154
Pumpkin Cheesecake, page 174

Dave's Baking Powder Biscuits

Ingredients:

2 packages active dry yeast
1 cup warm water (no hotter than 115 degrees)
6 cups flour
2 cups buttermilk
3/4 cup vegetable oil
1/4 cup sugar
4 teaspoons baking powder
1-1/2 teaspoons salt
1/4 teaspoon baking soda

- In a large bowl, dissolve yeast in warm water.
- Mix in flour, buttermilk, oil, sugar, baking powder, salt and baking soda by hand.
- Place dough in a greased bowl. Cover and refrigerate. (Dough will keep 3 days in refrigerator.)
- When needed, roll pieces of dough into balls and place on a greased cookie sheet. "No need to let rise."
- Bake in a preheated oven at 425 degrees for 20 to25 minutes.

Makes several dozen, as needed, or about 50 total

from **The Historical Hudspeth House**
1905 Fourth Avenue
Canyon, TX 79015
806-655-4168

Innkeepers Dave and Sally Haynie restored this 35-room mansion and opened an eight-guestroom inn and health spa in 1987. In addition to traditional B&B, they offer one to five-day spa packages and classes for small groups, including exercise, diet control, skin care, massage and stress management.

The inn is named after Mary Elizabeth Hudspeth, who joined the faculty of what is now West Texas State University in 1910 and boarded in this house. In 1913 she purchased it and had it moved closer to the college. As the story goes, local folks saw smoke coming from the chimney as a tractor pulled the house down the street because the cook was inside preparing lunch for Miss Hudspeth. One of Miss Hudspeth's friends and faculty colleagues, Georgia O'Keeffe, visited the home often, and the dining room where the Haynies serve breakfast is named in her honor.

Canyon, located 15 miles south of Amarillo, is also close to Palo Duro Canyon State Park, known as the Grand Canyon of Texas, 1,100 feet deep and 120 miles long. Visitors can ride a train along the canyon floor or watch an musical drama on the history of the Texas Panhandle. The play is presented in the outdoor amphitheater every night in the summer.

Fresh Apple Muffins

Ingredients:

1 cup sugar
3/4 cup vegetable oil
2 eggs
1 teaspoon vanilla extract
2 cups flour
1 teaspoon baking soda
1 teaspoon cinnamon
1/2 teaspoon salt
1-3/4 cups apples, peeled and chopped
1/2 cup raisins
1/2 cup pecans or walnuts, chopped

- With an electric mixer, beat sugar and oil for 2 minutes. Then beat in eggs and vanilla.

- In a separate bowl, combine the flour, baking soda, cinnamon and salt.

- Stir the dry ingredients into the oil mixture just until all are combined.

- Fold in apples, raisins and nuts.

- Fill 12 greased or paper-lined muffin cups. Bake in a preheated oven at 400 degrees for 20 to 25 minutes or until toothpick inserted in the center comes out clean.

Tester's Comments: These got "thumbs up" from veteran inn travelers/muffin eaters, even when the apples weren't peeled (but they were chopped fairly finely).

Makes 14 muffins

from **Durham House B&B**
921 Heights Boulevard
Houston, TX 77008
713-868-4654

"I have kept a muffin file for over 20 years," said Innkeeper Marguerite Swanson. "I call these muffins my 'Emergency Muffins' because I can make them for unexpected guests -- all the ingredients are available all year." The muffins freeze well if wrapped individually in plastic wrap, she said.

This school counselor-turned-innkeeper opened Durham House along with husband Dean in 1985. The restored Queen Anne Victorian is listed on the National Register of Historic Places. Swansons offer five antique-filled guestrooms to visitors, honeymooners and business travelers, who find the location in historic Houston Heights convenient, only five minutes from downtown. Swansons also specialize in romantic weddings in the garden gazebo and original murder mystery dinner parties for groups of 12 or more.

Another Durham House B&B recipe:
Peach Upside-Down French Toast, page 172

Galisteo Inn Cornmeal Scones

Ingredients:

2 cups unbleached flour
1 cup yellow or blue cornmeal
1/2 cup sugar
1 tablespoon baking powder
1/2 teaspoon baking soda
3/4 teaspoon cinnamon
3/4 cup butter, cold
1 cup buttermilk
1 cup pecans, chopped

Also:

Butter, preserves and/or honey

- In the food processor, combine flour, cornmeal, sugar, baking powder, soda, cinnamon and butter, "pulsing" until it resembles small peas.
- Pour the mixture into a large mixing bowl. Stir in the buttermilk and pecans.
- Lightly flour a board or counter-top. Roll out the dough to 1/2-inch thick.
- Using cookie cutters, cut the scones into shapes such as hearts, circles or diamonds.
- Place on ungreased cookie sheets.
- Bake in a preheated oven at 400 degrees for 12 minutes or until the scones are golden brown. Serve warm with butter, preserves and/or honey.

Makes 18 scones

from **The Galisteo Inn**
Off Highway 41
HC 75, Box 4
Galisteo, NM 87540
505-982-1506

Innkeeper Joanna Kaufman calls this recipe "by far our most popular breakfast pastry. Every time we bake these, several guests ask for the recipe." At the Galisteo Inn, these scones are part of a breakfast buffet that may start off with a "smoothie" juice drink and include granola and a fresh fruit platter.

Guests may also enjoy dinner at the inn, famous for its cuisine. Dinner might feature mint and jalapeno-glazed lamp chops, roasted corn chowder with cilantro and chile pestos, and a homemade margarita sorbet for dessert. Joanna and Wayne Aarniokoski hire local chefs and staff at this 12-guestroom adobe estate, where guests can take the horses on trail rides.

Other Galisteo Inn recipes:
Cranberry Smoothie Fruit Drink, page 23
Cranberry Raspberry Muffins, page 47
Chocolate Chip Banana Nut Bread, page 68
Galisteo Inn Cornmeal Waffles, page 154
Pumpkin Cheesecake, page 174

Healthy Muffins

Ingredients:

3 eggs
1 cup vegetable oil
2 cups flour
1-1/4 cups sugar
1 apple, grated
2 cups carrots, grated
1 cup zucchini, grated
3/4 cup golden raisins
3/4 cup coconut
1/2 cup pecans, chopped
1 tablespoon cinnamon
2 teaspoons baking soda
1-1/2 teaspoons orange peel, grated
1 teaspoon vanilla extract
1/2 teaspoon salt

Orange Glaze:
4 tablespoons orange juice
2 tablespoons coconut
2 tablespoons orange peel, grated
Powdered sugar

- In a large bowl, beat eggs and oil.

- In a separate bowl, mix remaining ingredients.

- Stir flour mixture into egg mixture.

- Fill greased or paper-lined muffin tins three-quarters full. Bake in a preheated oven at 375 degrees for 25 minutes or until a toothpick inserted in the center comes out clean.

- For Orange Glaze: Mix orange juice, coconut, orange peel and enough powdered sugar to form a thick glaze. Drizzle over the top of each muffin.

Makes 24 muffins

from **The Wild Flower Inn**
1200 West 22-1/2 Street
Austin, TX 78705
512-477-9639

These muffins were the result of combining favorite recipes of Innkeeper Kay Jackson. Kay is a creative muffin maker whose inventions come from stirring up two kinds of muffins every day. "You start out with an idea, and then you think, 'What if I put pineapple in with this?' or something like that," she said.
"You can kind of tell if it will work in the batter." Kay and co-innkeeper Claudean Schultz, who worked together in a Houston school district, decided to leave their long-time careers, move to Austin and try the B&B business as a second career. They opened four guestrooms in 1990.

Other Wild Flower Inn recipes:
Peach and Poppyseed Muffins, page 56
Wonderful Applesauce Muffins, page 61
Wild Flower Apple Bread, page 80

Lemon-Glazed Oat Muffins

Ingredients:

1-1/3 cups flour
2/3 cup Oat Flour
2/3 cup sugar
2 teaspoons baking powder
1 egg white, beaten
2/3 cup milk
1/4 cup unsweetened applesauce
1 teaspoon fresh lemon zest
1 tablespoon lemon juice
About 3 dozen berries (raspberries, blueberries or small strawberries)

Oat Flour:
    2/3 cup oatmeal, uncooked
    1/3 cup wheat bran

Lemon Glaze:
    2/3 cup sugar
    1/3 cup lemon juice

- For Oat Flour: Mix oatmeal and bran in a food processor until consistency of coarse flour.
- In a large bowl, combine flour, oat flour, sugar and baking powder.
- Mix in egg white, milk, applesauce, lemon zest and lemon juice, stirring just until combined.
- Pour into greased or paper-lined muffin tins. Place 3 berries in the top of each muffin.
- Bake in a preheated oven at 350 degrees for 15 to 20 minutes.
- For Lemon Glaze: Mix sugar and lemon juice in a microwave-safe bowl. Microwave for 1 minute, then stir. Dip tops of each muffin, hot from the oven, in glaze.

Makes 10-12 muffins

from **The McCallum House**
613 West 32nd Street
Austin, TX 78705
512-451-6744

To add fiber, Innkeeper Nancy Danley uses homemade oat flour as a substitute for one-third of flour in all her baking. She also tries to reduce cholesterol, often using just an egg white, as in this recipe she has modified.

Nancy and Roger Danley opened their B&B in 1983, when few B&Bs existed in Texas. Nancy worked as a conference planner at the University of Texas and Roger has a remodeling construction business, so their skills were perfect to turn the spacious 1907 home into a comfortable five-guestroom inn.

The house was built by Jane Y. and A.N. McCallum. Jane was a leader of the suffrage movement until women achieved the vote in 1920. Meetings of "suffragists" were held downstairs in the large living room. Today, the hallway walls are lined with newspaper clips about her efforts, and Nancy has been fortunate to find a suffrage banner and other memorabilia.

Other McCallum House recipes:
Oatmeal Breakfast Cake, page 39
Mexican Puff, page 125
Migas, page 126

Linzer Muffins

Ingredients:

    2 cups flour
    2/3 cup sugar
    1 tablespoon baking powder
    1/2 teaspoon salt
    1/2 teaspoon cinnamon
    1 egg, beaten
    1/3 cup butter, melted
    1 cup milk
    12 heaping teaspoons raspberry (or other favorite) jam
    12 teaspoons almonds, ground

- In a large bowl, sift together flour, sugar, baking powder, salt and cinnamon.
- Stir in the egg, butter and milk just until all ingredients are blended.
- Fill 12 greased or paper-lined muffin tins half-full with batter.
- Top batter with a spoonful of jam, then nuts, then other half of batter.
- Bake in preheated oven at 400 degrees for 20 minutes or until tops appear dry.

Tester's Comments: Wonderful with apricot, apple or raspberry butters as well as jam. Err on the small side when filling muffin tins with batter; fill them slightly less than half-full before adding jam and nuts or you can't cover the jam and nuts with the top layer of batter.

Makes 12 muffins

from **The Victorian Inn of Prescott**
246 South Cortez Street
Prescott, AZ 86303
602-778-2642

While Innkeeper Tamia Thunstedt calls these muffins "kissin' cousin to European Linzer torte," she notes "strawberry or apricot jams are good, too," instead of traditional raspberry. It just so happens, however, that raspberry matches the color theme of her breakfast table, echoed in placemats, linen napkins, the china pattern and even the flower vase.

Tamia opened this Queen Anne home as a four-guestroom inn in 1990. She "fell in love with the house. I considered a quilt or antique shop, but decided it was perfect for a B&B." Tamia makes it especially photogenic at Christmas, with help from Jaycees and firefighters who donate time to install thousands of Christmas lights outlining the house. The 1893 home is so picture-perfect it appears on a local postcard featuring Victorian architecture in Prescott.

🏠 *Other Victorian Inn recipes:*
Cashew Coconut Whole Wheat Muffins, page 46
Amaretto and Applesauce, page 100

Morning Glory Muffins

Ingredients:

- 1-1/2 cups whole wheat flour
- 1-1/2 cups flour
- 1 tablespoon baking soda   3/4 Tbs.
- 2-1/4 teaspoons cinnamon
- 1/2 teaspoon salt
- 2 whole eggs
- 2 egg whites
- 3/4 cup vegetable oil
- 3/4 cup honey
- 1/2 cup apple juice concentrate
- 2 teaspoons vanilla extract
- 2/3 cup crushed pineapple, drained
- 3/4 cup coconut
- 3 cups carrots, shredded
- 1-1/2 cups apples, diced
- 3/4 cup nuts, chopped

- Sift flours, baking soda, cinnamon and salt together. Set aside.
- In a large bowl, mix eggs, egg whites, oil, honey, juice concentrate and vanilla.
- Mix in the flours. Then stir in pineapple, coconut, carrots, apples and nuts.
- Fill greased and floured muffin tins two-thirds full.
- Bake in a preheated oven at 350 degrees for 15 to 20 minutes until muffins are golden brown.

Makes about 24 muffins

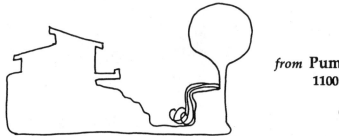

from **Pumpkinshell Ranch**
11005 East Johnson Road
HC 66, Box 2100
Cornville, AZ 86325
602-634-4797

"These delicious muffins have reduced egg yolks and no white sugar. And fruits, vegetables and whole wheat flour make them high in fiber," said Innkeeper Kay Johnson. Kay makes them in batches of 80 to serve guests before a full breakfast in her B&B. Kay and Terry, her husband, built their dream home on a hillside above a small waterfall, which the guestrooms overlook. Kay opened the B&B in 1989 to use her considerable cooking skills and to enjoy the company of visitors to the Cornville-Sedona area.

Other Pumpkinshell Ranch recipes:
Irish Coffee, page 27
Aunt Gladys' Buttermilk Biscuits, page 44
Zucchini Muffins, page 62
Hollandaise Sauce, page 90
Irish Soda Bread, page 171

Orange Mini-Muffins

Ingredients:

1 cup butter or margarine
1 cup sugar
2 eggs
1 teaspoon baking soda
1 cup buttermilk
2 cups flour
1/2 cup golden raisins
Grated peel of 2 oranges (about 5 tablespoons)

Glaze:
1 cup brown sugar, packed
Juice of 2 oranges (about 1/2 cup)

- In a large bowl, cream butter and sugar with an electric mixer.
- Add eggs and beat until fluffy.
- Dissolve baking soda in buttermilk.
- Add buttermilk to the egg mixture alternately with the flour.
- Stir in raisins and orange peel.
- Grease tiny tart or mini-muffin tins. Fill three-quarters full with batter. Bake in a preheated oven at 400 degrees for 15 minutes.
- For Glaze: While muffins are baking, mix brown sugar and orange juice. Pour a teaspoonful over each mini-muffin when it is still warm.

Makes 48 mini-muffins

from **Durant Star Inn**
519 East Highway 80
Sunnyvale, TX 75182
214-226-2412

Innkeeper Elaine Cromeens has made this tiny muffin recipe for years. "It's been a family favorite as well as a 'special' at bake sales," she said. "It needs to be made in the mini-pans" and isn't the same when full-sized, she said.

She and husband Jeff retired into the B&B business, naming theirs after the antique Durant and Star autos from the '20s that Jeff restores (Jeff gives guests a ride in one of his cars over to his Antique Auto Museum, located on the property). Their motto is, "Just a real good place to stay with a full breakfast."

Their restored home was built in the late 1930s and has five guestrooms, plus a honeymoon cottage, decorated with family antiques, brass and iron beds and lace curtains. Refinished wood floors, antique clawfoot tubs, crystal chandeliers and a baby grand piano are some of the home's features. The 16 acres includes a fishing pond where guests can use pedal boats, and dinner cruises at Lake Ray Hubbard are only 10 minutes away. Dallas is 16 miles west, making the B&B convenient for business and pleasure travelers.

Peach and Poppyseed Muffins

Ingredients:

2-1/2 cups puréed fresh peaches
1 teaspoon baking soda
10 tablespoons butter or margarine (1/2 cup plus 2 tablespoons)
1 cup sugar
2 eggs
1-1/4 cups flour
1/2 teaspoon vanilla extract
1/4 teaspoon salt
3 tablespoons poppyseeds

- Stir peaches and baking soda together.

- In a separate bowl, cream butter and sugar.

- Mix in eggs, flour, peach mixture, vanilla and salt, in that order.

- Add poppyseeds last.

- Fill greased or paper-lined muffin tins three-quarters full. Bake in a preheated oven at 350 degrees for 25 minutes or until a toothpick inserted in the center comes out clean.

Makes 12 muffins

from **The Wild Flower Inn**
1200 West 22-1/2 Street
Austin, TX 78705
512-477-9639

This treasured recipe was handed down to Innkeeper Kay Jackson from her 91-year-old Aunt Jewel. Kay advises using "junior" baby food peaches if fresh peaches are not available.

Kay, who former worked in special education, and Claudean Schultz, a textbook administrator, had started a small wooden crafts business together. Once while taking a business trip, they stayed in a B&B. "We really liked it and explored whether we could do that as a business," Kay said. Each ended a 24-year career to move to Austin and open their four-guestroom inn.

The two women bought a 50-year-old house that had been broken up into apartments. They removed walls and kitchen units, restored original floors, painted and began stenciling that is still going on today. They share an apartment they left intact in the back of the house. Well-mannered house dogs Samantha, a golden retriever/Australian shepherd, and Shorty, a terrier about whom, Kay said, "the name fits," also welcome guests.

Other Wild Flower Inn recipes:
Healthy Muffins, page 51
Wonderful Applesauce Muffins, page 61
Wild Flower Apple Bread, page 80

Pineapple Bran Muffins

Ingredients:

1/2 cup boiling water
1 cup Nabisco 100% Bran cereal
1/2 cup Kellogg's All-Bran cereal
1-1/2 teaspoons baking soda
1 cup buttermilk
1/4 cup canola oil
1 egg
3/4 cup brown sugar, packed
1/2 teaspoon salt
1-1/4 cups flour
1/2 cup fresh pineapple or half of an 8-ounce can crushed pineapple, in natural juice

- In a large bowl, pour boiling water over cereals to soften. Set aside.
- Add baking soda to buttermilk and stir. Set aside.
- In a large bowl, beat canola oil and egg. Mix in brown sugar, salt and flour.
- Stir in softened cereals and buttermilk.
- Mix in pineapple.
- Fill greased or paper-lined muffin cups. Bake in a preheated oven at 375 degrees for 20 minutes.

Tester's Comments: Batter can be kept, covered, in refrigerator for a week. Beat extra pineapple into softened cream cheese and spread on muffins, warm or cold.

Makes 15 muffins

from **Alexander's Inn**
529 East Palace Avenue
Santa Fe, NM 87501
505-986-1431

These muffins combine good-for-you fiber with great taste, said **Manager Mary Jo Schneider**, who, along with **Owner Carolyn Delecluse**, stirs up some type of muffin daily to serve guests. In the winter, breakfast is served by the woodstove. In the summer, guests eat outside on the garden-side deck.

Carolyn's son is probably the only pre-schooler around to have his own inn. Carolyn named it after Alexander after they moved from Paris to Santa Fe in 1987. "I wanted to do something that would allow me to provide for us while staying at home and caring for him myself," she said. She bought the house that fall and began renovation and improvements. The brick and wood two-story home has five guestrooms, including a guesthouse.

Another Alexander's Inn recipe:
Cheesy Artichoke Squares, page 197

Raisin Bran Muffins

Ingredients:

2 cups flour
3/4 cup whole wheat flour
1 tablespoon and 1 teaspoon baking soda
1/2 tablespoon salt
1/2 cup sugar
1/2 cup brown sugar, packed
2/3 cup vegetable oil
2 eggs
2 tablespoons molasses
2-1/2 tablespoons honey
2 cups buttermilk
1-1/2 cups raisin bran cereal
1 cup all-bran cereal
1/2 cup raisins

- In a large bowl, mix flours, baking soda and salt. Set aside.
- In a separate bowl, beat sugars, oil, eggs, molasses and honey.
- Beat buttermilk into egg mixture alternately with flour mixture.
- Stir in cereals and raisins.
- Put in a tightly-covered container and refrigerate overnight. "Keeps well for three to four weeks."
- In the morning, stir well. Place 1/4 cup batter into greased and floured or paper-lined muffin tins.
- Bake in a preheated oven at 375 degrees for 20 minutes.

Tester's Comments: Batter kept over long periods may darken; discard that portion. The molasses is a tasty and unusual addition and the buttermilk makes these bake up moist.

Makes about 36 muffins

from **Antik Haus Inn**
118 South Union Street
New Braunfels, TX 78130
512-625-6666

Innkeeper Loretta Dueweke doubles this recipe, then scoops out enough batter to make fresh-baked muffins every morning. Breakfast might be served in the two formal dining rooms of this 1907 house, or outdoors in the gazebo.

Loretta and Ralph bought this two-story brick home, built by one of New Braunfels' blacksmiths, while teachers in Michigan. They worked summers to restore the Victorian home to its early grandeur and are now year 'round innkeepers. The inn is steps from the Comal River tube chute for innertubing.

Another Antik Haus Inn recipe:
Tex-Mex Egg Casserole, page 136

Sour Cream Muffins

Ingredients:
1/2 cup butter or margarine
1-1/2 cups sugar
1/2 teaspoon salt
4 eggs
1 teaspoon baking soda
1/8 teaspoon nutmeg
1-1/2 cups sour cream
2-3/4 cups cake flour
1 to 2 cups fresh or frozen "dry pack" blueberries, optional

Also:
Sugar

- In a large bowl, cream butter, sugar and salt until light and fluffy.
- Add eggs, baking soda, nutmeg, sour cream and flour, beating well after each addition.
- Gently stir in blueberries by hand.
- Fill greased or paper-lined muffin tins three-quarters full. Sprinkle with sugar.
- Bake in a preheated oven at 450 degrees for 15 minutes.

Tester's Comments: Even better with streusel topping (1/2 cup flour, 1/2 cup brown sugar, 1/4 cup butter). You may substitute "lite" sour cream or part plain yogurt for sour cream, all-purpose unbleached flour for cake flour, or raspberries for blueberries.

Makes 21 muffins

from **Wild Briar Inn**
Farm Road 2339
P.O. Box 21
Edom/Ben Wheeler, TX 75754
903-852-3975

"Blueberry season in Edom is June 6-July 6," notes Innkeeper Mary Scott, who has been enjoying the East Texas fruit all her life. If she doesn't put them in muffins, fresh ones might show up in a fruit bowl for breakfast.

She and Max, who traveled extensively in Great Britain staying in country inns, came home to plan their own retreat. Wild Briar, set amid 23 acres, is a contemporary home with six guestrooms. Each is decorated in a British, Welsh, Scottish or French style, reflecting touches the Scotts recall from five years of travels. Like a traditional country inn, dinner is offered by reservation. During the day, guests can wander the grounds, visit antique or craft stores nearby or enjoy the East Texas piney woods.

Another Wild Briar Inn recipe:
Poppyseed Dressing, page 94

Sunday Morning Muffins

Ingredients:

1 cup sour cream
1/4 cup butter, melted
1 egg, beaten
1 cup bran flakes cereal
1/3 cup sugar
1 cup flour
1 teaspoon cinnamon
3/4 teaspoon baking soda
1/2 teaspoon salt
1 cup apples, chopped

- In a large bowl, mix sour cream, butter and egg.
- Stir in bran flakes. Let the mixture stand until the flakes absorb the moisture.
- Stir in sugar, flour, cinnamon, baking soda and salt. Mix only until all ingredients are moistened.
- Fold in the apples.
- Fill greased or paper-lined muffin tins nearly full.
- Bake in a preheated oven at 400 degrees for 20 minutes, or until a toothpick inserted in the center comes out clean. Let the muffins stand about 10 minutes. Serve warm.

Tester's Comments: Using bran flakes means these muffins don't seem like grainy bran muffins. The apples don't have to be peeled. Plain yogurt could be substituted for the sour cream.

Makes 10 muffins

from **Small Inn**
4815 West Bayshore Drive
Bacliff, TX 77518
713-339-3489

Innkeeper Harriet Small makes these muffins more often than just on Sunday. Her guests might enjoy them along with an egg dish, sausage or bacon and beverages, served poolside all year long, weather permitting. If, unfortunately, the weather doesn't permit, guests still enjoy breakfast with a view of the pool and Galveston Bay from the Small's dining area.

Harriet has a catering background and has served groups as large as 250. At the Small Inn, her talents are lavished on just two adult guests, and possibly their children, at a time, since she operates one guestroom. "My guests can contract for all meals and even meals where they invite guests, " she notes.

Other Small Inn recipes:
Pineapple Rum Punch, page 28
Persimmon Bread, page 73
Raisin Pumpkin Bread, page 76

Wonderful Applesauce Muffins

Ingredients:

1-1/2 cups oatmeal
3/4 teaspoon cinnamon
1 teaspoon baking powder ~reduce
1-1/4 cups flour
1/2 teaspoon nutmeg
3/4 teaspoon baking soda
1/4 cup butter
1/2 cup brown sugar, packed
1/2 cup sugar
1 egg
1 teaspoon vanilla extract
1/2 cup half-and-half
1 cup unsweetened applesauce

Topping:
1/3 cup brown sugar, packed
1/3 cup pecans, chopped
1/3 cup coconut

- In a large bowl, combine oatmeal, cinnamon, baking powder, flour, nutmeg and baking soda.

- In a separate bowl, cream butter, sugars, egg and vanilla.

- Mix sugar mixture into dry ingredients with the half-and-half and applesauce. Mix well.

- Fill greased or paper-lined muffin tins almost three-quarters full.

- For Topping: Combine brown sugar, pecans and coconut. Sprinkle each muffin with a heaping teaspoon of the mixture.

- Bake in a preheated oven at 400 degrees for 20 minutes or until a toothpick inserted in the center comes out clean.

Tester's Comments: Don't make these without the topping -- it's what makes them so wonderful!

Makes 18 muffins

from **The Wild Flower Inn**
1200 West 22-1/2 Street
Austin, TX 78705
512-477-9639

Innkeeper Kay Jackson created these in the kitchen one morning, and they turned out to be a hit. "Then I had to try to re-create them after I'd done it the first time!" She and co-innkeeper Claudean Schultz serve muffins as part of a full breakfast, and it's not uncommon to find Kay "ad libbing" with muffin recipes. Kay returned to her home town of Austin when the two opened this inn in 1990. It is located seven blocks from the University of Texas campus.

Other Wild Flower Inn recipes:
Healthy Muffins, page 51
Peach and Poppyseed Muffins, page 56
Wild Flower Apple Bread, page 80

Zucchini Muffins

Ingredients:

3 eggs
1 cup vegetable oil
1 cup sugar
1 cup brown sugar, packed
1 tablespoon maple flavoring
2 cups zucchini, shredded
2-1/2 cups flour
1/2 teaspoon baking powder
2 teaspoons salt
2 teaspoons baking soda
1/2 cup wheat germ
1 cup walnuts, chopped

Also:

Sesame seeds

In a large bowl, mix eggs, oil, sugars and maple flavoring. Beat until the mixture is thick, foamy and light in color. Stir in zucchini by hand.

In a separate bowl, sift flour, baking powder, salt and baking soda together. Mix in wheat germ and walnuts.

Stir flour mixture gently into zucchini mixture. Blend well.

Fill greased and floured muffin tins two-thirds full. Sprinkle tops of muffins with sesame seeds.

Bake in a preheated oven at 350 degrees for 20 to 25 minutes or until a toothpick inserted in the center comes out clean.

Makes 24-30 muffins

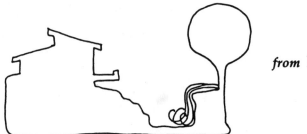

from **Pumpkinshell Ranch**
11005 East Johnson Road
HC 66, Box 2100
Cornville, AZ 86325
602-634-4797

These muffins freeze well if they are thoroughly cooled before freezing, said Innkeeper Kay Johnson. Kay, who studied cooking at Maxim's in Paris, often serves these muffins with coffee before guests sit down to a full breakfast that they've ordered off an extensive menu. She has an unique incentive to encourage long stays: "If you stay 10 days, you get 10 different muffins, 10 different breakfasts, and 10 different fancy napkin folds!"

Other Pumpkinshell Ranch recipes:
Irish Coffee, page 27
Aunt Gladys' Buttermilk Biscuits, page 44
Morning Glory Muffins, page 54
Hollandaise Sauce, page 90
Irish Soda Bread, page 171

Any way you slice it, absolutely *nothing* beats the smell of bread baking on a chilly morning. Well, perhaps the smell of cinnamon rolls baking. Some recipes for rolls and breads with yeast, requiring time to "rise," are included. Several recipes are for sweet breads that can be whipped up in a few minutes, and which would do justice served as dessert. (And many of those are so moist and flavorful they require no buttering.) No matter what side you butter your bread on, there's sure to be a recipe to please you. These creations run the gamut of traditional to creative, from basic bread to unusual persimmon bread, nutty beer bread or banana bread with chocolate chips.

Breads

Apricot Banana Bread

Ingredients:
2 cups flour
1 teaspoon baking powder
1/2 teaspoon baking soda
1/2 teaspoon salt
1 cup sugar
1/2 cup dried apricots, chopped
1/2 cup walnuts, chopped
3/4 cup ripe banana, mashed
1/2 cup milk
1 egg
1/4 cup butter or margarine, melted

Also:
Honey butter, whipped

- In a large bowl, mix flour, baking powder, baking soda, salt and sugar.
- Stir in chopped apricots and nuts, mixing until nuts and apricots are well-coated.
- In a separate bowl, combine banana, milk, egg and butter.
- Stir banana mixture into dry ingredients just until all are well-blended.
- Grease three small (3 x 5-1/2 inches) or one regular bread loaf pan. Pour in the batter, which will be fairly stiff.
- Bake in a preheated oven at 350 degrees for 45 minutes (for small loaves, longer for large loaf), or until bread begins to shrink from the sides of the pans.
- Let bread cool in pans for 10 minutes, then turn out onto a rack to cool. Freezes well
- Serve with whipped honey butter.

Tester's Comments: Outstanding toasted with butter (the apricot bits get warm and chewy). Try substituting 2/3 cup buttermilk for 1/2 cup milk. Apricots can be snipped with clean kitchen shears, instead of chopped.

Makes 3 mini-loaves or 1 bread loaf

from **Graham's B&B Inn**
150 Canyon Circle Drive
Sedona, AZ 86336
602-284-1425

Homemade bread is often on the menu for breakfast at Bill and Marni Graham's custom-built B&B. The Grahams serve a full breakfast poolside, weather permitting, or by the two-sided fireplace in the dining room. Marni and Bill got "red rock fever" and moved to Sedona in 1984. He was sales manager for a food company, she was a legal secretary in northern California, and it was time for a new challenge. They built a five-guestroom inn and opened in 1985. Each second-floor guestroom has a balcony overlooking Sedona's Bell Rock or other vistas. Guests are free to use the outdoor pool and hot tub. The Grahams have earned a four-star rating for several years.

Arizona Date Mini-Bread

Ingredients:

1/2 cup pitted Arizona dates, chopped
2 tablespoons vegetable oil
2 teaspoons baking soda
1 cup boiling water
2/3 cup brown sugar, packed
2 cups whole wheat flour
1 egg, beaten

- In a mixing bowl, combine dates, oil, baking soda and boiling water. Let stand 30 minutes.
- Stir in brown sugar, flour and egg just until all ingredients are moist.
- Pour batter into three greased mini-loaf pans, measuring 3-1/4 x 5-3/8 inches.
- Bake in a preheated oven at 350 degrees for 40-45 minutes or until a knife inserted in the center comes out clean. Remove bread from pans while still warm.

Tester's Comments: Easily made in one regular bread-loaf pan; bake about 10 minutes longer. Substituting 1-3/4 cups unbleached flour for same amount of whole wheat still makes a dark bread. Spread with cream cheese.

Makes 3 mini-loaves or 1 bread loaf

from **Maricopa Manor**
15 West Pasadena Avenue
Phoenix, AZ 85013
602-274-6302

Nell Dunn, a native Arizonan who cooked for cowboys on a ranch in the 1920s, devised this recipe, which has been modified a bit by Innkeeper Mary Ellen Kelley. At her Maricopa Manor, well-groomed business travelers might be enjoying this bread, rather than dusty cowhands. Mary Ellen and Paul bring the mini-loaves to the doors of their five guestrooms as part of a picnic basket. Guests may eat in the privacy of their suite or on one of several decks on the acre of lawn, perhaps by the fountain or under the orange trees.

Mary Ellen and Paul raised 11 children and foster children in this large Spanish-style home five miles from the heart of Phoenix. In 1989, they opened the manor house and a guesthouse as a B&B, and soon thereafter Paul was elected vice-president of the growing Arizona Association of B&B Inns. Today, their comfortable urban inn has accommodations appropriate for business travelers, traditional B&B-lovers and families.

Other Maricopa Manor recipes:
Mary Ellen's Apricot Breakfast Bars, page 187
Mary Ellen's Breakfast Cookies, page 188
Mexican Hors d'Oeuvres, page 205

Basque Sheepherder's Sourdough Bread

Ingredients:

3 cups milk
3 tablespoons butter or margarine
3/8 cup honey
1-1/2 ounces fresh baker's yeast (or active dry yeast)
2 tablespoons warm water
1-1/2 quarts active sourdough
6 cups whole wheat flour, freshly ground, if possible, and divided
3 tablespoons sugar
3 teaspoons baking soda
3 teaspoons salt
3/8 cup wheat germ, optional
3 cups white bread flour

In a large bowl, mix milk, butter and honey. Heat to 105 degrees in a microwave oven. Add fresh yeast (purchased in a block, like tofu, from a local bakery) or dry yeast and warm water.

In a larger bowl, put active sourdough culture. Stir in the milk mixture and 3 cups whole wheat flour. Mix in sugar, baking soda and salt.

Place in a warm oven with a pan of hot water and cover with a damp towel. (Do not have oven on a setting any higher than "warm" or dough will form a crust.) Let rise 30 minutes.

Remove from the oven and add remaining 3 cups whole wheat flour. (If not freshly ground, add wheat germ.) Add about 3 cups white flour until dough is "too stiff to stir with a spoon."

Turn dough out onto a floured board. Knead and add white flour until dough is just manageable.

Pat dough into a circle about two inches thick. Cut into four sections. Put each section into a greased and floured loaf pan. Spray the top of each loaf with non-stick cooking spray. Return pans to the warm oven and cover. Let rise to the top of the pan, 30 minutes for fresh yeast, 45-60 for dry yeast.

Bake in a preheated oven at 400 degrees for 18 minutes or until the crust is brown. Reduce temperature to 325 degrees and bake 10 more minutes or until bread shrinks from the sides of the pan.

Makes 4 loaves

from **Casita Chamisa**
850 Chamisal Road NW
Albuquerque, NM 87107
505-897-4644

Innkeeper Arnold Sargeant's sourdough was started by a Basque sheepherder in northern Idaho in 1880. Arnold and Kit make this bread part of breakfast in their Rio Grande River-valley home, which is more than 200 years old. It is the site of a 10-year archaeological dig, led by Kit, which has uncovered more than 150,000 pottery shards, plus tools and bones among the village site. Kit and Arnold, formerly in the Army, moved here so Kit could pursue archaeology at the university. Today their adobe home has one guestroom and a guesthouse. Travelers can pet the dogs, talk to the parrot, sit on the porch swing, learn about beekeeping or swim in the indoor pool.

Bear Mountain Guest Ranch Basic Bread

Ingredients:

1 egg
1/2 cup sugar
1/2 cup safflower or corn oil
4 cups warm water (no hotter than 115 degrees)
1 tablespoon salt
5 cups whole wheat flour, divided
1-1/2 tablespoons active dry yeast
3-1/2 cups white flour

Fillings (make 1/2 cup or more):
   Date: Chopped dates (or raisins)
   Cinnamon: Sugar and cinnamon
   Orange: 1/2 cup sugar and
        3/4 teaspoon grated rind
   Apple: 1 diced apple with 1/2 cup
        sugar, 1/2 cup raisins and
        1-1/2 teaspoons cinnamon

- In a large bowl, mix egg, sugar, oil, water and salt.

- Stir in 2 cups whole wheat flour and yeast. Mix well.

- Stir in remaining wheat flour and enough white flour so dough does not stick to sides of bowl.

- Turn dough out onto a floured board. Cover with cloth and let rest for 10 minutes.

- Knead dough about 10 minutes. Place dough in large, well-greased bowl. Cover with clean cloth and let rise until double in bulk (about 1 hour, or "when your finger, touching the dough, leaves a dent that remains"). Then punch down the dough and cut into five one-pound units.

- For unfilled bread, shape loaves and place in greased pans. Let rise until double in bulk (about 1 hour). Then bake in a preheated oven at 400 degrees for 35 to 40 minutes or until loaves are brown.

- For filled bread, roll each section into a rectangle 1/4-inch thick and as wide as the long side of the bread loaf pan. Spread the rectangle with one of the fillings.

- Roll from each end of the rectangle to the center. Place loaf seam-side down in the loaf pan. Repeat with other four units. Follow directions above for unfilled bread.

Makes 5 loaves

from **Bear Mountain Guest Ranch**
2251 Bear Mountain Road
P.O. Box 1163
Silver City, NM 88062
505-538-2538

"I made up the variations on a recipe that my mother handed down to me," said Innkeeper Myra McCormick. "I serve this bread at dinner and toasted at breakfast. Breakfast is served at 8 a.m., buffet style, in the birdwatching room. Unfilled bread is a special treat for picnic lunches."

Birdwatching is a favorite activity here, where migrating species can be spotted in the spring and fall. Myra has organized a monthly bird identification class, as well as wild plant and bicycle tours of the 3 million-acre Gila National Forest. The ranch house, built on 160 acres in 1928, is a two-story home to which she moved "because Albuquerque was getting far too big 32 years ago." Silver City (250 miles southwest of Albuquerque) has a population of about 11,000, and the ranch is at an elevation of 6,250 feet. Myra serves guests three meals a day.

Chocolate Chip Banana Nut Bread

Ingredients:

1 cup butter
1 cup sugar
2 eggs
1 cup ripe bananas, mashed (2 or 3 bananas)
1/4 cup buttermilk
1 teaspoon vanilla extract
1-1/2 cups flour
1/2 teaspoon salt
2/3 teaspoon baking soda
1 cup semi-sweet chocolate chips
1 cup favorite nuts, usually pecans or walnuts

- In a large mixing bowl, cream the butter and sugar until light and fluffy.
- Blend in eggs, bananas, buttermilk and vanilla.
- Mix in dry ingredients, just until blended. Then stir in chocolate chips and nuts by hand.
- Pour the batter into two greased bread loaf pans.
- Bake in a preheated oven at 350 degrees for 45 to 50 minutes, until golden brown, or until a toothpick inserted in the center comes out clean.

Tester's Comments: Adding the chocolate chips is one of those "how come nobody did this before?" ideas that makes perfect sense. Chocolate lovers won't make banana bread without chips again.

Makes 2 loaves

from **The Galisteo Inn**
Off Highway 41
HC 75, Box 4
Galisteo, NM 87540
505-982-1506

The owners of the Galisteo Inn pride themselves on providing an unusual haven for guests, and this banana bread with chocolate chips is an unusual breakfast treat. "This is a simple banana bread recipe, but adding the chocolate chips makes it totally irresistible to our guests, even at breakfast," said Innkeeper Joanna Kaufman. Breakfast is not the only irresistible offering of this inn. Irresistible dinners are served, too. Guests can horseback ride under the cottonwoods on the eight acres, or stroll down by the pond, or take a bike ride or a swim. Several of the 12 guestrooms have fireplaces.

Other Galisteo Inn recipes:
Cranberry Smoothie Fruit Drink, page 23
Cranberry Raspberry Muffins, page 47
Galisteo Inn Cornmeal Scones, page 50
Galisteo Inn Cornmeal Waffles, page 154
Pumpkin Cheesecake, page 174

Grandma's Date Nut Bread

Ingredients:

1 8-ounce package pitted Arizona dates
1-1/2 teaspoons baking soda
1 cup boiling water
1 tablespoon butter
3/4 cup sugar
1 egg
1/2 cup nuts, chopped
1 teaspoon vanilla extract
1/2 teaspoon salt
1-1/2 cups sifted flour

🥄 Spray a loaf pan with non-stick cooking spray. Set aside.

🥄 Place dates and baking soda in a bowl. Pour boiling water over them. Set aside.

🥄 In a large bowl or food processor, cream butter and sugar.

🥄 Beat in egg. Then beat in nuts, vanilla and salt.

🥄 Pour in the dates, soda and water. Mix well. Add the flour last. Pour the batter into the loaf pan.

🥄 Bake in a preheated oven at 350 degrees for 1 hour or until a toothpick inserted in the center comes out clean.

Makes 1 loaf

from **B&B at Saddle Rock Ranch**
255 Rockridge Drive
Sedona, AZ 86336
602-282-7640

"This recipe was given to me by my maternal grandmother," said Innkeeper Fran Bruno. "Her family was among the original pioneer settlers in Devil's Lake, North Dakota. She cooked without a written recipe, stirring in a bit of this, a pinch of that. It took me several weeks of 'assisting' in the bread's preparation in order to replicate the recipe."

Fran and Dan, a former Pittsburgh Steeler and professional Indy and Grand Prix driver, settled into innkeeping in this historic ranch home after managing the Ritz-Carlton. The main house, built in the '20s, is on three choice acres. The red stone floors and adobe walls were made on-site, and the wood beams were shipped down from Flagstaff. Nearly every room, including the two guestrooms and guest cottage, has a stone fireplace. Outside, a cascade connects the whirlpool and swimming pool, which guests are welcome to use. Breakfast may be served poolside or in the rock-walled breakfast room.

🏠*Other B&B at Saddle Rock Ranch recipes:*
Saddle Rock Ranch Jammie Cake, page 42
Peachy Wheat Germ Waffles, page 156

Nutty Beer Bread

Ingredients:

1-1/2 cups self-rising flour
1/2 cup wheat germ
1/3 cup pecans, chopped
1/4 cup sugar
10 ounces beer
1/4 cup butter or margarine, melted

- In a large bowl, mix flour, wheat germ, pecans and sugar.
- Add beer and mix lightly.
- Melt butter or margarine in a loaf pan. Spread bread batter over butter.
- Bake in a preheated oven at 350 degrees for about 50 minutes, or until golden brown.
- Remove bread from oven, turn out onto a rack and cool for a few minutes before slicing.

Makes 1 loaf

from **Westways Resort Inn**
Off Bell Road in Northwest Phoenix
P.O. Box 41624
Phoenix, AZ 85080
602-582-3868

"If there is any left over the next day, this makes the best French toast," said Innkeeper Darrell Trapp. Guests here may enjoy breakfast wherever they please -- in the formal oak-paneled dining room, in the Arizona Leisure Room by the fireplace, in the eat-in kitchen, or poolside on the patio.

Located adjacent to Thunderbird Park and Arrowhead Ranch in northwest Phoenix, Westways is a 5,000-square-foot inn on an acre of landscaped grounds. The inn, built in 1983, was completely renovated in 1987 as a private resort. Decor is "Arizona contemporary Spanish Mediterranean" and furnishings are leather, oak, wicker, rattan and antiques.

Six guestrooms, called "casitas," all have double or queen beds, private baths, TVs and amenities. Outdoors, guests can swim in the 40-foot pool, enjoy the fountain, relax in the whirlpool and soak up the sun. A fitness area has weights and other equipment. Guests may use bicycles and tennis racquets, or borrow a set of golf clubs to play at the nearby Arrowhead Country Club.

Other Westways recipes:
Westways Enchiladas de Zucchini, page 158
Keeper of the Inn Pinto Beans, page 163

Orange Walnut Bread

Ingredients:

2 eggs
1/2 cup vegetable oil
4 cups flour
1-2/3 cups sugar
1/2 teaspoon salt
2 tablespoons baking powder
1 large seedless orange, unpeeled
1-1/2 cups milk
1 cup walnuts, finely chopped

- In a large bowl, beat eggs and gradually add oil. Beat for 1 minute.

- In a separate bowl, sift together flour, sugar, salt and baking powder. Mix into egg mixture.

- Cut the orange into small pieces. Put pieces in a blender. Blend at high speed until finely chopped.

- Add orange to bread batter. Then slowly beat in milk. Beat for 2 minutes. Stir in nuts.

- Grease and flour two bread loaf pans. Pour in batter and let stand for 20 minutes.

- Bake in a preheated oven at 400 degrees for 20 minutes or until the dough has started to brown. Reduce heat to 300 degrees. Remove bread and score tops of loaves lengthwise. Return to oven and bake 40 minutes more or until a toothpick inserted in the center comes out clean. Let pans cool for 10 minutes before turning bread out onto a rack.

Tester's Comments: Using the whole orange really works, but I needed to add about 2 tablespoons of orange juice to get my blender to chop it finely. French toast made using this bread is tasty, too, and filling.

Makes 2 loaves, 24 slices

from **Orinda**
1 Orinda Lane
P.O. Box 4451
Taos, NM 87571
505-758-8581

Innkeeper Karol Dondero's bread often is used for French toast at this inn. Karol or Dave dip slices into an egg/cinnamon mixture. Of course, the bread is made the day before. "The breakfasts served at Orinda," they write in the forward to their own cookbook, "must fill one of two basic criteria: they must be able to prepared by a comatose innkeeper in less than 20 minutes...or they must be able to be made in large quantities ahead of time, and then completed and served in less time than it takes Spencer Christian to do the weather on 'Good Morning, America.'" The Donderos are fully awake when they welcome guests to the two suites, both with kiva fireplaces. Orinda is set in an open meadow close to Taos Plaza and five minutes from Taos Pueblo.

Another Orinda recipe:
Overnight Baked Apples, page 111

Pecan and Cinnamon Clusters

Ingredients:

1 loaf frozen white bread dough
1 cup butter or margarine, divided
1/2 cup brown sugar, packed
1/2 cup pecans, chopped
1/2 cup sugar
3/4 teaspoon cinnamon

- Defrost dough overnight in the refrigerator.

- Lightly grease 6 to 8 cupcake or muffin cups. Place 1 tablespoon butter and 1 tablespoon brown sugar in each. Top with 1 tablespoon pecans.

- In a separate bowl, melt remaining 1/2 cup butter or margarine. Set aside.

- In a separate bowl, mix sugar and cinnamon.

- Pinch off walnut-sized pieces of defrosted dough. Roll each piece in melted butter, then sugar cinnamon mixture. Place 3 pieces in each cupcake cups.

- Let rise about 40 minutes, then bake in a preheated oven at 350 degrees for 15 to 18 minutes. Or cover and refrigerate until the next morning (allow dough to come to room temperature and rise slightly in the morning before baking).

- Immediately after baking, invert pan on a serving plate and allow syrup to drizzle over the rolls.

Makes 6-8 rolls

from **White House B&B**
217 Mittman Circle
New Braunfels, TX 78132
512-629-9354

Hardly anyone has time to make from-scratch yeast rolls anymore, innkeepers included, and frozen dough often saves the day for Beverly White. Beverly has been baking since she was "12 or 13 years of age because my mother hated to bake, but was an excellent all-American cook." Every breakfast here includes homemade sweet rolls, muffins or breads, as well as a hearty entree.

Beverly and Jerry took early retirement and moved from Illinois to New Braunfels to open a B&B. They bought a Spanish-style home on more than an acre of grounds, complete with a small fishing pond and a row of fruit trees. They opened two guestrooms in 1987.

Guests often come to New Braunfels for innertubing through town on crystal-clear rivers, enjoying German restaurants and shopping in new outlet malls. The Natural Bridge Caverns are a short drive from this B&B.

Another White House recipe:
Sweet Thick Rice, page 177

Persimmon Bread

Ingredients:

2 eggs
1-1/2 cups sugar
1/2 cup vegetable oil
1 cup persimmon, puréed in the blender
1-3/4 cups flour
1 teaspoon baking soda
1 teaspoon salt
1/2 teaspoon cloves
1/2 teaspoon cinnamon
1/2 teaspoon nutmeg
1/2 teaspoon allspice
1/4 teaspoon baking powder
1/2 cup raisins

- In a large bowl, beat eggs.

- Mix in sugar, oil and persimmon purée.

- In a separate bowl, sift together flour, baking soda, salt, cloves, cinnamon, nutmeg, allspice and baking powder.

- Stir dry ingredients into persimmon mixture.

- Fold in raisins.

- Pour batter into a greased and floured loaf pan.

- Bake in a preheated oven at 350 degrees for 45 minutes or until a knife inserted in center comes out clean. Remove from oven and cool about 10 minutes before removing bread from pan to a wire rack.

Makes 1 loaf

from **Small Inn**
4815 West Bayshore Drive
Bacliff, TX 77518
713-339-3489

"I enjoy serving hot breads for breakfast, or with a sweet white wine or punch at 4 in the afternoon," said Innkeeper Harriet Small. She uses fresh Texas persimmons in this recipe.

Harriet, a caterer, and George, a chemical engineer, have enjoyed having guests since they opened one guestroom in 1981. The Smalls have traveled worldwide staying in B&Bs. They also enjoy the reaction of guests to their Galveston Bay-side home, complete with private dock and pool.

Other Small Inn recipes:
Pineapple Rum Punch, page 28
Sunday Morning Muffins, page 60
Raisin Pumpkin Bread, page 76

Pineapple Zucchini Bread

Ingredients:

3 eggs
1 cup vegetable oil
2 cups sugar
2 cups unpeeled zucchini, grated
3 teaspoons vanilla extract
3 cups flour
3 teaspoons cinnamon
1 teaspoon salt
1 teaspoon baking soda
1 cup pecans, chopped
1 8-ounce can crushed pineapple, with juice

In a large bowl, beat eggs, oil and sugar. Mix in the zucchini and vanilla.

In a separate bowl, combine the flour, cinnamon, salt and baking soda.

Stir the dry ingredients into the egg mixture. Then mix in pecans and pineapple.

Grease a Bundt pan or two bread loaf pans. Pour batter into prepared pan(s).

Bake in a preheated oven at 350 degrees for 45 to 60 minutes or until a knife inserted in the center comes out clean. Cool for a few minutes before inverting.

Tester's Comments: Moist and wonderful. Don't be afraid to use one-third whole wheat flour.

Makes 2 loaves

from **Carrington's Bluff B&B**
1900 David Street
Austin, TX 78705
512-479-0638

"This bread freezes well and tastes great with pineapple cream cheese," said Innkeeper Gwen Fullbrook, who makes this in a pretty Bundt ring. Homemade breads such as this always are a part of Gwen's breakfasts, served, weather permitting, on the large, roofed side porch. Guests can come out early, grab a rocking chair and sip fresh-squeezed orange juice, then dig into homemade granola and other treats. Gwen and David opened five antique-filled guestrooms in this 1877 home, located just a few minutes from the University of Texas and the state Capitol. This is the third inn for the couple, who also had a country inn in Vermont. "The third time is definitely the charm," Gwen noted.

Other Carrington's Bluff recipes:
Strawberry Pecan Bread, page 79
Apple Butter, page 84
Devonshire Cream, page 88
Homemade Granola, page 200

Poppyseed Bread

Ingredients:

3 eggs or 3/4 cup egg substitutes
2-1/4 cups sugar
1-1/2 cups vegetable oil
1-1/2 cups milk
3 cups flour
1-1/2 teaspoons baking powder
1-1/2 teaspoons salt
1-1/2 tablespoons poppyseeds
2 teaspoons almond extract

Glaze:
1/4 cup pineapple or orange juice
    concentrate
3/4 cup powdered sugar
1/2 teaspoon vanilla extract
1 teaspoon almond extract

- In a large bowl, beat eggs, sugar, oil and milk.

- In a separate bowl, combine the flour, baking powder and salt.

- Beat the dry ingredients into the egg mixture.

- Stir in poppyseeds and almond extract.

- Pour into two greased loaf pans or a greased Bundt pan. Bake in a preheated oven at 350 degrees for 45 to 60 minutes or until a toothpick inserted in the center comes out clean.

- For Glaze: While bread is baking, mix juice, sugar and extracts.

- Remove pans from oven and cool for 10 minutes, then run a knife around the edges of the pans. Invert pans and remove loaves to wire racks or to serving plates. Poke holes in the bread with a toothpick and spread or drizzle with glaze.

Tester's Comments: For lemon poppyseed bread, substitute 4 teaspoons lemon extract for almond. In the glaze, use lemon juice instead of pineapple or orange juice and lemon extract instead of almond. If on a cake plate, using all the glaze may result in the bottom becoming saturated (but yummy). Cake-like; good for dessert.

Makes 2 loaves

from **La Casa Muneca**
213 North Alameda Street
Carlsbad, NM 88220
505-887-1891

Innkeeper M.J. Lawrence makes this bread in a Bundt pan and mini-loaf pans. "The shape of the Bundt pan makes the bread look fancy when the glaze drips down the sides," she said. She often uses liquid egg substitutes and skim milk and swears "no one knows or can tell the difference." (But their arteries do.)

M.J. and Joseph moved to Carlsbad for retirement after 10 years in California. They bought a two-story house and named it "the doll house" in Spanish after M.J.'s handmade dolls and toys. In July 1990, they opened four guestrooms, two upstairs and two on the first floor, and a separate guesthouse.

Another La Casa Muneca recipe:
Pineapple-Kiwi Fruit Jam, page 93

Raisin Pumpkin Bread

Ingredients:

1 cup sugar
1/3 cup margarine
2 eggs
1 cup cooked pumpkin, mashed
1-2/3 cups flour
1 teaspoon baking soda
1/2 teaspoon cinnamon
1/2 teaspoon nutmeg
1/4 teaspoon baking powder
1/2 cup pineapple juice
1/2 cup raisins

- In a large bowl, cream margarine and sugar.
- Beat in eggs one at a time.
- Mix in pumpkin.
- In a separate bowl, sift together flour, baking soda, cinnamon, nutmeg and baking powder.
- Add dry ingredients to pumpkin mixture alternately with the pineapple juice.
- Fold in raisins.
- Pour batter into a greased and floured loaf pan.
- Bake in a preheated oven at 350 degrees for 60 minutes or a knife inserted in the center comes out clean. Cool a few minutes before removing from pan.

Makes 1 loaf

from **Small Inn**
4815 West Bayshore Drive
Bacliff, TX 77518
713-339-3489

Innkeeper Harriet Small has scaled down her recipes from her catering business. Small is better, you might say. That's one of the reasons she and husband George have only one guestroom in their B&B.

The guests who book the only room get a king-sized bed (or two twins) and a king-sized view of Galveston Bay. Guests can romp with the family dogs, swim in the private pool, fish from the dock, or get advice from George and Harriet about where to eat, fish, dance, sightsee, waterski or beachcomb. Bacliff is located between Houston and Galveston, not far from the Johnson Space Center and Houston Gulf airport.

Other Small Inn recipes:
Pineapple Rum Punch, page 28
Sunday Morning Muffins, page 60
Persimmon Bread, page 73

Schnecken (German Cinnamon Rolls)

Ingredients:

1 cup sugar
1 cup shortening
1 teaspoon salt
1 cup boiling water
2 packages active dry yeast
1 cup warm water, up to 115 degrees
2 eggs, slightly beaten
6-1/2 cups flour
Butter, melted

Filling:
2 cups brown sugar, lightly packed
1-1/2 teaspoons cinnamon
3/4 cup margarine or butter, melted
1 cup nuts, optional

☛ In a large bowl, cream sugar and shortening. One ingredient at a time, beat in salt, boiling water, yeast, warm water and eggs.

☛ Beat in 4 cups of the flour.

☛ Gradually add remaining flour, beating well after each addition.

☛ Cover and chill dough at least 4 hours, or overnight.

☛ In the morning, divide dough in half. On a lightly-floured surface, roll dough out to an 10 x 18-inch rectangle.

☛ Combine filling ingredients. Sprinkle half of the filling over rectangle.

☛ Starting with the 18-inch side, roll up jelly-roll fashion. Cut into 12 rounds 1-1/2 inches wide.

☛ Place rolls in greased 9-inch pie pans, sides not quite touching, or greased muffin tins.

☛ Repeat with second half of dough.

☛ Cover pan or tins with a towel and let rise in a warm place until dough has doubled, about 1 hour.

☛ Brush with melted butter. Bake in a preheated oven at 350 degrees for 20 to 25 minutes.

☛ Invert baking pans immediately after removing from the oven. Enjoy rolls warm. (Immediately after cooling, rolls can be frozen, then reheated when needed.)

Makes about 2 dozen rolls

from **The Oxford House**
563 North Graham Street
Stephenville, TX 76401
817-965-6885

"I grew up making a batch of these rolls with my mother for the family every week," said Innkeeper Paula Oxford. "Little did I know I would be making my own batch every week for a bed and breakfast!" "Schnecken" means "snail" for the swirl of the cinnamon roll. The homemade rolls are a favorite at this four-guestroom inn. Paula and Bill Oxford restored the 1898 mansion of Judge W.J. Oxford, Bill's grandfather, and opened their B&B in 1986.

🏠 *Other Oxford House recipes:*
Almond Tea, page 22
Raspberry Bars, page 190

Shredded Wheat Toasting Bread

Ingredients:

    2 cups boiling water
    2 shredded wheat cereal biscuits (not miniature-sized)
    1 tablespoon lard
    1 active dry yeast cake
    1 cup warm water
    1/2 cup molasses
    1 teaspoon salt
    6 cups flour

- In a large bowl, pour boiling water over shredded wheat and lard. Cool to less than 115 degrees.
- Dissolve yeast in warm water.
- Stir yeast, molasses and salt into cooled mixture.
- Mix in flour. The dough should be wet and sticky. Cover with a damp towel and let rise in a warm place overnight.
- In the morning, divide dough into two greased bread loaf pans. Let rise until the dough is a full loaf-size in the pan.
- Bake in a preheated oven at 350 degrees for 50 minutes. Turn bread out onto a rack and let cool.

Makes 2 loaves

from **The Brimstone Butterfly**
940 North Olsen Avenue
Tucson, AZ 85719
800-323-9157 or 602-322-9157

"This bread is only for toasting into a chewy, sweet, crunchy snack," said Innkeeper Maria Johnstone. "I learned this recipe from some old-timers in Brooklin, Maine, a childhood residence."

Maria bought this spacious adobe home in 1990 for a B&B, which she opened in 1991. "I've always felt a house is something that should be shared and also work for itself -- I like the old-fashioned, European idea of having your work and your house in the same location." Since she enjoyed cooking and entertaining, a B&B was a good option for her.

The guestroom in the main house has a four-poster bed. Two other suites are in adjacent adobe guesthouses. Guests enjoy the swimming pool, enclosed by an adobe wall and a hedge of fragrant jasmine. The University of Arizona and its medical center are within two blocks.

Another Brimstone Butterfly recipe:
Eggs Florentine, page 122

Strawberry Pecan Bread

Ingredients:

3 cups flour
2 cups sugar
3 teaspoons cinnamon
1 teaspoon salt
1 teaspoon baking soda
1 cup oil
1/2 cup butter, melted
4 eggs
2 10-ounce packages frozen strawberries, with syrup, defrosted
1 cup pecans, chopped

Also:

Cinnamon or nutmeg

🖝 In a large bowl, sift together the flour, sugar, cinnamon, salt and baking soda.

🖝 Blend in the oil and butter. Add eggs and beat well.

🖝 Stir in defrosted strawberries, "juice and all." Stir in pecans.

🖝 Grease a Bundt pan or two bread loaf pans. Sprinkle the pan(s) with cinnamon and/or nutmeg. Pour in the batter.

🖝 Bake in a preheated oven at 350 degrees for 45 to 60 minutes or until a knife inserted in the center comes out clean. Cool for a few minutes before inverting.

Makes 2 loaves

from **Carrington's Bluff B&B**
1900 David Street
Austin, TX 78705
512-479-0638

"This bread is wonderful served with strawberry cream cheese," said Innkeeper Gwen Fullbrook. Gwen makes this in a Bundt pan for spectacular presentation on the breakfast buffet, often served outdoors on the porch.

Gwen and David are experienced innkeepers, now operating their third inn. They call this 1877 home "an English Country Bed & Breakfast," in part because David is from England and Gwen adds the Texas "country." It's also called that because of the decor, which mixes fine antiques with comfortable country touches. It was the country home and farm of wealthy businessman L.D. Carrington, who also built a "city" house two blocks from the state Capitol. As it is, this home is only nine blocks from the Capitol.

🏠*Other Carrington's Bluff recipes:*
Pineapple Zucchini Bread, page 74
Apple Butter, page 84
Devonshire Cream, page 88
Homemade Granola, page 200

Wild Flower Apple Bread

Ingredients:

2 eggs
2 cups sugar
1/2 cup vegetable oil
1/2 teaspoon vanilla extract
2 cups apples, chopped
3 cups flour
2 teaspoons cinnamon
1 teaspoon baking soda
1/2 teaspoon baking powder
1/2 teaspoon salt
1 cup pecans, chopped

- In a large bowl, beat eggs. Blend in sugar and oil.
- Stir in vanilla and apples.
- In a separate bowl, mix flour, cinnamon, baking soda, baking powder and salt.
- Stir dry ingredients into apple mixture.
- Fold in nuts. "Batter will be extremely stiff."
- Divide batter into two greased loaf pans. Bake in a preheated oven at 350 degrees for 40 to 50 minutes or until a toothpick inserted in the center comes out clean.

Tester's Comments: A sweet, hard-crust bread that tastes a bit less sweet when served cold. Add 1/2 cup plain yogurt and increase baking time a few minutes for taller bread. Don't bother to peel the apples!

Makes 2 loaves

from **The Wild Flower Inn**
1200 West 22-1/2 Street
Austin, TX 78705
512-477-9639

"The apples will weep while cooking and it will be a delicious, moist bread," so don't worry about the very thick batter, said Innkeeper Kay Jackson. She and co-innkeeper Claudean Schultz bake breads or muffins every day. Guests are served family-style in the dining room.

Kay and Claudean knew this was the place for them soon after they saw it. It was the last property the realtor showed them, and the details worked out perfectly. They restored the 50-year-old home and opened their four-guestroom B&B in 1990.

Other Wild Flower Inn recipes:
Healthy Muffins, page 51
Peach and Poppyseed Muffins, page 56
Wonderful Applesauce Muffins, page 61

Zucchini Nut Bread

Ingredients:

2 eggs, well beaten
1/3 cup canola oil
1 cup honey
1 teaspoon vanilla extract
2 cups unpeeled zucchini, grated
2 cups whole wheat flour
1 teaspoon baking soda
1/2 teaspoon baking powder
1 teaspoon sea salt
1 teaspoon cinnamon
1 teaspoon allspice
1/4 teaspoon cloves
3/4 cup walnuts, chopped

- In a large bowl, beat eggs. Mix in oil, honey and vanilla. Then stir in zucchini.
- In a separate bowl, combine flour, baking soda, baking powder, salt and spices.
- Stir the dry ingredients into the zucchini mixture. Fold in nuts.
- Turn batter into a well-greased and floured bread loaf pan. Bake in a preheated oven at 350 degrees for no longer than 55 minutes or until a toothpick inserted in the center comes out clean.
- Cool before removing bread from pan, and cool completely before serving. Freezes well.

Makes 1 loaf

from **Country Elegance B&B**
Off Page Springs Road
P.O. Box 564
Cornville, AZ 86325
602-634-4470

Innkeeper Rita Sydelle believes this bread is even better if it's wrapped in plastic and allowed to sit overnight. She serves it warm or cold and uses it in baked stuffed French toast recipes, often part of her large, healthy breakfasts. "The only complaint so far is that I feed people too much!"

Rita moved to Cornville, 14 miles from Sedona and 10 miles from the historic copper mining town of Jerome, after 25 years in San Diego. "I wanted to slow down my life and get back to the country" after owning her own interior design firm. She rejuvenated a 13-year-old home into this country B&B, complete with free range chickens and an organic vegetable garden.

Other Country Elegance recipes:
Pumpkin Cream Cheese Roll-Up, page 175
Date Bars á la Bernice, page 182
Grandma's Noodle Kugel, page 184

There's nothing like homemade, and this chapter proves it. Still serving Hollandaise from a dehydrated mix or adding, heaven forbid, non-dairy topping to your fruit, or pouring imitation maple syrup on your pancakes? The extra effort to make homemade Hollandaise, Devonshire Cream or Whipped Maple Syrup really pays off. A number of fruit dips in this chapter transform a simple fruit plate into a spectacular fruit course. Blueberry Honey Butter is wonderful on hot muffins or biscuits. Spoon Blueberry Sauce on pancakes instead of traditional maple syrup. Homemade Salsa, Green Jalapeno Jelly and Prickly Pear Syrup bring a taste of the Southwest to the table.

Preserves, Butters, Spreads & Sauces

Apple Butter

Ingredients:

4 cups homemade or purchased unsweetened applesauce
1 cup sugar
2 teaspoons cinnamon
1/2 teaspoon allspice
1/8 teaspoon ginger
1/8 teaspoons cloves, ground

- In a large saucepan or kettle, combine applesauce, sugar and spices.
- Bring mixture to a boil, stirring constantly. Then simmer on low heat for 1 hour, stirring often as mixture thickens to avoid scorching.
- Cool apple butter. Store in a tightly-covered jar in the refrigerator.

Makes 1 quart

from **Carrington's Bluff B&B**
1900 David Street
Austin, TX 78705
512-479-0638

When Innkeeper Gwen Fullbrook is making apple butter, everyone knows it, even the neighbors, if the windows are open, because of the aroma. "This is excellent with apple, pear and peach muffins or breads," she said. She often serves it with her homemade breads and granola on the breakfast buffet.

Gwen, who is a native Texan, and David, who is British, opened this B&B, their third, in 1989. They had operated a B&B in Vermont and another one in Austin before finding what they considered the ideal inn. Located on Shoal Creek Bluff, the 1877 home is on an acre of tree-covered hillside in the heart of Austin. But you'd never know you were in the middle of town; the inn looks out over the lush grounds in a residential neighborhood. The state Capitol is nine blocks away and the University of Texas is seven blocks.

Four of the five guestrooms are located on the second floor with bluff views. The beds, often iron or brass, are covered with handmade quilts. Some of the guestrooms are named after the Carrington family, who purchased the original 22-acre farm in 1856. L.D. Carrington owned a general store, the water company and a newspaper. He had the front porch built facing the bluff to watch for Indians living along Shoal Creek, from whom Carrington, as a brigade commander, was supposed to protect Austin.

Other Carrington's Bluff recipes:
Pineapple Zucchini Bread, page 74
Strawberry Pecan Bread, page 79
Devonshire Cream, page 88
Homemade Granola, page 200

Blueberry Honey Butter

Ingredients:

1/2 cup butter, softened
1 cup honey
1 cup blueberries, crushed
1/4 teaspoon cinnamon
1/4 cup pecans, finely chopped

- When butter is at room temperature, beat in honey.
- In a separate bowl, crush blueberries. Then beat into honey butter.
- Stir in cinnamon and mix well.
- In a food processor, finely chop pecans. Stir into honey butter.
- Cover and refrigerate honey butter until a few minutes before ready to use.

Makes 2 cups

from **Rosevine Inn B&B**
415 South Vine Avenue
Tyler, TX 75702
214-592-2221

Innkeeper Rebecca Powell takes advantage of Tyler's fresh blueberries for this summer treat, which she might serve to guests with homemade beer bread.

Rebecca and Bert built this home in 1986 on a brick street lined with large oak trees. On the site, Dr. Irwin Pope, Jr., once had his home. His father was one of Tyler's first physicians, and this entire block of Vine Avenue was home to Dr. Pope's family. Unfortunately, the 1934 home was burned to the ground in 1969. The lot, still with the foundation and oak trees intact, stood vacant until Powells bought it and built their inn.

The four guestrooms are furnished with antiques and country collectibles. Guests might enjoy a full breakfast in the inn's dining room before heading out for a busy day exploring the area. Antique and craft shops are within walking distance of the inn. Visitors shouldn't miss the Municipal Rose Garden, the nation's largest with 38,000 rose bushes. Tyler also is well-known for its azaleas (in the spring there is an "azalea trail" to follow in the inn's neighborhood), and peach production is the second-largest in the state (behind Gillespie County where Fredericksburg is located). Tyler also has a zoo, museums and the Carnegie History Center.

Other Rosevine Inn B&B recipes:
Blueberry Peach Coffeecake, page 34
Rosevine Breakfast Bake, page 131

Blueberry Sauce

Ingredients:

2 cups fresh or frozen dry-pack blueberries
1/2 cup sugar
Pinch of salt
1 tablespoon cornstarch
2 tablespoons lemon juice
2 tablespoons water

- Rinse fresh berries. Set aside.
- Mix sugar, salt and cornstarch in a saucepan. Stir in lemon juice and water until smooth.
- Stir in blueberries. Stirring constantly, bring mixture to a boil. Cook until clear and thick, about 2 minutes, stirring constantly. Serve warm over pancakes or cold over vanilla ice cream.

Makes about 2 cups

from **Red Rooster Square B&B**
Highway 314 North
Route 3, Box 3387
Edom/Ben Wheeler, TX 75754
903-852-6774

Innkeeper Doris Moore picks gallons of fresh Edom blueberries in June and July, when the pick-your-own farm is open from 7 a.m. to 7 p.m. Then she freezes the berries for use all year. The Edom area is well-known for its fruit.

Doris and Bob opened the doors to their neo-Victorian home in 1985. "We built a too-big house, with all local labor, because our girls and their families are just two hours away," Doris said. "We wanted a place big enough for them to come home. Bob suggested bed-and-breakfast, and we have enjoyed it. You meet lots of real neat people in this world."

Doris and Bob serve a hearty breakfast that includes eggs, breakfast meat, fruit, cereal, and homemade muffins, coffeecake or pancakes. Breakfast is set out buffet-style on the breakfast bar, and guests eat with Moores at the oval dining room table. The B&B's decor is "country," with antiques and reproductions, country wallpaper, and ruffled curtains throughout.

The B&B is always full for "First Monday Trade Days" in nearby Canton. As far back as 1873, the first Monday of each month was when the judge held court and when stray horses were auctioned. Trading grew, and now "First Monday" begins on the Friday before and runs for a four-day weekend. As many as 4,000 flea market booths are rented in what may be the country's biggest flea market, covering 100 acres and drawing 50,000 bargain hunters.
"We have 'show and tell' when they get back," Doris said. "We've had everything from old wooden wagons to a Greta Garbo nightie made of silk."

Creamy Fruit Dip

Ingredients:

6 ounces cream cheese, softened
1 cup brown sugar, packed
2 cups sour cream
1 teaspoon vanilla extract

Also:

Strawberries or other fresh fruit for dipping

- In a food processor or with an electric mixer, blend cream cheese and brown sugar.
- Mix in sour cream and vanilla.
- Serve in a pretty bowl accompanied by fresh fruit for dipping.

Tester's Comments: This easy caramel sauce can be used on top of strawberry shortcake or fruit cups, too.

Makes 3 cups

from **Crystal River Inn**
326 West Hopkins Street
San Marcos, TX 78666
512-396-3739

"After seven years of innkeeping, I learned the quick and easy recipes are usually my favorites," said Cathy Dillon. She makes this dip often, especially for weekend brunches, and serves it with a variety of fresh Hill Country fruit.

Mike and Cathy found refuge from big city life in Houston while canoeing on the rivers in the area, including the San Marcos, Blanco, Comal and Guadelupe. In 1984, they made San Marcos officially their home when they opened the Inn. The 1883 home, which they restored, is easy to find on one of San Marcos' main streets. They also have opened the Young House, across the street, with three guestrooms there. Breakfast is served in the sunny dining room of the main inn.

Each of the eight guestrooms is named after a favorite Texas river. The Medina serves as the honeymoon suite, complete with a fireplace and four-poster bed. The Colorado is done in "contemporary Texas decor" with a canopy over the bed made from rope and cactus in planters. The Frio, done in blue, has white wicker furnishings. All rooms have designer decor that has earned feature presentation in many magazines.

Other Crystal River Inn recipes:
Scrambled Eggs with Chive Cream Cheese, page 133
Herbed Broiled Tomatoes, page 161
Hot Crab Dip, page 201

Devonshire Cream

Ingredients:

1 cup heavy cream
1/2 cup powdered sugar
1-1/2 teaspoons vanilla extract
1 cup sour cream

- In a large, chilled bowl, beat whipping cream, powdered sugar and vanilla until soft peaks form.
- Beat in sour cream, blending well.
- Refrigerate in a covered container. Serve as a topping for fruit, or pile it on split scones and then top with jam, as the British do.

Tester's Comments: If you're watching your diet, this is dangerous to leave hanging around in the refrigerator!

Makes 2 cups

from **Carrington's Bluff B&B**
1900 David Street
Austin, TX 78705
512-479-0638

"This is America's answer to English clotted cream, which I can't seem to find," said Innkeeper Gwen Fullbrook. "If it's not sweet enough for you, keep adding powdered sugar until it is. My English husband, as well as guests, love this."

L.D. Carrington purchased 22 acres here in 1856, when the land was part of the Republic of Texas. Carrington was a wealthy man who owned a general store, the water company and a newspaper, and who served as city alderman and county commissioner. "His true love was being was commander of the brigade that guarded Austin from the Indians who roamed along Shoal Creek," located below the bluff, Gwen said. "That's why the front porch faces bluff -- to watch for the Indians." The 1877 house had been restored in 1980 so all Gwen and David had to do before opening their inn was decorate it.

David and Gwen met in 1982 when Gwen owned a decorative hardward and interior design business. He needed 800 cabinet knobs for a condominium project he was working on -- she sold him 2,500. They married in 1984. They have since operated two other B&Bs, one in Austin and one in Vermont. Gwen lasted a year in Vermont, where record snowfalls and a long winter "were a little much for a native Texan," she said.

Other Carrington's Bluff recipes:
Pineapple Zucchini Bread, page 74
Strawberry Pecan Bread, page 79
Apple Butter, page 84
Homemade Granola, page 200

Green Jalapeno Jelly

Ingredients:

1 4-ounce can jalapeno peppers, chopped
1 green bell pepper, chopped
2-1/4 cups cider vinegar, divided
6 cups sugar
1 6-ounce bottle fruit pectin
6 drops green food coloring

- In a food processor, blend jalapeno and bell peppers and 1/4 cup of the vinegar.
- In a large saucepan, mix remaining 2 cups vinegar with sugar. Stir over medium heat until mixture boils.
- Stir in pepper mixture and bring to full, rolling boil.
- Stir in fruit pectin and bring back to a boil.
- Remove from heat. Stir in food coloring. Skim foam off the top. Pour into six hot, sterilized 4-ounce or three 8-ounce jelly jars, leaving 1/2-inch space at the top. Immediately cover with sterilized, tight-fitting lids and bands (for more detailed directions, read the pectin package). Let jars cool.
- Serve on crackers with softened cream cheese.

Makes 3 8-ounce jars

from Dierker House
423 West Cherry Avenue
Flagstaff, AZ 86001
602-774-3249

Innkeeper Dorothea "Dottie" Dierker serves this southwestern jelly as hors d'oeurves in the afternoon. It can also be served over cream cheese spread on toast. Many people are surprised by the sweet-sour taste, thinking pepper jelly would be hot and spicy.

Dottie opened her B&B in 1984 as an "empty nest" business after raising her six children in this home. The house, listed on the National Register of Historic Places, was built in 1914 as a summer home for the LaBaron family, who were sheep farmers in the Flagstaff area. It is located about five blocks from downtown, in a location Dottie thought would be ideal for travelers.

A veteran B&B traveler herself, Dottie stayed in B&Bs while traveling in Europe. She enjoyed meeting other international travelers, so the combination of her large home, her B&B experience, and her love for people and cooking got her thinking about opening her own place. She has three antique-filled guestrooms upstairs with a private entrance.

Another Dierker House recipe:
Relleno Casserole, page 130

Hollandaise Sauce

Ingredients:

2 eggs (or 4 egg yolks for more color)
1/2 cup butter, melted and cooled
2 tablespoons lemon juice
Dash of salt
Dash of white pepper
1/4 cup boiling water

- In a blender, blend eggs, butter, lemon juice, salt and pepper at "stir" speed.
- While mixture is moving, slowly pour in 1/4 cup boiling water.
- Pour the sauce into the top of a double boiler. Set it above hot, not boiling, water.
- Constantly whisk the sauce until thickened.
- Remove top of double boiler from heat and continue to whisk for 1 to 2 minutes.
- If not immediately used, refrigerated sauce can be "gently" reheated in the microwave.

Makes 2 servings, enough to cover 4 Eggs Benedict

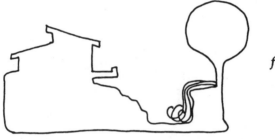

from **Pumpkinshell Ranch**
11005 East Johnson Road
HC 66, Box 2100
Cornville, AZ 86325
602-634-4797

Innkeeper Kay Johnson makes this homemade Hollandaise to serve over Eggs Benedict. Or she will substitute steamed fresh spinach leaves for the Canadian bacon in the Benedict to create Eggs Florentine.

Opening a B&B was "a natural," said Kay, who opened two guestrooms in 1987. "I love to entertain and cook for people," she said. She and Terry had built two extra guestrooms in the contemporary solar home to be used by their five grown children returning for visits. The hillside home overlooks a waterfall and creek and is at the end of their own road.

In the Cornville and Sedona area, Kay also is known as a cooking instructor. She studied French cooking at Maxim's in Paris, and teaches gourmet and international cooking. When she and Terry built their home, Kay designed an enviable commercial kitchen. It's complete with stainless steel flour bins, two refrigerators, a convection oven and special floors to prevent fatigue.

Other Pumpkinshell Ranch recipes:
Irish Coffee, page 27
Aunt Gladys' Buttermilk Biscuits, page 44
Morning Glory Muffins, page 54
Zucchini Muffins, page 62
Irish Soda Bread, page 171

Homemade Salsa

Ingredients:

3 28-ounce cans stewed tomatoes
15 fresh jalapeno peppers, chopped
3 large yellow onions, chopped
3 tablespoons vegetable oil
1/4 cup chili powder
1/2 teaspoon cumin, freshly ground
3 or 4 garlic cloves
Salt to taste
Juice of 3-1/2 limes

Also:

1/2 cup fresh cilantro, chopped

- Chop tomatoes in a food processor. Set aside.
- In a large kettle, sauté jalapenos and onion in oil until onions are clear but still crisp.
- Stir in chili powder and cumin. Cook and stir for 4 minutes.
- Stir in garlic. Immediately add tomatoes and cook 5 more minutes.
- Mix in salt and lime juice.
- Pour into three quart jars and cool. Store in the refrigerator.
- So the hot salsa won't cook the cilantro and destroy its flavor, add cilantro just before serving.

Makes 3 quarts

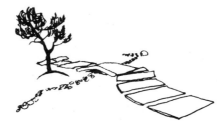

from **La Posada de Taos**
309 Juanita Lane
P.O. Box 1118
Taos, NM 87571
505-758-8164

This spicy salsa appears on the side of Innkeeper Sue Smoot's breakfast burrito, a tortilla stuffed with scrambled eggs, bacon and pinto beans. She often serves southwestern dishes with a bite. One reviewer noted, "Sissy breakfasts are served on request."

Sue first came to Taos more than 30 years ago. She came back in 1983 as a graduation present to herself when she earned her architecture degree. That was in August. By November, she had sold her New York City co-op and had driven her furnishings west in a 30-foot rental truck to move into a delapidated 75-year-old adobe home. By January, she had turned the home into a picture-perfect southwest B&B with five guestrooms and a courtyard less than three blocks from Taos Plaza.

Other La Posada de Taos recipes:
Cactus Quiche, page 121
Shirred Eggs with Green Chili Sauce, page 134

91

Pear Preserves

Ingredients:

Keifer or other hard fall pears
Sugar

☛ Wash, peel and slice pears.

☛ In a kettle, alternate a layer of pears with a layer of sugar. "I suppose it amounts to about half and half."

☛ Cover with a cloth and let stand overnight.

☛ In the morning, stir and cook on medium heat until the pears turn clear. "They will be light in color. If they get dark, you have cooked them too long."

☛ Remove from heat and skim off foam. Ladle pears into sterilized, hot jelly jars, leaving 1/2-inch space at the top. Immediately cover with sterilized, tight-fitting lids and bands and process in a hot water bath for 5 minutes. Remove and invert for about 15 minutes. Then retighten bands.

☛ "The syrup left after putting the pears in hot, sterilized jars is delicious on pancakes or waffles."

from **Ash-Bowers-Jarrett House**
301 South Magnolia Street
Palestine, TX 75801
903-729-1935

"I grew up helping my mother make pear preserves" without a written recipe, said Innkeeper Lee Jarrett. "It's a regular thing in September or early October at our house today and guests may arrive smelling the wonderful aroma in the kitchen." She might serve the preserves on hot, from-scratch biscuits along with a bacon-and-eggs breakfast. The mahagony table and chairs in the dining room are original pieces and had been stored in the carriage house.

"We got into innkeeping because our house is large and very lovely and historical," she said. "We live alone so we wanted to share the house." In 1986, she and Jim opened their B&B. They offer three guestrooms in the main house and two in the carriage house. There are other out-buildings: a greenhouse, smokehouse and servant's house. Lee said the property is one of the last complete Victorian homesteads in East Texas. Henry Ash, a local merchant, built the home in 1878. Six years later, it was purchased and subsequently enlarged by Andrew Bowers, an entrepreneur. Some original Bowers family furniture still remains, as do the heavy damask drapes from 1897 and leaded glass windows installed the same year.

Four miles out of town is the Texas State Railroad, which runs popular weekend excursions March through October. The 50-mile round-trip is over the route begun in 1896 by inmates to serve the industries of the state prison system. The train chugs through the Piney Woods and over 30 bridges.

🏠*Another Ash-Bowers-Jarrett House recipe:*
Cornflake Waffles, page 153

Pineapple-Kiwi Fruit Jam

Ingredients:

4 ripe kiwi fruit, peeled and sliced 1/8-inch thick
3 cups sugar
1/4 cup lime juice
1 8-ounce can crushed pineapple, undrained
1 3-ounce package liquid fruit pectin
3 drops green or yellow food coloring

☛ In a two-quart, microwave-safe bowl, combine kiwi slices, sugar, lime juice and pineapple.

☛ Microwave on high for 12 to 16 minutes or until mixture comes to a full, rolling boil, stirring every two minutes.

☛ Mix in liquid pectin. Microwave on high for 2 to 3 minutes or until mixture comes back to a full, rolling boil.

☛ Microwave on high for 1 minute. Skim off foam on top. Stir in food coloring.

☛ Spoon jam into 5 sterilized, hot 8-ounce jelly jars, leaving 1/2-inch space at top. Cool slightly and cover with sterilized, tight-fitting lids (for more detailed directions, read the pectin package).

☛ Cool several hours. Store jam in refrigerator for up to 3 weeks or freeze up to 3 months.

Makes 5 eight-ounce jars

from **La Casa Muneca**
213 North Alameda Street
Carlsbad, NM 88220
505-887-1891

Innkeeper M.J. Lawrence uses four-ounce jars "to be able to give them as gifts -- people just love to take a little bit of our B&B home with them." The jam is served every morning with English muffins or on her homemade nut breads.

"My husband has three children and I have four. With all their friends, we were operating a B&B, but just didn't know it." She and Joseph "retired" to Carlsbad. She is active in the Chamber of Commerce and he is a handyman.
"When we saw the house we now call our B&B, we just knew it would be perfect," she said. The stucco home, built in 1929, has four guestrooms, and an adjacent casita serves as a private guesthouse. A stone wall makes the courtyard private, and guests may choose to have breakfast there under the pecan trees. Guests also may use the common room in the main house, which has a fireplace. The Lawrence's poodle, named "Bob," may join them there.

Carlsbad Caverns National Park is 27 miles away. The Lawrences say it draws 700,000 visitors a year, many to see the nightly bat flight from mid-May through October.

🏠 *Another La Casa Muneca recipe:*
Poppyseed Bread, page 75

Poppyseed Dressing

Ingredients:

1-1/2 cups sugar
2 to 3 teaspoons prepared mustard (not Dijon)
2 teaspoons salt
2/3 cup white vinegar
2 cups corn oil
3 tablespoons poppyseeds

- With an electric mixer, mix sugar, mustard and salt.
- Beat in vinegar. Then slowly beat in oil.
- Add poppyseeds and mix just once.
- Store in a covered jar in the refrigerator. Shake well before using. Use as a dressing for fruit or fruit salad.

Tester's Comments: I make this often using canola oil and a prepared honey mustard. It has an absolutely wonderful sweet-sour tang.

Makes about 3-1/2 cups

from **Wild Briar Inn**
Farm Road 2339
P.O. Box 21
Edom/Ben Wheeler, TX 75754
903-852-3975

Innkeeper Mary Scott uses this dressing with fruit plates, but says it is especially good poured over grapefruit. There is no shortage of fruit here, and the Edom area is especially well known for its blueberries. Pick-your-own farms and seasonal fruit stands abound.

Fresh fruit is always on the breakfast table at this country inn, which Mary and Max opened in 1988. Both native East Texans, they decided to open their own inn after five years of travels in Great Britain. Inside their contemporary home, guests can stay in the Harrogate, Tresanton, Glebe or Thakeham rooms, plus two others, each with British, Scottish, Welsh or French decor.

The inn has a gathering room with a fireplace, and guests can wander out onto the deck by the garden or over the 23 acres on which the inn is set. There's also a small room called "the snug," with patterned carpet and an antique tin ceiling, where guests can store drinks in a refrigerator. Finally, to make guests' relaxation complete, Mary and Max offer dinners with a room reservation, so guests don't have to leave the inn once they've arrived.

Another Wild Briar Inn recipe:
Sour Cream Muffins, page 59

Prickly Pear Syrup

Ingredients:

2 cups juice from prickly pear fruit (see directions below)
2 cups sugar
Juice of 1 lemon (2 to 3 tablespoons)

🍐 To make prickly pear juice: Wear rubber gloves to avoid getting thorns in fingers. Cut the cactus fruit in half and put it in a food processor. ("Do not peel because the thorns will be removed during the straining.") "Pulse" until fruit is puréed. Place purée in a large kettle and add 1/2 cup water for each 2 cups of purée. Bring to a rolling boil. Boil for 5 minutes. Strain through cheesecloth.

🍐 In a kettle or large saucepan, stir together prickly pear juice, sugar and lemon juice.

🍐 Bring to a full rolling boil. Boil for 1 minute.

🍐 Pour syrup into sterilized jars. Immediately place sterilized caps and rings on top and invert until syrup has cooled. Refrigerate until use.

Makes 4 cups

from **Peppertrees B&B Inn**
724 East University Boulevard
Tucson, AZ 85719
602-622-7167

"I like to keep a large jar of syrup in the refrigerator -- lemon, bitter orange, prickly pear or pomegranate -- to use either to season fruit plates and keep them fresh, or to use as a syrup for pancakes, waffles or crepes," said Innkeeper Marjorie Martin. The red prickly pear fruit in southern Arizona makes "a wonderful vermillion syrup that has a very delicate flavor." She also may use it as the basis for a fruit drink, adding soda water.

Marjorie gets her fresh lemons from "a wonderful lemon tree outside my kitchen window that grows lemons the size of grapefruit." Her yard is also blessed with two large peppertrees, believed to be as old as the 1905 brick house, and after which her B&B is named.

Peppertrees B&B was opened in 1988. Marjorie has two guestrooms in the main house, decorated with family antiques brought from her native England. Across the patio are two southwest-style guesthouses. Guests are served breakfast on the patio near the fountain, surrounded by blooming plants. Marjorie's breakfasts include fresh fruit, a coffeecake or muffins, and a hearty entree. Guests also are treated to afternoon tea on the patio or front porch.

🏠*Other Peppertrees B&B Inn recipes:*
Peppertrees' Coffee Coffeecake, page 41
Bananas and Strawberry Cream, page 101
Peppertrees' Scottish Shortbread, page 173

Spinach Dill Sauce

Ingredients:

- 1/4 cup butter
- 2 cups milk, half-and-half or heavy cream
- 1/4 cup flour
- Salt to taste
- 3 large sprigs fresh dill, finely chopped
- 4 to 6 fresh spinach leaves, finely chopped
- 4 to 6 sprigs fresh parsley, finely chopped

Also:

- 6 to 8 poached eggs
- 6 to 8 halves of English muffins, toasted, or homemade biscuits
- Dash of cayenne pepper

- In a large non-stick saucepan, melt butter.

- Whisk the flour into the butter. Stir constantly over low heat until the mixture is thick and bubbly.

- Slowly stir the milk into the flour mixture. Bring the mixture to a boil, stirring frequently.

- Stir salt and the chopped dill, spinach and parsley into the white sauce.

- Place each poached egg on half of a toasted English muffin or a biscuit. Spoon the hot sauce over each poached egg. Top with a dash of cayenne pepper.

Makes 6-8 servings

from **Sipapu Lodge**
65 Piki Drive
P.O. Box 552
Sedona, AZ 86336
602-282-2833

"A guest told me his favorite herb was dill," said Innkeeper Lea Pace, and that's all the inspiration she needed to create this sauce. "What a hit! I use this recipe frequently. The dash of cayenne on top adds a Southwest zest." For a different flavor, she sometimes substitutes 1 cup of the marinade drained from marinated artichoke hearts for 1 cup of the milk.

The dill grows in Lea's herb garden. She and son Vince Mollan opened their home as a five-guestroom B&B, named "Sipapu" after the opening in a Hopi Kiva. The Hopi believe it is a passageway for enlightened beings to enter this dimension, Lea said. Lea and Vince like to think they help their guests enter another dimension of sorts, one full of relaxation and restoration.

Other Sipapu Lodge recipes:
Fruit Frappé, page 25
Fruit Tacos, page 104
Hot, Spiced Melon, page 108
Southwest Egg and Bean Burritos, page 135
Spaghetti Squash Supreme, page 157

Whipped Maple Syrup

Ingredients:

1/2 cup pure maple syrup
1/4 cup water
1/2 cup heavy cream, whipped
2 egg whites
1 teaspoon lemon juice

☛ Put small bowl of an electric mixer in the freezer to chill.

☛ Mix maple syrup and water in a small saucepan.

☛ Bring to a boil, turn the heat to medium, and let the syrup boil about 5 minutes, or to "soft ball" stage (236 degrees on a candy thermometer).

☛ Meanwhile, whip cream in the chilled bowl. Remove it to a mixing bowl.

☛ Beat the egg whites and lemon juice in the chilled bowl. Whites should form stiff peaks but remain moist.

☛ When the syrup reaches the soft ball stage, slowly beat it into the egg whites. When thoroughly mixed, fold in whipped cream. Serve on Blue Corn Buttermilk Pancakes or other favorite pancakes.

☛ Cover and store in the refrigerator. "This mixture keeps well for a few days, although it does lose some of its air. Stir it well before you use it to combine the liquid on the bottom with the lighter mixture on top."

Makes about 3 cups

from **A Touch of Sedona**
595 Jordan Road
Sedona, AZ 86336
602-282-6462

"This is great on a waldorf salad or any fruit salad -- it's a good way to use it up," said Innkeeper Doris Stevenson. That is, if there are any leftovers. Dick and Doris serve it on their Blue Corn Buttermilk Pancakes and the combination has been their most-requested breakfast entree.

Breakfast is served family-style at 8 a.m. Guests gather at the large round dining room table with a Lazy Susan in the middle. Home-baked bread also might be on the breakfast menu.

Dick and Doris discovered Sedona in the early '80s and moved to town in 1986. Dick plays with the local Rim Country Band and Doris collects works of local artists. Their contemporary home, with four guestrooms, is "furnished with stained glass lamps, antiques, but with a mix of contemporary."

Another Touch of Sedona recipe:
Blue Corn Buttermilk Pancakes, page 144

OK, fruit may be good for us, but we don't have to *like* it. These clever innkeepers have figured out how to dress up, spice up or soup up ordinary fruit and, as one said, have guests who swear they're not fruit eaters asking for seconds. They've even made fruit *fun*. Fruit is tucked into sugared tortilla shells for fruit tacos. Substitute fruit and yogurt for ice cream and you've got breakfast banana splits. Cantaloupe, strawberries and other melons turn up in unusual soups. Fresh berries become spirited when soaked in plum wine. Even in the "off-season," there's no reason to give up the fruit. Baked, poached, marinated, sautéed or simmered in a slow-cooker, fruit is as adaptable as the innkeepers who perfected these recipes!

Fruits

Amaretto and Applesauce

Ingredients:

1 cup golden raisins
2 cups chunky applesauce
1 cup crushed pineapple, drained
1/4 cup brown sugar, packed
1 tablespoon cinnamon
1 tablespoon Amaretto liqueur

🥄 The night before, boil raisins in enough water to cover for 5 minutes. Remove from heat and allow raisins to sit in the water overnight to "plump."

🥄 In the morning, drain raisins. Pour into a slow cooker or saucepan.

🥄 Stir in applesauce, pineapple, sugar, cinnamon and liqueur.

🥄 Heat on low until sugar is dissolved and aroma fills the house. Serve warm.

Makes 8 servings

from **The Victorian Inn of Prescott**
246 South Cortez Street
Prescott, AZ 86303
602-778-2642

Innkeeper Tamia Thunstedt starts her original side-dish early so "guests enjoy the aroma as they approach breakfast time," she said. "I serve this with muffins and baked strata on snowy winter mornings."

Snow in winter is one of the pleasures of living in Prescott, which, along with Denver, is known as "the mile-high city." The hilly town has a moderate climate all year 'round, attracting outdoor enthusiasts who come up from the desert to the pines.

Tamia loves sharing the history of this house, built in 1893 by John Herndon, the district attorney. Guests might get a tour and history lesson from her, or from other family members, who all help with the B&B. Her mother may have helped prepare breakfast for the guests, and the guests may have made reservations on the phone with her dad. Daughter Eve may have checked the guests in, and sister Judy refinished the antiques in their room.

Tamia, who also works as a childbirth educator and obstetrical nurse, opened the downtown B&B in 1990. When she had an opportunity to purchase the Queen Anne Victorian, she thought of opening a quilt or antique shop there, but opted for the B&B. She hasn't regretted her choice. "I love the wonderful people I meet who come here to stay," she said.

🏠 *Other Victorian Inn recipes:*
Cashew Coconut Whole Wheat Muffins, page 46
Linzer Muffins, page 53

Bananas and Strawberry Cream

Ingredients:

1 pint fresh strawberries
1/2 cup sugar
3 bananas
2 cups egg custard

Egg Custard:
1-1/2 cups milk, scalded
3 tablespoons butter
3 tablespoons flour
1/4 cup sugar
1 teaspoon vanilla extract
1 egg, beaten

🍂 To make Egg Custard: Scald the milk; set aside. Melt butter in a saucepan over low heat. Whisk in the flour and cook, stirring constantly, until bubbly. Slowly add the hot milk, stirring constantly, until thick. Stir in the sugar and vanilla. In a separate bowl, add 1/2 cup custard to the beaten egg. Then pour the egg mixture back into the rest of the custard. Stir and remove from heat. Cover pan or bowl with plastic wrap and cool thoroughly.

🍂 Wash the strawberries. Set aside 6 good ones, preferably with leaves, for garnish.

🍂 Remove hulls from remaining strawberries. Crush or purée in a blender.

🍂 Slice the bananas into fruit bowls. Spoon the cold egg custard over one side and the puréed strawberries over the other side. Garnish with strawberries and serve.

Makes 6 servings

from **Peppertrees B&B Inn**
724 East University Boulevard
Tucson, AZ 85719
602-622-7167

"Bananas and Strawberry Cream was created when I had unexpected guests," said Marjorie Martin. "I had not been grocery shopping for a couple of days and was wildly looking around for fruit that was presentable enough for a fruit plate. The bananas were OK, the strawberries had seen better days, and I was out of yogurt!" Marjorie, who is British, often makes egg custard, which she called "a standard English dessert...It is more bland than ice cream and goes well with any tart fruit pie," as well as with most fruit dishes.

This innkeeper has been cooking for crowds "ever since my first love, a Frenchman, gave me a cookbook and suggested that maybe I should learn to cook!" She started on a gourmet dinner for 25. Later, she perfected from-scratch cooking as a way to stretch the budget while raising four children. When she opened her B&B in 1988, she continued her use of fresh ingredients, no artificial sweeteners or preservatives, and use of natural herbs and spices.

🏠*Other Peppertrees B&B Inn recipes:*
Peppertrees' Coffee Coffeecake, page 41
Prickly Pear Syrup, page 95
Peppertrees' Scottish Shortbread, page 173

Breakfast Banana Splits

Ingredients:

2 bananas
2 apples, diced
2 cups fresh strawberries, blackberries and/or raspberries
1 cup grapes or fresh peaches, sliced
2 cups mixed berry flavor yogurt
4 tablespoons wheat germ
1 kiwi fruit, peeled and sliced

- In each banana split bowl, place half of a banana, split lengthwise.
- Cover with half an apple, diced.
- Wash and drain berries. Mound 1/2 cup berries in the middle of each bowl.
- Place washed and drained grapes or peach slices around berries.
- Top with 1/2 cup yogurt, then 1 tablespoon wheat germ. Place a kiwi slice on top.

Makes 4 servings

from **Das College Haus**
106 West College Street
Fredericksburg, TX 78624
512-997-9047

"The fruit and yogurt combination is appetizing, even to non-yogurt lovers," said Innkeeper Bebe Curry, who has an abundance of fresh Hill Country fruit from which to choose all spring, summer and fall. She may vary the flavor of yogurt, depending on fruit used, but has found guests prefer the mixed berry.

Guests may begin a leisurely breakfast sipping coffee and chatting in the kitchen, which Bebe has decorated with antique utensils. Then guests move into the old-fashioned dining room. Bebe has a display of her Flow Blue china on the antique buffet, and she's also collected some Depression Glass. Other antiques are from farm auctions she attended in Kentucky and Indiana and brought to the 80-year-old home.

Das College Haus has two guestrooms upstairs, each with a private entrance off the veranda, and one guestroom downstairs. The L-shaped veranda, either upstairs or down, is ideal for setting a spell in this residential neighborhood. Teddy bears in the guestrooms help make visitors feel at home. Bebe has left many of the home's assets intact, including original wallpaper in the suites. She moved here in 1988, specifically to open an inn. She enjoys meeting interesting guests and offering them her version of B&B hospitality: "more than just a room in a house."

Cantaloupe Soup

Ingredients:
    2 ripe cantaloupes
    1/2 cup orange juice
    1 tablespoon orange liqueur

⚓ Cut cantaloupes in half and carefully remove seeds.

⚓ Make cantaloupe bowls from each half by cutting out triangle-shaped wedges all around the edge of the fruit. On the bottom of each half, cut off a very thin slice so it will sit flat on the serving plate.

⚓ Scoop out the fruit, without disturbing the zig-zag edges, leaving at least 1/4 inch near rind.

⚓ Combine fruit, orange juice and liqueur in blender. Blend thoroughly. Taste and add a little sugar, if necessary.

⚓ Chill in the freezer, then give one short twirl in the blender just before serving. Pour soup into bowls and "garnish with strawberry and parsley or whatever you have on hand for color."

Makes 4 servings

from **Yacht-O-Fun**
2216 Windsor Drive
Richardson, TX 75082
214-238-8224

"Most people think Cantaloupe Soup sounds awful but are pleasantly surprised to find out that it is actually very good and refreshing, especially on a hot summer Texas day," said Yachtkeeper Diana Greer. "I serve it as the first course for breakfast/brunch. We serve on board our 51-foot Yacht-O-Fun Bluewater Coastal Cruiser on Lake Texoma, along the Texas/Oklahoma border, after a morning cruise."

Diana and Buddy, businesspeople from Richardson, operate bed-and-brunch on weekends. Guests may opt to come aboard for dinner, or board later in the evening for a moonlight cruise. The cruiser is docked at night. Guests overnight in one of two staterooms, then resume cruising in the morning.

Diana, a former caterer, devised this original recipe as a surprise refreshment. She's been cooking since grade school and first got interested watching her grandmother cook for her family and for boarders. "Since B&Bs are our favorite way to travel, we wanted to return that hospitality to others by sharing the boat and our cooking with guests," she said. She and Buddy have been cruising with guests since 1985 "and we still love it!"

🏠 *Another Yacht-O-Fun recipe:*
Breakfast Appetizer Cheese Spread, page 194

Fruit Tacos

Ingredients:

2 cups mixed fresh fruit of 3 or 4 varieties (honeydew, cantalope, watermelon, grapes, peaches, kiwi, strawberries and/or pineapple suggested), cubed
1 cup favorite flavored yogurt
6 to 8 small flour tortillas (1 per person)
1/4 cup vegetable oil
1/4 cup granola

Also:

Sugar, optional
Fruit slices and parsley

- Mix cubed fruit with yogurt. Set aside.
- Heat vegetable oil in a non-stick skillet and fry tortillas for 5 seconds, on one side only.
- While still soft, remove tortillas from hot oil, fold in half and drain on a rack or paper towels. Optional: dip the outside of each hot taco shell in sugar.
- Spoon the fruit mixture into the taco shells.
- Sprinkle granola over the fruit in each taco.
- Arrange the tacos on the platter and garnish with fruit slices and parsley and serve.

Makes 6-8 servings

from **Sipapu Lodge**
65 Piki Drive
P.O. Box 552
Sedona, AZ 86336
602-282-2833

"Fruit Tacos are my most requested dish from returning guests," said Innkeeper Lea Pace. It's no wonder guests love this dish, and it's no wonder they return to Sipapu Lodge. Lea and son Vince Mollan turned their home in West Sedona into a warm five-guestroom inn. The light guestrooms and the large living room have Southwest Indian decor and family antiques.

While fruit tacos are a popular summer breakfast treat, guests come to Sipapu Lodge year 'round to enjoy Sedona's outdoors. Famous for its scenic red rocks, Sedona's often-photographed Chimney Rock formation is just a short drive from this B&B. Hiking trails dot the hillsides for those who want to breathe the fresh air, take in a glowing sunset, or find the electromagnetic vortexes that some believe give off energy and provide healing.

Other Sipapu Lodge recipes:
Fruit Frappé, page 25
Spinach Dill Sauce, page 96
Hot, Spiced Melon, page 108
Southwest Egg and Bean Burritos, page 135
Spaghetti Squash Supreme, page 157

German Sautéed Apples

Ingredients:

3 tablespoons butter
3 tablespoons brown sugar, loosely packed
3 large green apples, MacIntosh preferred, washed, cored and sliced thinly
Dash or 2 of cinnamon

- In a non-stick skillet, melt butter and stir in brown sugar.
- Mix in thinly-sliced apples and a dash or two of cinnamon.
- Cook over low heat, stirring with a heat-resistant spatula, until apple slices are soft. This only takes a few minutes; be careful not to burn.

Tester's Comments: For more caramelized apples, add 1-2 tablespoons corn syrup with butter and brown sugar. This recipe is flexible enough to add other ingredients, such as firm pear slices. Pecans stirred in at the last minute also are a nice addition. Good served over German oven pancake.

Makes 4 servings

from **Davanna House**
107 East Clarksville Street
Jefferson, TX 75657
903-665-8238

"My father served this dish with pork, sausage or ham. He had a restaurant in a small town in Indiana for 40 years," said Innkeeper Pat Tuttle. Working in the restaurant was Pat's first experience in the hospitality business. She's chosen to continue in that industry as an innkeeper. "I know how important it is to please a guest. It is a lot of work, but rewarding."

Pat and Dave, who is a mechanical-engineer-turned-wood carver, opened this two-guestroom B&B in 1991. The house is Greek Revival style and it had been restored when they purchased it. The exterior is cypress, which is weather-resistant. Inside, guests find wood floors, antique furnishings, and plenty of rabbits, angels, cats and dogs that Dave carved and Pat painted.

"Breakfast is served in the dining room at 9 a.m.," Pat said, a time that seems to be agreeable to most. "Some guests have already had a pot of coffee before breakfast. Then others barely make it to the table by 9." But they don't want to miss a large, homemade breakfast of pancakes, sausage and these apples, or perhaps an egg dish, bacon, grits and fruit bread.

Other Davanna House recipes:
Layered Scrambled Eggs, page 123
Riced Potato Croquettes, page 164

Grandmother's Spirited Berries

Ingredients:

  1 pint fresh raspberries, blueberries, blackberries or sliced strawberries
  1/4 cup Japanese plum wine, Gekkeikan preferred

Also:

  Sugar or honey

🍓 As soon as you bring the berries home from the market, wash, drain and "place them in a glass bowl and pour the plum wine over them, folding gently. This will prevent them from molding in the refrigerator."

🍓 Fold in honey or sugar to taste.

🍓 Cover and store in the refrigerator. Serve straight, with milk or cream, or heap the berries over melon or grapefruit halves.

Makes 2-3 servings

from **La Mimosa B&B**
1144 Andrews Lane
P.O. Box 2008
Corrales, NM 87048
505-898-1354

"I learned this trick from my grandmother, who, when she came home with the berries, would call to my grandfather, 'Alfred, bring me some spirits,'" said Innkeeper Glorya Mueller.

Glorya and Joachim, a graphics designer and painter, opened one guest suite on the side of their home in 1989. They had moved back to Albuquerque after 15 years in New York state, where Glorya owned an art gallery. She opened another one in Albuquerque's Old Town. "One day I was standing there and I thought, 'What am I doing here? I've done this before.' Actually, I was working to pay someone to work in the garden and do the things I loved to do." She had read about a woman in a similar circumstance who opened a B&B, and she knew her home would be perfect for it.

The private suite is part of the original adobe home, built in the 1920s. Muellers have two acres of land, one of which is enclosed in a walled courtyard. Under the mimosa and cottonwood trees, guests can enjoy the flowers and fruit trees Glorya now tends herself. Or they can throw sticks to Sammy, the effervescent blue tick dog whose hefty canine sidekick, 125-pound Moses, would rather be petted. The rural town of Corrales, 15 miles north of downtown Albuquerque in the rich Rio Grande valley, has many galleries and boutiques within walking distance of the B&B.

🏠*Another La Mimosa recipe:*
Poached Pears, page 112

Honeydew Compote

Ingredients:

1 honeydew melon, cut in half and seeds removed
2 or 3 limes (to make 1/2 cup juice)
1/2 cup sugar
1/3 cup water
1 tablespoon gingerroot, peeled and grated
1 tablespoon fresh mint leaves (about 6-7 small leaves)

- Use a melon scoop to make honeydew balls. Place balls in a bowl and set aside.
- Remove the rind of 1 lime in strips with a vegetable peeler. Set aside.
- Squeeze out the juice of as many limes as necessary to make 1/2 cup.
- In a small heavy saucepan, mix the lime peel, lime juice, sugar, water and gingerroot.
- Boil mixture, stirring until the sugar is dissolved, at least 5 minutes total.
- Pour lime syrup through a sieve into a bowl and let cool.
- When cool, pour syrup over the melon balls. Mix in the mint leaves. Cover and chill for at least an hour or overnight.

Tester's Comments: Good over other fruit, too. Add a little cornstarch before boiling for a fruit salad dip.

Makes 4-6 servings

from **Adobe Abode**
202 Chapelle Street
Santa Fe, NM 87501
505-983-3133

"Such a simple but refreshing treat for a summer morning," said Innkeeper Pat Harbour. "Even guests who swear they don't like honeydew will ask for more." As director of advertising for a large company, Pat traveled extensively, but began avoiding monotonous hotel chains. For the past 15 years, she's been a B&B guest across the U.S. and abroad. "The lifestyles of the owners seemed so appealing and I vowed I would one day have my own B&B." She discovered Santa Fe on a business trip. "It took me six years to wait for my children to graduate high school, quit my job, move to Santa Fe and find the ideal house and location -- but here I am! I wake up every day to interesting conversation with my guests, blue skies and the best life anyone could want." After spending six months restoring this historic adobe home in downtown Santa Fe, Pat opened two guestrooms and a guesthouse in 1989.

Other Adobe Abode recipes:
Santa Fe Cheese Casserole, page 132
Caramelized French Toast, page 137
Apple Skillet Cake, page 142
Fiesta Baked Tomatoes, page 160

Hot, Spiced Melon

Ingredients:

1 cup honeydew
1 cup casaba melon
1 cup cantaloupe
1/2 teaspoon nutmeg
1/2 teaspoon ginger
1/2 teaspoon cloves

Also:

Whipped cream
Fresh mint leaves

- Cut melons into bite-sized pieces or scoop into melon balls.
- Place in a microwave-safe dish.
- Mix the spices and sprinkle over melon pieces.
- Heat in the microwave 1 or 2 minutes until hot but not mushy.
- Top each serving with a dab of whipped cream and garnish with a mint leaf. Serve immediately.

Tester's Comments: Hot melon may not sound appealing at first, but this dish is surprisingly good, mostly due to the whipped cream and spices. Don't substitute or make it without them!

Makes 6 servings

from **Sipapu Lodge**
65 Piki Drive
P.O. Box 552
Sedona, AZ 86336
602-282-2833

Innkeeper Vince Mollan created this recipe as a way to use leftover melon. "Vince became a creative cook when he was in charge of preparing family dinners when he was in the sixth grade," said mother and co-innkeeper Lea Pace. His experimentation has paid off handsomely at this busy Sedona B&B.

Vince and Lea prepare breakfast while talking with guests in the first floor dining area. Guests often share information about their visit with other guests and the innkeepers. One of the advantages of staying in a B&B is having time with the resident innkeepers, and these know Sedona well. "Vince is very knowledgeable about special places to hike. He gets people off the beaten track and into the hidden nooks and crannies of our red rocks," Lea said.

Other Sipapu Lodge recipes:
Fruit Frappé, page 25
Spinach Dill Sauce, page 96
Fruit Tacos, page 104
Southwest Egg and Bean Burritos, page 135
Spaghetti Squash Supreme, page 157

Indian Fruit

Ingredients:

4 large pears, sliced, or 1 12-ounce can, undrained
1 pineapple, cut in chunks, or 1 12-ounce can, undrained
6 to 8 apricots, sliced, or 1 12-ounce can, undrained
3 to 4 peaches, sliced, or 1-12-ounce can, undrained
1 cup sugar, if using fresh fruit above
1 12-ounce package frozen or 1 16-ounce can tart cherries, undrained
1/2 cup butter
1-1/2 teaspoons curry powder
3/4 cup brown sugar, packed

Also:

Whipped cream

- In a 9 x 12-inch baking dish, combine fresh or canned fruits and juice. If using fresh or frozen fruit not in syrup, stir in 1 cup sugar and mix well.
- In a saucepan, melt butter. Stir in curry powder and brown sugar.
- Bring curry mixture to a slow boil over medium heat, stirring constantly.
- Drop spoonfuls of thick curry mixture over fruit.
- Bake in a preheated oven at 300 degrees for up to 1 hour, until bubbly and the fruit is "tender."
- Let stand for a few minutes, then serve warm with dollops of whipped cream.

Makes 8 servings

from **Casa de Leona**
1149 Pearsall Highway
P.O. Box 1829
Uvalde, TX 78802
210-278-8550

Innkeeper Carolyn Durr serves a taste of India often during the winter when a warm dish of fruit is a welcome treat at breakfast. She may serve it with muffins and Eggs Benedict and suggests it as a sidedish to roast pork.

Guests at this four-guestroom B&B step into a hacienda built on the Leona River amid 17 private acres. Fort Inge, located a few miles south, was the site of the first white settlers in 1849, but these lush river flats have been home to Native Americans and soldiers and hunters for many more years. Deer inhabit the riverflats and guests often can get a glimpse of them at sunset. Wood ducks are happy to be fed breadcrumbs by guests. Guests are happy to be fed by Carolyn. She and Ben have a courtyard and a music room for guests' use. They have traveled in B&Bs for years.

Another Casa de Leona recipe:
Raspberry Rouser, page 29

109

Morning Surprise Pears or Apples

Ingredients:

 1/2 cup applesauce
 1/2 cup pecans or walnuts, chopped
 1/2 cup heavy cream
 1 cup mincemeat
 4 pears or apples, cored

Also:

 Heavy cream
 Cinnamon

▪ Mix applesauce, nuts, cream and mincemeat.

▪ Remove cores of apples or pears.

▪ Stuff mincemeat mixture into center of fruit.

▪ Place stuffed fruit in a baking pan. Spoon any remaining mincemeat mixture into the pan.

▪ Microwave on "high" for 8 to 10 minutes or until fruit is "tender." Or bake in a preheated oven at 325 degrees for 1 hour or until fruit is tender.

▪ Serve warm. Spoon extra mincemeat mixture in pan over top of fruit. Then pour heavy cream over each pear or apple. Sprinkle top with a dash of cinnamon.

Makes 4 servings

from **The Bonnynook B&B Inn**
414 West Main Street
Waxahachie, TX 75165
214-938-7207

"My mom said to never experiment on guests, but this one worked out," said Bonnie Franks. After she and Vaughn opened their B&B in 1989, "we were working through a lot of procedures -- one of them was the grocery list. Vaughn thought I had gotten the fruit for breakfast and I thought he had." Turned out neither had (thus the "morning surprise"), but Bonnie had these ingredients on hand. "Everybody loves this dish, much to my surprise," and she makes it frequently now, on purpose.

Many guests come to Waxahachie to see homes like this one, trimmed in gingerbread, because the town has the state's largest concentration of gingerbread-trimmed Victorian architecture. The Bonnynook has been one of six homes featured, along with the courthouse, auditorium and museums, on the annual Gingerbread Home Trail tour the first full weekend in June.

🏠 *Other Bonnynook B&B Inn recipes:*
Blueberry Pudding, page 35
Pennsylvania Shoofly Squares, page 40
Applesauce Pancakes and Syrup, page 143

Overnight Baked Apples

Ingredients:

 4 apples
 1 cup raisins
 1 teaspoon brown sugar
 1 teaspoon butter
 2 teaspoons pine nuts or walnuts

Also:

 Orange peel, ground
 Cloves
 Nutmeg
 Cinnamon
 Orange juice, reconstituted from concentrate only
 Sour cream or yogurt

- The night before serving, core apples almost to the bottom, removing seeds and creating a cavity.

- Set apples in a baking dish. Place 1/4 cup raisins in each cavity. Add a pinch of orange peel, cloves, nutmeg and cinnamon to each. Then add 1/4 teaspoon brown sugar and butter to each. Top with 1/2 teaspoon nuts.

- Pour enough orange juice in the baking dish to fill half-way up the sides of the apples.

- Cover with lid or foil. Place in a 150 or 175-degree oven overnight. (Editor's Note: Many ovens are unreliable below 200 degrees, so you may wish to prepare apples, then set "timed bake" clocks to switch on and bake apples at 250 degrees for about 90 minutes before breakfast time.)

- In the morning, serve with a dollop of sour cream or yogurt, topped with a sprinkle of cinnamon.

Makes 4 servings

from Orinda
1 Orinda Lane
P.O. Box 4451
Taos, NM 87571
505-758-8581

Anything that can be made overnight is appreciated by Innkeepers Karol and Dave Dondero, who don't want to skimp on taste in breakfast haste. The smell of cinnamon and the other spices is an added benefit to this recipe.

Breakfast is served family-style in the large sunroom, which has a 20-foot open ceiling and a Navajo rug from Buffalo Bill Cody's Scout Rest Ranch. Dave and Karol opened the adobe estate in 1988 after leaving California's Silicon Valley for the gentle lifestyle here. They like Taos' "charm of a New Mexico village from earlier in the century" and lovingly describe it as "an hour north of Santa Fe and 50 years behind!"

Another Orinda recipe:
Orange Walnut Bread, page 71

Poached Pears

Ingredients:

1 cup dark brown sugar, packed
1 cup dark rum
1 cinnamon stick
3 two-inch strips of fresh orange peel, or 2 teaspoons grated peel
2 ripe, firm pears, peeled but with stem left on

Also:

Water
Mint sprigs or fresh berries

- In a large saucepan, mix sugar, rum, cinnamon and orange peel.
- Add enough water, about 4 cups, so there are about 5 cups of liquid.
- Bring to a boil and simmer for 10 to 15 minutes.
- Add the pears and simmer for about 5 minutes or until fruit is soft, but not mushy. "Be sure to turn two or three times so all sides of the pears are infused with the liquid."
- Serve warm with mint sprigs or berries. Pour some of the rum sauce over all. Or cover the saucepan and refrigerate pears in the liquid overnight, then serve cold with same garnishes.

Makes 2 servings

from **La Mimosa B&B**
1144 Andrews Lane
P.O. Box 2008
Corrales, NM 87048
505-898-1354

"The poaching liquid can be refrigerated in a covered glass jar and re-used." Innkeeper Glorya Mueller keeps hers at least a month and said the rum-based sauce improves with age. "When the produce stores look grim, I will poach banana halves in the pear liquid and garnish with berries." Glorya's showcase course is the fruit. She might purée berries and place the pears atop the purée for a dramatic color effect. Warm muffins, baguettes and cheese with grapes or cherries also are served. Guests might enjoy breakfast in their private suite or on the courtyard patio amid the lilacs, garden flowers and cherry and apple trees. The mimosa tree blooms from late spring through September and attracts hummingbirds to its pink blossoms.

Glorya and Joachim, who lived in the area after they first married, returned after many years in New York state. The B&B is one suite on the side of their adobe home, set on two acres in the lush Rio Grande valley.

🏠*Another La Mimosa recipe:*
Grandmother's Spirited Berries, page 106

Spiced Peaches

Ingredients:

1 1-pound, 13-ounce can peach halves, undrained
1/2 cup vinegar
1/4 cup brown sugar, packed
1 teaspoon whole cloves or 1/2 teaspoon ground cloves
1 cinnamon stick

- In a saucepan, gently mix peaches, vinegar, brown sugar, cloves and cinnamon stick.
- Bring to a boil, then simmer 15 minutes.
- Pour into a tightly-covered container and refrigerate. Serve hot or cold, but remove whole cloves and cinnamon stick before serving.

Tester's Comments: Good "tang" from the vinegar. True comfort food when served hot in the winter. You may substitute 3 large fresh peaches, peeled and thickly sliced, and 2 tablespoons sugar for the canned peaches. Consider adding a dash of ground cinnamon and 1/2 teaspoon or more of ginger, or a slice of ginger root. Simmer 5-8 minutes; don't let peaches get mushy.

Makes 4 servings

from **The Norton-Brackenridge House**
230 Madison Street
San Antonio, TX 78204
512-271-3442

These easy and aptly-named peaches often are on the breakfast buffet served on the white-railed veranda. Owner Carolyn Cole or Manager Nancy Cole may serve an egg dish, pastries and fruit such as this to guests in the five guestrooms. Carolyn, who earned a home economics degree, has also used her cooking expertise in teaching and as a former employee for Magic Chef.

The Norton-Brackenridge House, named after former owners, was built in 1906, but moved to 230 Madison Street in 1985. Carolyn bought it, restored the former apartment building and opened it as an inn less than a year later. It won an award in 1987 from the San Antonio Conservation Society for restoration and adaptive use of the property.

Located in the King William Historic District, six blocks from the Alamo, the two-story home has southern verandas on each story, divided by intricately-carved columns. Inside, guestrooms have hand-crocheted bedspreads and are furnished with Carolyn's family heirloom antiques.

Another Norton-Brackenridge House recipe:
Blintz Souffle, page 120

Strawberry Soup

Ingredients:

4 cups frozen, sliced strawberries
1 cup sugar
1 cup sour cream
1/2 cup cold water

Also:

Mint leaves

- Defrost strawberries, saving the juice with the berries
- Purée strawberries in the blender, then mash purée through a sieve. Discard any pulp that remains.
- In a saucepan, whisk sugar and sour cream into strawberry purée. Stir in cold water.
- Stir constantly over low heat until mixture is heated through, but do not boil.
- Cover and chill thoroughly, preferably overnight.
- To serve, pour into soup bowls and garnish with mint leaves.

Tester's Comments: Substitute "lite" sour cream, if you wish. Either way, it's better than a strawberry milkshake!

Makes 4 servings

from **The McKay House**
306 East Delta Street
Jefferson, TX 75657
903-665-7322

"Enjoy this on a hot summer day," advises Innkeeper Peggy Taylor, who has been refreshing guests since 1985 at this 1851 home, on the National Register of Historic Places. She might serve the soup in her Depression Glass bowls.

A "gentleman's breakfast" is served in the conservatory, a lovely room Peggy and Tom added in 1991. Several dining tables are situated to enable guests to look out four sets of French doors at the lush garden while they feast. The large garden is full of blooming perennials, and the local birds and squirrels are as well-fed as McKay House guests.

While that room is new, the rest of the McKay House "experience" is old-fashioned. Peggy or other servers wear Victorian gowns and aprons while serving a homemade breakfast. Guests may have indulged in period dress themselves the night before, as Taylors have hung antique dressing gowns for women and night shirts for men in each of their eight guestrooms. Vintage hats also are for trying on or wearing for afternoon refreshments.

Other McKay House recipes:
Summer Melon Soup, page 115
Orange French Toast, page 138

Summer Melon Soup

Ingredients:

    2 cups ripe cantaloupe pieces
    2 cups ripe casaba pieces
    1 cup ripe honeydew pieces
    1/3 cup lime juice, freshly squeezed (2 or 3 limes)
    1/4 cup plain non-fat yogurt
    1 teaspoon honey

Also:

    Mint leaves
    Lime slices

- In a blender or food processor, purée the melon pieces.
- Mix in lime juice, yogurt and honey. Blend again.
- Cover and chill thoroughly, preferably overnight.
- To serve, pour into soup bowls and garnish with mint leaves and a lime slice.

Makes 6 servings

from **The McKay House**
306 East Delta Street
Jefferson, TX 75657
903-665-7322

Innkeeper Peggy Taylor takes full advantage of the variety of East Texas fruit, and summer melons are one of the best crops from the sandy soil.

In 1984, Tom and Peggy found this Greek Revival home languishing and in need of loving restoration. Thirteen months later, they opened six guestrooms in an inn with refinished floors, new bathrooms, fresh wallpaper, a porch swing and picket fence, and antique furnishings gathered all over the U.S.

A few years later, the Dallas couple moved a Sunday House to the property. Sunday Houses were owned by farmers who came into town on Saturday to do business, then stayed in their small houses for church on Sunday. Taylors created two guestrooms here. One is particularly unique as a replica of a log cabin. It has a big stone fireplace, a clawfoot bathtub in one corner, and the corner commode is concealed in a wooden outhouse replica, complete with half-moon cut out on the door. Likewise, touches in the other house are unusual, like the bathroom with twin "his and hers" clawfoot bathtubs. But there is no shortage of romance or comfort, with Amish quilts and electric blankets on all the beds and fireplaces in some guestrooms.

Other McKay House recipes:
Strawberry Soup, page 114
Orange French Toast, page 138

Spicy-hot. Gooey-rich. Tasty vegetarian. Old-fashioned hearty. All the breakfasts that mom made, or wishes she could have, are here. As might be expected at these B&B inns, amazing things are done daily with the ordinary, inexpensive, always-on-hand egg. Likewise, innkeepers have a way of making elegant creations out of what used to be rather mundane French toast, pancakes or waffles. And many of their ideas are time-savers, to boot -- dishes that are made ahead the night before, refrigerated overnight and baked in the morning. No need for plain-old-bacon-and-eggs again!

Entrees

Aunt Tommy's Sausage Quiche

Ingredients:

12 slices bread
Butter, softened
1/2 pound bulk pork sausage
1/4 cup onion, chopped
2 tablespoons pimientos
1 cup favorite cheese, grated
4 eggs
2 cups milk
1 teaspoon salt

- Trim crusts from the bread. Butter each slice.
- Grease a 7 x 11-inch baking pan. Place 6 slices of the bread, buttered-side down, in the pan.
- Cook sausage and onion, breaking up sausage as it cooks. Drain.
- Stir in pimientos.
- Spread meat mixture evenly over bread slices.
- Top with half the cheese.
- Place other 6 slices of bread, buttered-side up, on top of the cheese layer.
- In a large bowl, beat eggs, milk and salt. Pour egg mixture over bread.
- Top with remaining half of cheese. Quiche may be covered and refrigerated for up to 18 hours.
- Bake in a preheated oven at 325 degrees for 50 minutes. Serve immediately.

Makes 6 servings

from **Magnolia House**
101 East Hackberry Street
Fredericksburg, TX 78624
512-997-0306

Innkeeper Geri Lilley credits this recipe to her Aunt Tommy Roberts. Geri often serves it as part of a large country breakfast.

For Geri , innkeeping "came naturally." She had entertained business associates at a ranch every weekend for years. She bought this 1925 home in the Hill Country town of Fredericksburg and began major restoration. In 1991, she opened it as a six-guestroom inn.

Outdoors, guests can enjoy the porches or sit under the magnolias by a limestone waterfall. Indoors, guests will appreciate the woodwork, hand-selected by the architect owner who had the house built.

Other Magnolia House recipes:
Cinnamon Nut Coffeecake, page 37
Apple Brown Betty, page 180

Baked Deviled Eggs

Ingredients:
6 eggs, hard-boiled
1/2 cup mayonnaise or salad dressing
4 English muffins, split
8 slices Canadian-style bacon
1/2 cup Cheddar cheese, grated

Also:
Black pepper, freshly ground

- In a large bowl, chop hard-boiled eggs with a pastry cutter until the pieces are very small.

- Combine eggs and mayonnaise and blend well.

- Top each muffin half with Canadian bacon, then 1/4 cup of egg mixture. Sprinkle cheese on top.

- Bake in a preheated oven at 350 degrees for 6 to 8 minutes or until thoroughly heated and cheese is melted. Before serving, sprinkle with a touch of freshly ground black pepper.

Tester's Comments: Add 1/2 teaspoon prepared mustard to egg mixture for more morning zip. Lean, round deli slices of corned beef or pastrami instead of the Canadian bacon are also very tasty.

Makes 4 servings

from **The White Horse Inn**
2217 Broadway Avenue
Galveston, TX 77550
800-76-B AND B (800-762-2632)

An egg and meat dish is always on the breakfast menu at this Galveston inn, and this recipe fills the bill. Innkeeper Robert Clark serves it with fresh fruit and homemade muffins or bread at 9 a.m. in the formal dining room.

Many of the guests in this 1884 home come for getaways from Houston, only 50 miles away. They come to relax on the beach, 11 blocks away, where the water reaches 92 degrees in the summer. Or they'll walk eight blocks to shop and dine in the Strand Historic District, the restored downtown section that was a lively commercial center when Galveston's port was in its heydey.

Robert bought this home on Oct. 6, 1988, and opened for business Dec. 1. "It had been vacant for two years. It needed no structural work, just cosmetic." The 14-foot-high walls were wallpapered, floors refinished and carpeted, and the entire house and carriage house were furnished in Victorian antiques or reproductions. While the job might have daunted most, Robert had restored five other proud Galveston homes and knew what he was undertaking. He also knew B&Bs, having stayed in a number during business travels.

Another White Horse Inn recipe:
Peach or Pear Kuchen, page 189

Blintz Souffle

Ingredients:

1-1/2 cups sour cream
1/2 cup orange juice
6 eggs
1/4 cup margarine, softened
1 cup flour
1/3 cup sugar
2 teaspoons baking powder
1/2 teaspoon cinnamon

Filling:

16 ounces small curd cottage cheese
2 egg yolks
1 tablespoon sugar
1 teaspoon vanilla extract
1 8-ounce package cream cheese

Also:

Sour cream and apricot preserves OR
Fresh fruit and powdered sugar

- For Filling: In a small bowl, beat cottage cheese, egg yolks, sugar, vanilla and cream cheese until well blended. Set aside.
- In a blender, combine sour cream, orange juice, eggs, margarine, flour, sugar, baking powder and cinnamon.
- Cover and blend well, scraping sides occasionally.
- Pour half of batter into a greased 9 x 13-inch pan.
- Drop filling by spoonfuls over the batter. Spread evenly.
- Pour remaining batter on top of filling. Cover and refrigerate at least 2 hours, or overnight.
- Bake in a preheated oven at 350 degrees for 50-65 minutes or until puffed and light-golden brown.
- Serve hot, topped with sour cream and apricot preserves or fresh fruit and powdered sugar.

Tester's Comments: Sweet and rich, this was a big hit at a buffet brunch.

Makes 12 servings

from **The Norton-Brackenridge House**
230 Madison Street
San Antonio, TX 78204
512-271-3442

"This is a great recipe for making the night before -- there's no preparation in the morning," said Owner Carolyn Cole, a home economics major who enjoys finding recipes for her inn. Breakfast is served buffet-style here. Guests may eat on the front veranda, sitting on twisted willow furniture.

This 1906 home, once an apartment building, was turned into a five-guestroom inn in 1986. Carolyn discovered it after the building had been moved to its Madison Street location in 1985. Located in San Antonio's King William Historic District, it is a short walk to the River Walk and the Alamo.

Another Norton-Brackenridge House recipe:
Spiced Peaches, page 113

Cactus Quiche

Ingredients:

Enough canned cactus to cover the bottom of a 7-inch casserole dish
2 tablespoons red onion, very thinly sliced
1 cup Gruyere cheese, grated
1/2 cup cottage cheese
5 eggs
2 dashes white pepper

- Generously grease a 7-inch round casserole dish.
- Layer cactus, red onion slices and Gruyere cheese, in that order.
- In a food processor, blend cottage cheese until creamy. Add eggs and white pepper and blend.
- Pour egg mixture over other ingredients. Bake in a preheated oven at 350 degrees for 25 to 30 minutes.

Makes 4 servings

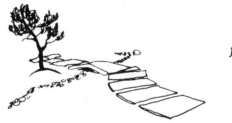

from **La Posada de Taos**
309 Juanita Lane
P.O. Box 1118
Taos, NM 87571
505-758-8164

A hearty quiche or other Southwestern-style entree is part of the breakfast Innkeeper Sue Smoot serves every day before guests head off to ski or explore Taos art galleries. Breakfast is served at 8 a.m. at the long dining room table, on blue-and-white dishes thrown by a local potter.

That Sue Smoot, who lived in New York for 20 years and earned a degree in architecture there, is running her own inn is no surprise, really. The surprise is that she's doing it in Taos. She always wanted to own a New England inn, but found real estate too pricey. She was able to trade her 450-square-foot New York apartment for nearly 3,500 square feet in this adobe home.

Of course, it cost her plenty, and more than just money. Turning the 75-year-old handyman's special into a welcoming and functioning B&B also cost her five broken ribs. During a busy renovation, completed in a mere two months, she took one very long step backward and fell into the basement. But the effort has resulted in a lovely living room with a log-beamed viga ceiling and kiva fireplace, a sunny dining room with French doors, and four guestrooms in the main house, plus a honeymoon cottage. She's also landscaped, adding a Japanese garden and a dry river bed that runs through the courtyard.

Other La Posada de Taos recipes:
Homemade Salsa, page 91
Shirred Eggs with Green Chili Sauce, page 134

Eggs Florentine

Ingredients:

1/4 cup butter, melted
1/3 cup flour
1 cup milk, warmed
1 cup half-and-half, warmed
2 cups white sharp Cheddar cheese, grated
1 pound spinach, washed and stems removed, or frozen chopped spinach, defrosted
Pinch of nutmeg
4 eggs, poached

Also:

Paprika

▶ In a non-stick skillet or saucepan, melt butter. Whisk in flour, then milk and cream. Cook, stirring constantly, until thick. Stir in cheese. Remove from heat. Cover and keep warm.

▶ Drop spinach (fresh or frozen) into boiling water with a pinch of nutmeg. (Frozen spinach needs to be in water only long enough to heat, fresh spinach slightly longer, until wilted.) Drain well. Chop fresh spinach finely.

▶ Poach eggs.

▶ Arrange spinach on four plates. Place one poached egg in the middle of the spinach and top with cheese sauce. Sprinkle with paprika.

Makes 4 servings

from **The Brimstone Butterfly**
940 North Olsen Avenue
Tucson, AZ 85719
800-323-9157 or 602-322-9157

"This makes an excellent light, yet fancy, breakfast," said Innkeeper Maria Johnstone. "It's easy to prepare on order." Maria's guests might select this entree the night before, then enjoy it at her 10-foot table in the large eat-in kitchen. Maria jokes that she bought this house "because I had to find a house that would accommodate that table!" But she really bought it because it made an ideal B&B. "It has a delightfully tranquil feeling to it. People immediately feel they're at home." An open area looks out onto the pool.

One guestroom is located in the main house, and two others are in adjacent guest cottages. The original part of the adobe home was built in the 1930s. Guests are welcome to swim in the pool, enjoy a fire in the living room fireplace or use the study in the main house, where they gather for breakfast. Breakfast may include homemade bread, fresh fruit and a made-to-order entree, served on linen and china and with crystal. Maria enjoys talking with guests while she's working on breakfast and they're enjoying coffee or juice.

🏠*Another Brimstone Butterfly recipe:*
Shredded Wheat Toasting Bread, page 78

Layered Scrambled Eggs

Ingredients:

8 eggs, beaten
8 tablespoons sour cream
4 tablespoons Cheddar cheese, grated
4 tablespoons Monterey Jack cheese, grated
12 strips bacon, fried crisp

Cream Sauce:
2 tablespoons butter
2 tablespoons flour
1 cup milk, heated
Dash of salt and white pepper

- To make Cream Sauce: Melt butter in a non-stick pan. Whisk in flour. Stir over low heat until bubbly. Slowly whisk inhot milk, and stir over medium heat until bubbly and thick. Boil 1 minute. Add salt and pepper to taste.
- In a separate pan ("I use a double boiler"), scramble eggs, but leave moist.
- Mix in Cream Sauce. Then divide eggs between four greased ramekins.
- On top of the egg layer, spread 2 tablespoons sour cream per ramekin.
- Crumble 3 strips bacon per ramekin as the third layer. Top with 1 tablespoon each type of cheese.
- Bake in a preheated oven at 350 degrees for 15-20 minutes.

Tester's Comments: These eggs lend themselves well to experimentation and personal preferences. Add layers of sautéed onions, chilies, sliced ripe olives, diced tomatoes and/or hot pepper cheese. Top with salsa and sour cream or plain yogurt.

Makes 4 servings

from **Davanna House**
107 East Clarksville Street
Jefferson, TX 75657
903-665-8238

"We started this by trying to hold eggs for late breakfast arrivals," said Innkeeper Pat Tuttle. "A cream sauce always helps" eggs stay moist. "So does the sour cream." Mosts guests can manage to get to the dining room by 9 a.m. Breakfast is served at the mahogany table with highback chairs, on Blue Danube blue-and-white china. It might include these eggs, grits, homemade muffins or fruit bread, and, at guest's request, chicory coffee.

This cypress clapboard house sits on a corner under large trees. Only Tom Sawyer would want to paint the long white picket fence that stretches around the corner. The Greek Revival-style home, circa 1860, has earned a Texas State Historical Marker. Tuttles opened two antique-filled guestrooms here in 1991. Guests enjoy walking Jefferson's quiet streets to take in the many outstanding restored examples of 19th century architecture.

Other Davanna House recipes:
German Sautéed Apples, page 105
Riced Potato Croquettes, page 164

Megetas

Ingredients:

1/3 cup onion, chopped
2 small garlic cloves, minced
8 to 10 small corn tortillas, torn into tiny pieces
6 to 8 eggs, beaten
1 7-ounce can Herdez or Embasa-brand Mexican red picanté sauce
1 to 2 cups favorite cheese, grated

Also:

Butter
Vegetable oil
Salt and pepper
Optional ingredients: Cooked sausage, diced potatoes, cherry tomatoes, halved

■ In a skillet, melt a little butter and oil. Sauté onion and garlic (and optional potatoes).

■ As mixture cooks, stir in tortilla pieces. "Add oil as needed to keep from burning. Fry until tortillas are crisp." (Add optional sausage now.)

■ Stir in beaten eggs, picanté sauce and salt and pepper to taste. Cook over low heat as a scrambled egg dish.

■ Stir in cheese at the last minute. Serve after cheese has melted.

Makes 4-6 servings

from **The Brenham House**
705 Clinton Street
Brenham, TX 77833
409-830-0477

Guests might enjoy Megetas on the sun porch of this home, along with fruit and homemade bread. The recipe is from Janice and David Phillips' son-in-law, who has relatives in Mexico.

Janice and David dreamed of owning their own B&B for more than 10 years before selecting this Brenham home. David, a book salesman who traveled extensively, and Janice visited B&Bs in six states before taking the plunge. They opened four guestrooms in 1991 in a home which had been restored as a B&B. It has a 55-foot-long hallway, hung with family heirloom quilts, and two library/sitting rooms for guests' use.

"Since Brenham is the home of Blue Bell Ice Cream, arriving guests have their choice of nearly a dozen flavors of this National Ice Cream of Texas, kept in a special freezer," David said. (Indeed, weekday guests can tour the creamery.) The Phillips serve the ice cream with brownies or cookies, and encourage guests to unwind from big-city life. Houston is only 70 miles away, and many guests come to relax and browse for antiques in Brenham's antique shops.

Mexican Puff

Ingredients:

3 eggs
2 cups sharp Cheddar cheese, grated
1 cup cooked white or brown rice
2 tablespoons mild picanté sauce

Also:

Paprika

➤ In a large bowl, beat eggs, cheese, rice ("brown is best") and picanté sauce.

➤ Spray a one-quart casserole dish with non-stick cooking spray. Pour in egg mixture. Sprinkle with paprika.

➤ Bake in a preheated oven at 350 degrees for 30 to 35 minutes, or until casserole is still "a bit runny in the middle -- use this as a topping as it's passed around." Serve hot.

Makes 4-6 servings

from **The McCallum House**
613 West 32nd Street
Austin, TX 78705
512-451-6744

This dish, along with homemade muffins and fresh fruit, might grace the breakfast table at this five-guestroom inn. Guests gather for a family-style breakfast, joined by Innkeepers Nancy and Roger Danley.

"We got into innkeeping by accident," said Nancy. "We read a column in the paper about B&Bs and decided to use our spare bedroom." That was in 1983. Today, Danleys have three guestrooms on the second floor, a garden apartment on the property, and a large suite in the dormered third floor called "Jane's Loft," which Roger built. Nancy works at innkeeping full-time and is active in professional organizations, and she and Roger are now "hooked" on B&Bs. "We love it because of the interesting guests, many from all over the world visiting UT-Austin, just a few blocks from here," Nancy said.

Danleys bought this 1907 home from the heirs of Jane and A.N. McCallum. A.N. was Austin's school superintendent for 39 years. Jane was a suffrage leader who helped organize the "Petticoat Lobby" for human service reforms in Texas. She served under two governors as secretary of state. They also raised five children in this house, which Jane designed while pregnant with her fifth child. The large house has earned a state historical marker.

🏠*Other McCallum House recipes:*
Oatmeal Breakfast Cake, page 39
Lemon-Glazed Oat Muffins, page 52
Migas, page 126

Migas

Ingredients:

1 heaping cup broken tortilla chips
1/2 cup Cheddar cheese, grated
1/2 cup Monterey Jack cheese, grated
3 eggs
2-3 green onions, chopped
2-3 strips of red bell pepper, chopped
2 small tomatoes, chopped

Also:

Paprika, parsley or cilantro
Picanté sauce
Plain yogurt or sour cream

- In a large bowl, mix chips, cheeses and eggs. Let stand until chips soften, at least 10 minutes.
- In a non-stick skillet, sauté onions, pepper and tomato until crisp-tender.
- Stir in egg mixture. Scramble until eggs are just done --"solid but soft."
- Place in a serving bowl. Garnish with paprika, parsley or cilantro. Serve with picante´sauce and yogurt or sour cream.

Makes 4-6 servings

from **The McCallum House**
613 West 32nd Street
Austin, TX 78705
512-451-6744

"We tasted this at a local Tex-Mex restaurant and figured out the recipe," said Innkeeper Nancy Danley. "It's great with corn muffins or just a coffeecake." Every morning, guests gather at the long dining room table for fresh Texas fruit, an entree such as this, muffins or coffeecake and good conversation.

Four of the guestrooms here are in the main house, with a fifth called the "Garden Apartment." The most lavish and newest is "Jane's Loft," which takes up the entire third floor. Roger Danley designed and constructed the suite, which has dormered windows in the sitting area, a queen-sized bed, an outdoor porch with a swing, a large bathroom, a kitchen area and white wicker furniture. It's popular for honeymoons or longer stays. Roger, who makes a living renovating historic homes, has worked on their home's gradual conversion to an inn since they opened one guestroom in 1983. The McCallum House is located about eight blocks from the University of Texas.

Other McCallum House recipes:
Oatmeal Breakfast Cake, page 39
Lemon-Glazed Oat Muffins, page 52
Mexican Puff, page 125

Mushrooms with Eggs

Ingredients:

2 eggs
2 tablespoons butter or margarine
1 pound fresh mushrooms, washed or peeled
1/2 cup heavy cream, half-and-half or low-fat milk
Crust for a one-crust pie

- Boil eggs for 15 to 20 minutes until "hard boiled." Rinse under cold water, peel and slice.
- Melt the butter in a saucepan. Add the mushrooms and simmer gently for 10 minutes.
- Stir in the egg slices and cream.
- Pour the mixture into a one-quart casserole dish or deep-dish pie plate and cover with the pie crust.
- Bake in a preheated oven at 350 degrees for 15 minutes or more, until the crust is slightly browned.

Makes 6 servings

from **The Delforge Place**
710 Ettie Street
Fredericksburg, TX 78624
512-997-6212

Innkeeper Betsy Delforge literally "discovered" this recipe. It was in a recipe collection she found in family's sea captain's trunk she inherited. She's adapted several of the antique recipes for use in her B&B in historic Fredericksburg. Likewise, many family heirlooms are in use there, as well. In the Map Room, for instance, a seven-foot mural map of her great-grandfather's hangs on the wall. He traveled with Admiral Perry and opened up many harbors of the world in the 1800s. Other family antiques can be found throughout the inn and in the four guestrooms.

Their inn itself is a carefully-restored antique. The dining room was built in 1898 as a one-room "Sunday house," commonly built by farmers who needed accommodations while in town to attend church services or do business. German pioneer Ferdinand Koeppen built this one on a tract of land set aside by the German Emigration Company for a communal garden. It was moved to its present site on Ettie Street, seven blocks from Main Street, and restored in 1975. Betsy and George settled here after George retired from a long career as an aeronautical engineer and Betsy as a dress designer and food consultant for major food companies. They have a very active second career as innkeepers, and Betsy also makes and sells "special day" gift baskets.

Other Delforge Place recipes:
Fresh Peach Soup, page 24
Belgium Torte, page 33
Cornmeal and Rice Griddle Cakes, page 147
Chocolate Potato Drop Cakes, page 181

Omelette Fleur de Courges

Ingredients:

4-1/2 ounces squash blossoms (about 8 medium blossoms)
1/4 cup butter
16 eggs, well beaten
1/4 cup fresh parsley and chives, chopped
Salt and white pepper
Pinch of garlic powder
Pinch of nutmeg

🌶 Wash squash blossoms without bruising and allow to dry. Then shred blossoms and set aside.

🌶 In a large, heavy omelette pan, melt butter over high heat until butter turns light brown and has a slightly nutty fragrance. Reduce heat.

🌶 Pour beaten eggs into hot butter. Stir once without scraping the bottom.

🌶 Shake pan briskly to distribute eggs evenly. Stir in squash blossoms, parsley and chives, salt, pepper, garlic powder and nutmeg, again without disturbing the bottom.

🌶 When edges are set, tilt the pan and fold the upper third of omelette over the squash blossoms. Do the same for the other side. Turn omelette over while sliding it onto a plate, so it is served with the folded side down. Garnish with a ribbon of chive and parsley.

Makes 8 servings

from **Salsa del Salto B&B Inn**
Highway 150, 1 mile north of Arroya Seco
P.O. Box 1468
El Prado, NM 87529
505-776-2422

Innkeeper and French chef Dadou Mayer developed this recipe for his French cooking school, and a similar version is in his cookbook, "La Cuisine A Taos." Now the giant omelette graces the dining table in the two-story common room with a huge stone fireplace. Breakfast may include homemade preserves and croissants, as well.

Dadou and Mary Hockett had this six-guestroom-inn custom-designed by architect Antoine Predock. "We had a vision of creating a place where visitors could stay in luxury while experiencing the rugged, historic Taos that we love," Mary said. Their inn opened in 1988.

Located on the mesa seven miles from Taos Plaza and seven miles from Taos Ski Valley, the inn has an outdoor pool, hot tub and tennis court for guests' use. Summertime croquet tournaments are held on the lawn. Each guestroom has views of the mesa or the Sangre de Cristo Mountains, location of Taos Ski Valley, where Dadou doubles as ski instructor. Each guestroom also has a king-sized bed with cozy down comforter and Southwest decor.

Potato Quiche Ranchero

Ingredients:

1 32-ounce package frozen "Southern style" hash browns, thawed
1/4 cup vegetable oil
1 cup salsa
1/4 cup ranch dressing
4 eggs, lightly beaten
1 cup milk
1 cup shredded white cheese, such as Monterey Jack or Swiss
1 cup shredded yellow cheese, such as Cheddar or Colby

Also:

Sour cream, salsa, paprika and fresh cilantro

- Put thawed potatoes into a large bowl lined with four layers of paper towels (or clean kitchen towels). Place two layers on top and squeeze out excess water.

- Remove paper towels. Stir in oil to coat potatoes.

- Spray a 9 x 13-inch baking dish with non-stick cooking spray. Arrange potatoes evenly on bottom.

- Bake in a preheated oven at 450 degrees for 45 minutes or until potatoes are golden brown.

- While potatoes are baking, mix salsa and ranch dressing.

- In a separate bowl, mix eggs and milk.

- When potatoes are done, turn oven to 350 degrees. Spread salsa mixture evenly over potatoes. Cover with egg mixture. Top with white cheese layer, then yellow cheese layer.

- Bake for 45 minutes "or until cheese bubbles but isn't too brown." Let stand 5 minutes. Serve with a generous dollop of sour cream, salsa, a sprinkle of paprika and a sprig of cilantro.

Tester's Comments: Long baking time makes this best for brunch. Try hot salsa or hot pepper cheese, or Greg's suggestions, below, to spice it up. Serve with fruit and brunch is complete.

Makes 8 servings

from **Lynx Creek Farm**
Off Highway 69
P.O. Box 4301
Prescott, AZ 86302
602-778-9573

"This dish can be embellished with a layer of green chilies or chorizo between the potatoes and cheese," said Innkeeper Greg Temple (if you use chorizo sausage, brown and drain it first). Greg often serves it to guests who come to hike or picnic on the 25 acres, pick their own apples or fruit, or soak in the spa overlooking Lynx Creek. Greg and Wendy offer B&B in the main house or in two antique-filled guest suites, each with a view of the creek or valley.

Another Lynx Creek Farm recipe:
Blue Corn Pineapple Muffins, page 45

Relleno Casserole

Ingredients:

1 27-ounce can chopped green chilies, rinsed
1-1/4 pound Monterey Jack cheese, sliced
1-1/4 pound medium Cheddar cheese, sliced
4 cups sour cream
12 eggs
1 teaspoon salt

🥄 Butter a 9 x 13-inch pan. Layer chilies on the bottom. Then arrange a layer of cheese slices on top in a checkerboard pattern by alternating slices of yellow and white cheese.

🥄 Repeat layers until all chilies and cheese are used, about three layers of each.

🥄 In a large bowl, beat sour cream, eggs and salt.

🥄 Pour egg mixture over cheese and chili layers. Bake in a preheated oven at 350 degrees for 50 minutes. Let stand for 10 minutes before serving.

Tester's Comments: I used only 8 ounces of chilies; the result still was good. Using Co-Jack cheese (Colby and Monterey Jack, mixed) means no checkerboarding, which can't be seen, anyway, once it's covered with eggs. This rich casserole can easily be cut in half; use an 8-inch square pan. "Lite" sour cream can be substituted.

Makes 8-10 servings

from **Dierker House**
423 West Cherry Avenue
Flagstaff, AZ 86001
602-774-3249

Innkeeper Dorothea "Dottie" Dierker serves this casserole with sausage, fresh fruit and sweet rolls for a filling breakfast. Breakfast is served in the formal dining room of this National Register home, which was built in 1914 as a summer home for a ranching family. Dottie raised her children here, and decided after staying in B&Bs in Europe to open her own once the children were grown. She opened three guestrooms in 1984.

The guestrooms are located upstairs in the two-story home. Guests have a private entrance, sitting area and sunny kitchen upstairs for their use. Dottie has decorated the guestrooms and home with antiques.

Many guests come to Flagstaff as the gateway to the south rim of the Grand Canyon. Others come to hike in the Ponderosa pine forests, cross-country or downhill ski, or escape the summer heat in other parts of the state. Dierker House is within walking distance of downtown.

🏠*Another Dierker House recipe:*
Green Jalapeno Jelly, page 89

Rosevine Breakfast Bake

Ingredients:

2 cups frozen hash brown potatoes, grated
1 cup seasoned croutons
1-1/2 cups Cheddar cheese, grated
1 cup ham, diced
1 4-ounce can sliced mushrooms
1-1/2 cups Swiss cheese, grated
10 eggs
2 cups milk
Salt and pepper to taste
1 teaspoon red pepper flakes, or to taste
1 cup corn flakes, crushed

- Spray a 9 x 13-inch baking pan with non-stick cooking spray.
- Sprinkle frozen potatoes evenly over bottom of pan.
- Top with layers of croutons, Cheddar cheese, ham, mushrooms and Swiss cheese, in that order.
- In a large bowl, beat eggs, milk, salt and pepper and red pepper flakes until frothy.
- Pour egg mixture over layers.
- Sprinkle crushed corn flakes on top.
- Cover pan and refrigerate overnight.
- In the morning, bake in a preheated oven at 350 degrees for 1 hour, or until eggs have set. Cool slightly before serving.

Tester's Comments: This is a flexible recipe that can accommodate preferences. For more "zip," add 2 tablespoons minced onion, or delete red pepper flakes and use part hot pepper cheese, or add a 4-ounce can of green chilies over ham layer. Sprinkling on corn flakes in the morning makes them a little crispier.

Makes 8-10 servings

from **Rosevine Inn B&B**
415 South Vine Avenue
Tyler, TX 75702
214-592-2221

Innkeeper Rebecca Powell appreciates the ease of night-before preparation of this egg casserole. She might serve it with fresh fruit and hot, homemade muffins. She and Bert Powell built and opened this four-guestroom inn on the site of a former physician's home, which had burned down decades ago. The inn is set under oak trees, well back from the brick street near Tyler's "azalea district" and quaint antique shops.

🏠 *Other Rosevine Inn B&B recipes:*
Blueberry Peach Coffeecake, page 34
Blueberry Honey Butter, page 85

Santa Fe Cheese Casserole

Ingredients:

2 cups Monterey Jack cheese, grated
2 cups Cheddar cheese, grated
2 4-ounce cans green chilies, drained and chopped (save some for garnish)
4 eggs, separated
2/3 cup evaporated milk
1 tablespoon flour
1/2 teaspoon salt
1/8 teaspoon pepper
2 medium tomatoes, sliced

Also:

Cilantro sprigs
Salsa

- Combine the cheeses and chilies in a buttered 3-quart casserole dish.

- Beat egg yolks, milk, flour and seasonings.

- In a separate bowl, beat egg whites until stiff, but not dry. Fold into the egg yolk mixture.

- Fold the egg mixture into the cheeses and chilies in the casserole.

- Bake in a preheated oven at 325 degrees for 30 minutes. Arranged sliced tomatoes on top and bake for 30 minutes more.

- Remove from oven. Garnish with cilantro sprigs and green chilies. Serve with salsa on the side.

Tester's Husband's Comment: "Boy, I hope you make this again!"

Makes 8 servings

from **Adobe Abode**
202 Chapelle Street
Santa Fe, NM 87501
505-983-3133

Innkeeper Pat Harbour often serves this as an entree with hot flour tortillas. "My guests rave about the combination of green chilies and cheese," she said. She serves it in a cactus-shaped casserole dish that holds a pink flower-shaped dish for the salsa. What else for someone who has enough linens and china to change the entire table daily? A full breakfast is served in the dining room of the 1907 adobe home. "Everyone eats together at the table while I cook in the adjoining kitchen." Pat opened two guestrooms and a separate guest house in 1989. Lively breakfast conversation is one reason she enjoys innkeeping.

Other Adobe Abode recipes:
Honeydew Compote, page 107
Caramelized French Toast, page 137
Apple Skillet Cake, page 142
Fiesta Baked Tomatoes, page 160

Scrambled Eggs with Chive Cream Cheese

Ingredients:

1/4 cup milk
2 dozen eggs
Salt and pepper to taste
2 tablespoons butter
12 ounces chive or chive-and-onion cream cheese (can be purchased in a plastic tub, softened)

Also:

Fresh chive strips for garnish

🖙 In a large bowl, whisk milk and eggs until eggs are well-beaten. Add salt and pepper to taste.

🖙 Melt butter in a large skillet. Pour in eggs. Scramble eggs over medium heat, until almost set. Then stir in cream cheese.

🖙 Serve hot, garnished with garden-fresh chives cut in long strips.

Tester's Comments: Also good with plain cream cheese and basil flakes, to taste, instead of chive cream cheese.

Makes 12 servings

from **Crystal River Inn**
326 West Hopkins Street
San Marcos, TX 78666
512-396-3739

"This recipe is one of our stand-bys for a busy morning and the guests always adore it," said Innkeeper Cathy Dillon. She serves it with herbed broiled tomatoes, fresh fruit and croissants. The recipe is easily cut down.

At their 1883 inn, Cathy and Mike specialize in creative weekend packages. River Weekends are a natural because of the four crystal-clear area rivers for canoeing and innertubing. River packages include itinerary planning, an innertube and shuttle service to and from any of the four rivers. Murder Mysteries also include a tubing trip, but add dinner, and costumes for guests who are participants in the mystery, based on real people, places and events in San Marcos. Romantic Interlude packages combine hot-air ballooning, breakfast in bed, champagne and truffles and "his and her" massages or other options with the B&B stay. Ladies Escape Weekends are especially for friends who want to shop-til-they-drop at San Marcos' new designer outlet mall, then return to the Inn for a stress-relieving massage, facial or pedicure. Dillons also will arrange bike touring, gourmet weekend and golf packages.

🏠*Other Crystal River Inn recipes:*
Creamy Fruit Dip, page 87
Herbed Broiled Tomatoes, page 161
Hot Crab Dip, page 201

Shirred Eggs with Green Chili Sauce

Ingredients:

8 eggs
2 cups sharp cheddar cheese, grated
8 strips bacon, fried crisp
Red and green bell pepper strips
Fresh parsley

For Green Chili Sauce:
1 pound ground beef, "not too lean"
2 cups fresh roasted green chilies, chopped
1 cup onion, chopped
2 cups hot water
1 49-ounce can chicken broth
1 tablespoon prepared mustard
1/2 teaspoon cumin
1 tablespoon oregano
2 tablespoons flour or cornstarch

- For Sauce: Brown ground beef. When almost brown, add chilies and onion.

- Stir in water, broth, mustard, cumin and oregano. Simmer for 15 to 20 minutes (while eggs bake).

- Mix flour or cornstarch with 3/4 cup cold water. Stir in enough to thicken sauce after cooking for a few minutes. Keep warm while eggs finish baking.

- For Shirred Eggs: Grease individual ramekins. Break in two eggs per serving.

- Bake in a preheated oven at 300 degrees for 15 to 20 minutes. "Perfect shirred eggs should have firm whites and yolks should just be set."

- Remove from oven. Sprinkle with cheese and top with two strips of bacon per serving. Reheat to melt cheese.

- Garnish with strips of pepper and parsley. Serve warm Green Chili Sauce on the side.

Makes 4 servings

from **La Posada de Taos**
309 Juanita Lane
P.O. Box 1118
Taos, NM 87571
505-758-8164

"If you can't get fresh, medium-hot chilies that have been roasted, you may use canned chilies, but your sauce will not be very spicy," said Innkeeper Sue Smoot. Sue cooks like a native, though she's only lived here since 1983.

She bought this sprawling, 75-year-old adobe home, with a view of the mountains, when it had seen better days. An intensive, two-month restoration involved moving walls, changing doorways, installing guest bathrooms and recovering from broken ribs she suffered after falling into the basement. In 1984, she opened four guestrooms and a honeymoon cottage. In addition to the view, the inn enjoys a location three blocks from Taos Plaza.

Other La Posada de Taos recipes:
Homemade Salsa, page 91
Cactus Quiche, page 121

Southwest Egg and Bean Burritos

Ingredients:

2 cups pinto, Anasazi or black beans
1/4 cup onion, diced
1/4 teaspoon cayenne pepper
8 to 10 eggs
1/4 cup water
1/2 teaspoon cumin
2 crushed garlic cloves or 1/2 teaspoon garlic powder
2 ounces (half a can) green chilies, chopped
1/4 cup green onion, chopped
8 to 10 small flour tortillas
1 cup Cheddar cheese, grated

Also:

Sour cream, sliced ripe olives, and paprika

- Cook beans according to package directions with diced onion and cayenne pepper. (Lea Pace cooks hers all night in a slow-cooking crock.)
- Combine eggs, water, cumin and garlic. Beat with a wire whisk until blended.
- Add green chilies and green onion and blend again.
- In a frying pan over medium heat, scramble the eggs until they are cooked but not dry.
- On a tortilla, place a spoonful of eggs on one side and a spoonful of beans on the other side.
- Roll the tortilla into a burrito. Place seam-side-down on a baking dish. Sprinkle with cheese.
- Heat in a 300 degree oven until the cheese is slightly melted, about 15 minutes.
- Top each burrito with sour cream and olives and sprinkle with paprika. Serve immediately.

Makes 8-10 servings

from **Sipapu Lodge**
65 Piki Drive
P.O. Box 552
Sedona, AZ 86336
602-282-2833

"I invented this burrito recipe for guests from New York who wanted to experience a special Southwest breakfast," said Innkeeper and native-Arizonan Lea Pace. She serves the burritos with a special Mexican coffee spiked with cinnamon. All Lea's breakfasts have some Southwestern flavor. Many feature herbs from her herb garden, right next to the house.

Other Sipapu Lodge recipes:
Fruit Frappé, page 25
Spinach Dill Sauce, page 96
Fruit Tacos, page 104
Hot, Spiced Melon, page 108
Spaghetti Squash Supreme, page 157

Tex-Mex Egg Casserole

Ingredients:

    6 slices bread, toasted
    Butter or margarine
    1 pound hot breakfast or Italian bulk sausage
    12 ounces Cheddar cheese, grated
    6 ounces jalapeno cheese, sliced
    6 eggs, beaten
    2 cups milk

Also:

    Warmed tortillas, optional
    Picanté sauce

- Toast bread. Trim crusts and butter each slice.

- Grease an 8 x 11-inch baking pan. Place bread slices of the bread, buttered-side down, in the pan.

- Cook sausage, breaking up sausage as it cooks. Drain.

- Spread sausage evenly over bread slices.

- Top with grated Cheddar cheese, then jalapeno cheese slices.

- In a large bowl, beat eggs and milk. Pour mixture over cheese. Cover and refrigerate overnight.

- In the morning, bake in a preheated oven at 350 degrees for 35 minutes. Remove cover and bake 10 minutes more or until firm. Remove from oven and let sit for 10 minutes before serving. Serve with warm tortillas and top with picanté sauce. Or cut casserole into 2 x 4-inch pieces and wrap in tortillas.

Tester's Comments: This is probably the "hottest" recipe in the book and is the spicy version of Aunt Tommy's Sausage Quiche. Offer hot picanté sauce for the masochists; the wimps may appreciate sour cream topping.

Makes 6-8 servings

from **Antik Haus Inn**
118 South Union Street
New Braunfels, TX 78130
512-625-6666

Innkeeper Loretta Dueweke notes that should there be any leftovers, this dish can be reheated in the microwave or a warm oven. Guests at this 1907 home may fill up on this breakfast entree before spending a leisurely day floating the Comal or Guadelupe Rivers on innertubes. New Braunfels visitors also like to check out the town's authentic German restaurants and the outlet malls on the outskirts. Loretta and Ralph have four guestrooms in their inn, which are decorated in antiques ("antiks," for the German heritage). The home's interior, which they restored, has 12-foot ceilings and lots of natural woodwork. Outdoors is the garden gazebo with hot tub.

Another Antik Haus Inn recipe:
Raisin Bran Muffins, page 58

Caramelized French Toast

Ingredients:

6 eggs
1 cup milk or half-and-half
1 tablespoon sugar
1 teaspoon vanilla extract
1/2 teaspoon cinnamon
1/4 cup unsalted butter
1 cup brown sugar, not packed
1/2 cup light corn syrup
6 slices French or sourdough bread, cut on a slant 1-inch thick

- In a large bowl, whisk eggs, milk, sugar, vanilla and cinnamon. Set aside.
- Melt butter. Swirl around the bottom of a 9 x 13-inch baking pan.
- Crumble brown sugar on top of the butter, covering as much of the pan as possible.
- Drizzle corn syrup over sugar.
- Dip each side of bread slices in the egg mixture. Place dipped bread on top of ingredients in pan.
- Bake in a preheated oven at 400 degrees for 20 to 25 minutes, until top of bread is lightly browned and the sauce underneath is bubbling.
- To serve, flip each slice over on a plate. "Best served right away as the sauce caramelizes."

Tester's Comments: Sprinkle on chopped pecans for a sinful French toast version of pecan "sticky buns."

Makes 6 servings

from **Adobe Abode**
202 Chapelle Street
Santa Fe, NM 87501
505-983-3133

"This is by far the easiest dish I make," revealed Innkeeper Pat Harbour. "While it's definitely not for dieters, there's very little ever left on the plates."

Pat's tan adobe home on the corner of Chapelle and McKenzie streets is only a few blocks from Santa Fe's Plaza, reknowned art galleries and 190+ restaurants. Guests may return to Adobe Abode and relax on the porch, overlooking the cactus garden, or in the common room, which has a fireplace, log-beamed ceiling and Southwest decor. Pat's two guestrooms in the main house have antique quilts, writing desks and hand-painted furniture. She also has a guesthouse with handcrafted twin platform beds.

Other Adobe Abode recipes:
Honeydew Compote, page 107
Santa Fe Cheese Casserole, page 132
Apple Skillet Cake, page 142
Fiesta Baked Tomatoes, page 160

Orange French Toast

Ingredients:
    4 eggs
    2/3 cup orange juice, freshly squeezed
    1/2 cup milk
    1/4 cup sugar
    1/2 teaspoon vanilla extract
    1/4 teaspoon nutmeg
    1 loaf French bread, sliced 1-inch thick
    1/3 cup butter, melted
    1/2 cup pecans, chopped

Also:
    Powdered sugar
    Maple syrup

- Whisk together eggs, orange juice, milk, sugar, vanilla and nutmeg.
- In a greased 9 x 13-inch pan, place a single, tight-fitting layer of bread slices.
- Pour egg mixture over bread. Cover and refrigerate overnight, turning once.
- In the morning, pour melted butter evenly over bread. Sprinkle with chopped pecans.
- Bake in a preheated oven at 400 degrees for 20 to 25 minutes or until golden brown.
- To serve, sprinkle each slice with powdered sugar. Serve with syrup and fresh fruit.

Tester's Comments: To increase the orange taste, hold off on pecans; melt orange marmalade in the microwave and brush on a layer before serving, then sprinkle with powdered sugar and the pecans.

Makes 4-6 servings

from The McKay House
306 East Delta Street
Jefferson, TX 75657
903-665-7322

At breakfast, guests relax in the conservatory, sitting on wicker chairs and looking out four sets of French doors to the large garden. They are served by Innkeeper Peggy Taylor or helpers, wearing outfits from the 1800s. Here, guests can dress up, too: vintage hats are in their rooms, and antique sleeping gowns for men and women are in the armoires.

After having stayed in B&Bs during 20 years of travel, Peggy and Tom spent more than a year restoring this 1851 home. They combined the best of the past with modern amenities, like electric blankets, thick towels, skylights and modern bathrooms. In addition to six guestrooms in the main house, a whimsically-decorated Sunday House has two more.

Other McKay House recipes:
Strawberry Soup, page 114
Summer Melon Soup, page 115

Pecan French Toast

Ingredients:

1 cup margarine, melted
1 cup brown sugar, packed
1 cup pecans
8 eggs, beaten
1-1/2 cups milk
1 loaf of French bread, cut into 1-1/2-inch-thick slices

- In a 12 x 15-inch jelly roll pan, melt margarine as oven preheats.

- Stir in brown sugar. Sprinkle with pecans.

- In a separate bowl, beat eggs and stir in milk.

- Dip slices of bread into egg mixture. Arrange slices over brown sugar mixture in jelly roll pan. Pour any remaining egg mixture over bread.

- Bake in a preheated oven at 350 degrees for 35 to 40 minutes. Invert each slice onto plates.

Makes 6-8 servings

from **Villa Cardinale**
1315 West Oracle Ranch Road
P.O. Box 649
Oracle, AZ 85623
602-896-2516

Innkeeper Judy Schritt's French toast needs no syrup, but choose maple if you wish. Guests here might be served this breakfast outdoors in the courtyard by the copper fountain. Judy serves a full breakfast with farm-fresh eggs, homemade breads and muffins and seasonal fruit.

"Our B&B was designed and built by my husband and myself," Judy said. She and Ron opened four guestrooms in 1989 with log-beamed ceilings, kiva fireplaces and a private entrance to each room from the courtyard. They also added an antique shop, where Ron repairs and restores antique clocks. The home is decorated in antiques they have discovered on their travels.

At 4,500 feet in the Santa Catalina Mountains, the Oracle area enjoys comfortable temperatures year 'round. Guests often come from Tucson, only 35 miles away, to relax and to hike or birdwatch. Nighttime stargazing in the courtyard is popular. Biosphere 2, where eight "citizens of the biosphere" are living in a miniature controlled environment, is nearby, and guests may take the "world of discovery" tour there.

Pineapple Stuffed French Toast

Ingredients:

12-14 thick slices cinnamon raisin bread, crusts removed
4 eggs, beaten
2-1/2 cups milk
1 teaspoon almond or vanilla extract
1 teaspoon cinnamon
4 ounces cream cheese, cut into small pieces
1 8-ounce can crushed pineapple, drained
3 tablespoons grated orange rind, optional

Also:

Fresh berry syrup or maple syrup

- Spray an 8 x 12-inch baking pan with non-stick cooking spray, or grease well.

- In a large bowl, mix eggs, milk, extract and cinnamon.

- Dip half of the bread slices in the egg mixture. Place in the baking pan to cover the bottom.

- Arrange cream cheese pieces evenly over the bread slices.

- Spoon pineapple onto each piece of bread, on top of the cream cheese.

- Sprinkle with orange rind, optional.

- Dip rest of the bread slices in egg mixture. Places slices on top of the other slices, like a sandwich.

- Pour remaining egg mixture carefully over all the bread. Cover the pan with foil.

- Refrigerate for at least 30 minutes. Can be refrigerated overnight.

- Bake in a preheated oven at 350 degrees for 45 to 50 minutes or until bread is not mushy. Serve with warm syrup.

Makes 6 servings

from **Birch Tree Inn**
824 West Birch Avenue
Flagstaff, AZ 86001
602-774-1042

"This is the most-often requested recipe we have," said Sandy Znetko. It's easy on co-innkeepers Sandy and Donna Pettinger because it can be made the night before. Mornings find them busy cooking bacon or sausage and setting the table with one of several sets of china for a different "look" each day. They and their husbands opened this five-guestroom inn in 1989.

Other Birch Tree Inn recipes:
Spiced Peach Punch, page 30
Hoogie Googie Cake, page 186
Saucy Spice Bars, page 191
Hearty Vegetable Soup, page 199
Layered Mexican Dip, page 203

Strawberry Stuffed French Toast

Ingredients:

1 8-ounce package cream cheese, softened
2 tablespoons strawberry jam
1 loaf French bread, sliced in half lengthwise
6 eggs, beaten
1 cup low-fat milk
1 teaspoon sugar
1 teaspoon vanilla extract

Also:

Cinnamon
Low-sugar strawberry jam or syrup

- In a food processor or with a mixer, beat cream cheese and jam.

- Spread jam mixture on one cut-side of the bread. Top with other half. Wrap in plastic wrap and refrigerate overnight.

- In the morning, unwrap the bread and slice about 1/2-inch thick.

- In a large bowl, beat the eggs, milk, sugar and vanilla.

- Dip both sides of the bread slices into egg mixture. Then brown on a non-stick griddle or a pan sprayed with a non-stick cooking spray. Before turning to brown the other side, sprinkle with cinnamon.

- Serve with low-sugar strawberry jam or fruit spread, or with syrup.

Makes 6-8 servings

from **Bartram's White Mountain B&B**
Woodland Lake Road
Route 1, Box 1014
Lakeside, AZ 85929
602-367-1408

Homemade strawberry jam, made each year in season by Innkeeper Petie Bartram, is used in place of syrup on hot slices of this French toast. No one leaves Petie's breakfast table hungry. Her family-style breakfast might include this entree, fruit, home-fried potatoes and a breakfast meat.

Cooking such a feast is no feat for Petie, who is co-owner of a catering business. She and a friend decided to start one in this resort area, so she is operating two businesses heavily dependent on food. Petie opened three guestrooms in 1987 after she and her husband semi-retired here. The rooms are full of homecrafted touches, such as needlework or other country crafts Petie somehow found time to complete.

Other Bartram's White Mountain B&B recipes:
German Pancake, page 148
Home-Fried Potatoes, page 162

Apple Skillet Cake

Ingredients:

    1/4 cup unsalted butter
    3 large eggs
    3/4 cup flour
    2 tablespoons sugar
    3/4 cup milk
    1 teaspoon cinnamon
    1 teaspoon vanilla extract
    2-3 green apples, such as Granny Smith, thinly sliced to make 2 cups

Also:

    Maple syrup

- In a 9 or 10-inch cast iron skillet, melt butter as oven preheats.

- In a large bowl, whisk eggs, flour and sugar until smooth.

- Whisk in milk, cinnamon and vanilla. Then stir in apples.

- Pour the batter over the butter in the skillet. Spread apples evenly.

- Bake in a preheated oven at 375 degrees for 30 minutes, or until cake is puffed and begins to pull away from the sides of the skillet.

- Transfer quickly to breakfast table, then cut into pie-shaped wedges. Serve with syrup.

Makes 4-6 servings

from **Adobe Abode**
202 Chapelle Street
Santa Fe, NM 87501
505-983-3133

This oven pancake is served on weekends at Pat Harbour's adobe B&B. "One morning at breakfast, a guest mentioned her grandmother's recipe for a skillet cake she often serves on the coldest winter days. I remembered that my great-aunt used to serve an apple cake when we would visit her. Luckily, my mother remembered the ingredients and this is the result of the two ideas."

Pat, a former advertising director for a large company, turned CEO of Adobe Abode in 1989. But she had made up her mind years before to have an inn of her own. She traveled extensively, often seeking out "alternative lodgings" to unremarkable hotels, and admired the life of the innkeeper. When the children had grown, she moved to Santa Fe and began a search for the right property. She then restored this 1907 adobe home and guesthouse.

Other Adobe Abode recipes:
Honeydew Compote, page 107
Santa Fe Cheese Casserole, page 132
Caramelized French Toast, page 137
Fiesta Baked Tomatoes, page 160

Applesauce Pancakes and Syrup

Ingredients:

1 egg
3/4 cup milk
1 tablespoon vegetable oil
1 cup applesauce
2 cups flour
1 teaspoon baking soda
1/2 teaspoon baking powder
1/8 teaspoon salt

Syrup:
1 cup apple jelly
1 cup applesauce
1/2 teaspoon cinnamon
1/4 teaspoon cloves
1/8 teaspoon salt

- For Pancakes: Mix egg, milk, oil and applesauce.
- In a separate bowl, sift together flour, baking soda, baking powder and salt.
- Stir dry ingredients into applesauce mixture. Mix well.
- Pour batter on a hot, greased griddle. Turn when bubbles appear. Cook other side until golden brown.
- For Syrup: Heat jelly until it "melts" and turns syrupy. Stir in applesauce, cinnamon, cloves and salt. Serve warm.

Tester's Comments: If using maple syrup instead of this apple syrup, add the cinnamon and cloves to the pancake batter. These pancakes turn a lovely golden brown.

Makes 6-7 servings

from **The Bonnynook B&B Inn**
414 West Main Street
Waxahachie, TX 75165
214-938-7207

"My mom made this as a special treat on Saturday mornings when we were kids," said Innkeeper Bonnie Franks. Now she serves it to guests who find it as appealing as she did as a kid.

Bonnie and Vaughn bought this home in 1983 and opened their four-guestroom inn six years later. They spent much time restoring the sunburst, fish scales, bullseyes and other gingerbread that trims the two-story home, one of many gingerbread homes in Waxahachie. In fact, it is one of more than 225 homes in town on the National Register of Historic Places. Guests may enjoy the antique-filled parlor, dining room, porches or sitting areas.

Other Bonnynook B&B Inn recipes:
Blueberry Pudding, page 35
Pennsylvania Shoofly Squares, page 40
Morning Surprise Pears or Apples, page 110

Blue Corn Buttermilk Pancakes

Ingredients:

 1 cup buttermik
 1 egg, room temperature (but not out of refrigerator for more than 2 hours)
 3 tablespoons butter, melted
 1/2 cup flour
 1/4 cup blue cornmeal
 1 teaspoon baking soda
 1/2 teaspoon salt

Also:

 Maple syrup

- In a large bowl, stir the buttermilk, egg and melted butter until smooth.

- In a separate bowl, mix flour, cornmeal, baking soda and salt.

- Stir the dry ingredients into the buttermilk mixture "only until the dry ingredients are moistened -- leave the lumps."

- Pour about 1/4 cup batter per pancake onto a hot, greased skillet or griddle. Spread batter with the back of the spoon so it is thinned out. Cook until bubbles appear, then flip and cook the other side briefly. Serve with maple syrup.

Tester's Comment: If you can't crack your own blue corn, this also is good using plain old yellow cornmeal.

Makes 3-4 servings

from **A Touch of Sedona**
595 Jordan Road
Sedona, AZ 86336
602-282-6462

"This is our most requested breakfast," said Innkeeper Doris Stevenson. "Dick experimented with blue corn until he got it perfect." Instead of using prepared cornmeal, they crack blue corn in a blender until it reaches "meal" consistency. Stevensons serve these topped with Whipped Maple Syrup.

Doris and Dick have traveled all over the U.S. and Canada, much of it by motorcycle over the past 10 years. They moved to Sedona in 1986 and opened their B&B three years later in this contemporary home. The four guestrooms each have different themes. There are eagle figurines in the Contemporary Eagle Suite and stained glass, blown glass or painted hummingbirds in the suite by that name. The Roadrunner Room has pictures featuring roadrunners, and the Kachina Suite's carved kachina "the headman" guards sleeping guests.

Another Touch of Sedona recipe:
Whipped Maple Syrup, page 97

Buttery Pancakes

Ingredients:

1 cup flour
1 teaspoon baking powder
3/4 teaspoon salt
2 eggs
1-1/2 cups half-and-half
1/2 cup butter, melted

- Stir together flour, baking powder and salt.
- In a separate bowl, beat eggs with the half-and-half.
- Pour egg mixture into flour mixture and stir. Then blend in melted butter. Batter will be thin.
- Pour about 1/3 cup batter for each pancake onto a hot griddle. When bubbles appear, flip and cook other side until golden brown.

Tester's Comments: Aptly named (don't grease a non-stick griddle). Crepe-like pancakes are wonderful with fruit syrup or preserves. For Scandinavian pancakes, serve these pancakes, rolled up like cigars, topped with whipped cream into which lingonberry jam or sauce has been folded.

Makes 4 servings

from **Rowell House**
301 South Alley Street
Jefferson, TX 75657
903-665-2634

Innkeeper Collie Parker often serves these pancakes to guests, knowing they are a sure-fire winner. "In trying to decide what I would serve guests, I thought about what even my pickiest eaters in the family would eat," she said. These are served for Christmas breakfast as a family tradition.

Collie, a librarian, and Brooks, an engineer, fell in love with Jefferson and decided it was where they wanted to "retire." After two years of searching, they found this restored circa 1858 home. "We had stayed in many B&Bs in this country and abroad and knew that we wanted to have a couple of rooms for that." They opened two guestrooms in 1990. They decided to continue operating the gift shop that was established in the white wood-sided house.

Guests may play the grand piano in the living room, under the impressive 14-foot ceiling. Refreshments are served in the afternoon, and in temperate weather, guests might enjoy them in the front porch rocking chairs. Walking the red-brick streets is a favorite pastime, taking in some of the 40 or so homes owned by that many millionaire residents of Jefferson prior to the Civil War. At that time, steamboats still were able to chug up from New Orleans. Today, the restoration makes visitors feel the clock has been turned back. This home has earned both a Texas and a national historic marker.

Cathy's Finnish Pear Pancakes

Ingredients:

    5 eggs
    1-1/2 cups milk
    1/2 teaspoon salt
    4 tablespoons sugar
    2 cups flour, sifted
    4 ripe pears, peeled, cored and thinly sliced
    4 tablespoons lemon juice
    1 cup butter, melted
    2 cup brown sugar, packed
    2 tablespoons cinnamon

Also:

    Sweetened whipped cream

- In a mixing bowl, beat eggs slightly. Stir in milk, salt and sugar.

- Sift in flour, mixing well. Set aside.

- Butter two 9-inch glass pie pans. Arrange pears in a fan shape in pans. Sprinkle with half of the lemon juice.

- In a separate bowl, mix remaining lemon juice, melted butter and brown sugar.

- Spread sugar mixture over pears. Then pour pancake batter over sugar mixture.

- Bake in a preheated oven at 400 degrees for 30 minutes, or until golden brown.

- Cut each "pie" into four or five wedges. Serve with whipped cream sprinkled with cinnamon.

Tester's Comments: Rich, gooey and sure to delight a sweet tooth or someone who is "not a breakfast eater."

Makes 8-10 servings

from **Grant Corner Inn**
122 Grant Avenue
Santa Fe, NM 87501
505-983-6678

"Cathy Wright visited the Inn a month before we opened," which would have been November 1982, recalled Innkeeper Louise Stewart. "During the stay, she made these wonderful pancakes." Louise and Pat Walter have incorporated them into the inn's breakfast menu. The hosts' friend visited during one of nine very hectic months in which their 1905 Colonial house, set amid adobes in Santa Fe, was restored. Today, the Inn has 13 guestrooms.

Other Grant Corner Inn recipes:
Grant Corner Inn Orange Frappé, page 26
Cheese Danish Coffeecake, page 36
Plum Cottage Cheese Pancakes, page 149
Cortés Hot Chocolate, page 168
Sour Cream Ambrosia, page 176

Cornmeal and Rice Griddle Cakes

Ingredients:
1 cup cooked white rice
1/2 cup cornmeal
1/2 cup flour
2 teaspoons baking powder
1/2 teaspoon salt
2 eggs, separated
1 cup milk

Also:
Maple syrup, warmed

- Cook raw rice according to package directions to obtain 1 cup ("instant" rice can be used).
- In a large bowl, mix cornmeal, flour, baking powder and salt.
- In a separate bowl, beat the egg yolks with the milk. Stir in cooked rice.
- Pour the rice mixture into the dry ingredients and mix.
- In a separate bowl, beat egg whites until stiff peaks form. Fold egg whites into pancake batter.
- Pour batter onto a hot, greased griddle, turning when bubbles appear.
- Serve with warmed maple syrup.

Makes 4 servings

from **The Delforge Place**
710 Ettie Street
Fredericksburg, TX 78624
512-997-6212

This "heirloom recipe" often is part of Innkeeper Betsy Delforge's seven-course breakfast. It was among a recipe collection she discovered in one of her family's sea captain's trunks. During the cooler months, Betsy may cook these pancakes on the woodstove. Then, guests enjoy breakfast in the dining room, which was the original one-room "Sunday house," built in 1898.

Whipping up elaborate breakfasts are all in a day's work for Betsy, who enjoyed a career developing new food products for several major food companies. She still enjoys trying new versions of old recipes, much to the benefit of guests here. Betsy handles the kitchen preparation while George, a retired aeronautical engineer, makes guests comfortable and serves the meal. They became innkeepers in 1985 and offer four antique-filled guestrooms. Breakfast might be brought to the suites or served to guests outdoors on the flower-filled patio, where herbs used in many recipes are grown.

Other Delforge Place recipes:
Fresh Peach Soup, page 24
Belgium Torte, page 33
Mushrooms with Eggs, page 127
Chocolate Potato Drop Cakes, page 181

German Pancake

Ingredients:
1/4 cup butter or margarine
3 eggs
3/4 cup milk
3/4 cup flour
2 tablespoons powdered sugar
1/2 teaspoon cinnamon

Also:
Favorite fruit topping or syrup

- In a cast iron frying pan, melt butter or margarine while preheating oven.
- Meanwhile, in a blender, mix eggs, milk, flour, powdered sugar and cinnamon.
- Pour blended mixture into the hot frying pan and return pan to the oven.
- Bake in the preheated oven at 425 degrees for 25 minutes or until golden brown and puffed.
- Serve with fruit pie filling, sugar and cinnamon or syrup.

Tester's Comments: Beautiful presentation, but falls quickly, so have guests seated when it's served! For homemade fruit topping, sauté 2 sliced apples in 2 tablespoons orange juice, 2 tablespoons margarine, 2 heaping tablespoons brown sugar, and 1/2 teaspoon cinnamon until apple slices are tender and sauce thickens.

Makes 5-6 servings

from **Bartram's White Mountain B&B**
Woodland Lake Road
Route 1, Box 1014
Lakeside, AZ 85929
602-367-1408

Innkeeper Petie Bartram often serves this oven pancake to guests. She may use apple pie filling sprinkled with cinamon and sugar for guests to use as a topping, instead of syrup.

Breakfast here is served family-style in the country-style dining room. Guests might eat on placemats Petie made herself, with linen napkins and crystal glasses. The emphasis here is on homey hospitality, and Petie will vary the menu according to guest's dietary needs. They may have to say "uncle" or she will fill them up with her homecooking, good enough to be sustain her local catering business. A refugee to the 7,000-foot-high pine country from the heat below, Petie gladly suggests where to hike to overlook the Mogollon Rim. Guests also come to ski at nearby Sunrise Park Resort near Show Low. Petie opened three guestrooms in 1987.

Other Bartram's White Mountain B&B recipes:
Strawberry Stuffed French Toast, page 141
Home-Fried Potatoes, page 162

Plum Cottage Cheese Pancakes

Ingredients:

6 eggs
2-1/2 cups cottage cheese
1/4 cup vegetable oil
1/2 cup flour
1/2 teaspoon salt
1 tablespoon sugar
3 fresh purple plums, coarsely chopped

Also:

3 plums, sliced and warmed
Maple syrup, warmed

- In a large mixing bowl, beat eggs with cottage cheese.
- Add the remaining ingredients, one at a time, beating well after each addition.
- Pour batter by the half-cupful onto a hot, greased griddle. Cook until golden brown or bubbles appear, then flip and cook other side until golden brown.
- Garnish each serving with sliced plums and serve with warmed maple syrup.

Makes 6 servings

from **Grant Corner Inn**
122 Grant Avenue
Santa Fe, NM 87501
505-983-6678

"These are the favorite at the Inn," said Innkeeper Louise Stewart. "Because of the many eggs and little flour, they are exceptionally light and not filling like most traditional pancakes. They are also delicious with peaches, apples or cherries." The pancakes often are one of two entree choices on the menu.

Louise knows good food. She grew up at the Camelback Inn in Scottsdale, which her father built and her family owned and managed until 1969, when Marriott Corporation purchased the resort. Her years at the family-run resort and Cornell Hotel School were well-spent. Grant Corner Inn is her family-run inn, with husband Pat Walter and daughter Bumpy. The Inn has first floor dining rooms and second and third floor guestrooms. The decor includes antiques, Indian art and bunnies (every type except the live kind), which have multiplied wildly and are everywhere from tea pots to door stops.

Other Grant Corner Inn recipes:
Grant Corner Inn Orange Frappé, page 26
Cheese Danish Coffeecake, page 36
Cathy's Finnish Pear Pancakes, page 146
Cortés Hot Chocolate, page 168
Sour Cream Ambrosia, page 176

Zucchini Hotcakes

Ingredients:

1-1/2 cups zucchini, grated (about 2 small or 1 medium zucchini)
2 tablespoons onion, grated
1/3 cup Parmesan cheese
1/4 cup flour
2 eggs
1 tablespoon mayonnaise
1/4 teaspoon oregano
Salt and pepper to taste

Also:

Sour cream with chives

- Pat grated zucchini dry with paper towels. Then mix all ingredients until smooth.

- Spoon 2 tablespoons batter per hotcake on a greased griddle or skillet. Spread with the back of the spoon. Cook on medium-low heat until golden brown, then flip and cook other side.

- Serve with sour cream with chives.

Tester's Comments: Simply delicious. For a change (gardeners, use that squash up!), add some ground cumin.

Makes 2-3 large servings

from **The Marks House**
203 East Union Street
Prescott, AZ 86303
602-778-4632

"I've had raves on the different flavors" combined in this recipe, said Innkeeper Dottie Viehweg. Her guests are pleasantly surprised to find something different on the breakfast menu. These also can be dinner fare.

This 1894 Queen Anne Victorian on Knob Hill above downtown was built by Jake and Josephine Marks. Jake was a rancher, had mining claims and was a merchant at various times in his professional life, but he was perhaps most successful as owner of the largest liquor distributorship in Arizona Territory.

The home, which had been converted to apartments, was restored in 1980 and opened as a B&B in 1987. Harold and Dottie Viehweg moved here from Scottsdale in 1991 to semi-retire as innkeepers. Their daughter, Beth Maitland Banninger, who stars as Traci on "The Young and the Restless," bought the B&B as a getaway and found the perfect "managers" in her parents.

Other Marks House recipes:
Impossible Coconut Pie, page 170
Buffet Salami, page 195

Blue Corn Waffles

Ingredients:

2 eggs, separated
1-1/2 cups milk
1/2 cup vegetable oil
1 teaspoon vanilla extract
1-1/2 cups blue cornmeal
1/2 cup flour
2 tablespoons sugar
1 tablespoon baking powder
1/2 teaspoon salt

Also:

Maple syrup

- Beat egg whites until stiff. Set aside.

- In a large bowl, mix egg yolks, milk, oil and vanilla.

- In a separate bowl, sift together the blue cornmeal, flour, sugar, baking powder and salt.

- Stir the dry ingredients into the egg mixture.

- Fold in beaten egg whites.

- Let waffle batter stand for 15 to 20 minutes.

- Pour onto a hot, greased waffle iron. Bake 3 to 5 minutes, until steaming stops. Keep waffles warm in the oven until all servings are ready. Serve with maple syrup.

Makes 10 servings

from **The Jones House**
311 Terrace Avenue
P.O. Box 887
Chama, NM 87520
505-756-2908

"Blue corn's flavor is slightly different," said Innkeeper Sara Jayne Cole. But she notes that rice flour may be substituted for the cornmeal and the waffles will still be light and very tasty. She serves them with warm maple syrup.

Sara Jayne and Phil Cole moved to Chama specifically to open this B&B. Sara Jayne had watched B&Bs boom in popular Santa Fe, where they were living, and she had taken hospitality management classes at the community college. They bought this 1926 home close to the Cumbres and Toltec Scenic Railroad station for their B&B, which they opened in 1988.

Other Jones House recipes:
Hurry Up Cake, page 38
Carrot Cake, page 196
Picnic Basket Quiche, page 208

151

Copper Bell's Favorite Waffles

Ingredients:
1/2 cup plus 3 tablespoons butter
2/3 cup sugar
3 eggs
1/2 teaspoon vanilla extract
2-1/4 cups flour
1/2 teaspoon baking powder
1/2 teaspoon cinnamon
1-1/4 cups milk

Also:
Maple or fruit syrup, whipped cream or fruit

- In a large bowl, cream butter, sugar, eggs and vanilla.
- Stir together flour, baking powder and cinnamon.
- Mix flour into butter mixture alternately with milk.
- Pour about 1/2 cup batter onto a hot, greased waffle iron. Bake until golden brown or the steaming stops, about 3 minutes. Serve with syrup or whipped cream and fruit.

Tester's Comments: Not as light as waffles with beaten egg whites, but taste doesn't suffer. One-bowl preparation a real plus.

Makes 6-7 waffles

from **Copper Bell B&B**
25 North Westmoreland Avenue
Tucson, AZ 85745
602-629-9229

Innkeeper Gertrude Eich-Kraus remembers these waffles as a childhood favorite in Germany. They were made by her grandmother who "made them with a real waffle iron, not with an electric one. And she baked them on an oven fired with wood or coal." Without modern conveniences, Grandma cooked a lot of waffles for the 13 grandchildren to munch on all day.

Gertrude and Hans moved to Tucson in 1989 from their German home near the border of France and Luxembourg. They moved to be near their children, who are a sculptor and a goldsmith. The large house, which was built in 1902 and completed in 1920, was purchased to open a B&B "like you can find in Germany." Guests have a choice of an American, German or French breakfast. Homemade preserves go with whichever is chosen. Guests eat breakfast in the home's large dining room.

Another Copper Bell recipe:
Cornflake Macaroons, page 198

Cornflake Waffles

Ingredients:

1-1/4 cups flour
3/4 cup finely crushed cornflakes (about 3 cups uncrushed)
1 tablespoon baking powder
1/4 teaspoon salt
2 eggs, separated
1-3/4 cups milk or buttermilk
1/2 cup vegetable oil

- In a large bowl, combine flour, cornflakes, baking powder and salt.

- In a separate bowl, mix egg yolks, milk and oil. Save egg whites.

- Stir egg mixture into cornflake mixture.

- In a separate bowl, beat egg whites until stiff peaks form. Fold into the batter without over-mixing.

- Oil and preheat a waffle iron. Pour approximately 1/2 cup batter onto the hot waffle iron. Remove when steaming has stopped.

Makes 6-7 waffles

from **Ash-Bowers-Jarrett House**
301 South Magnolia Street
Palestine, TX 75801
903-729-1935

Innkeeper Lee Jarrett serves these waffles with sliced strawberries and warm Pear-Butter Sauce. She uses about 2 cups of the pear syrup left over from making pear preserves (see page 92), adds 1/4 cup butter, 1/4 teaspoon cinnamon and a dash of nutmeg, and heats until the butter is melted.

A Texas State Historical Marker designates this Queen Anne Victorian as an historic landmark. It was built in 1878, and has the original carriage house, greenhouse, smokehouse and servant's house on the property. The exterior is loaded with gingerbread trim and a cupola crowns the roof. Inside, some of the doorways were carved in Eastlake design in 1886. The twin parlors have identical fireplaces with mirrors that reach the ceiling.

In 1986, the Jarretts opened three guestrooms in the main house and two in the carriage house in order to share their large home with others. A number of other Victorian homes are in the neighborhood, which makes for a fine walking tour, especially up Sycamore Street. Palestine is popular for antiquing and the spring-through-fall weekend excursions of the Texas State Railroad, which runs from Palestine to Rusk and back.

Another Ash-Bowers-Jarrett House recipe:
Pear Preserves, page 92

Galisteo Inn Cornmeal Waffles

Ingredients:

1/4 cup butter, melted
2 cups buttermilk
4 eggs, separated
3 tablespoons sugar
2 cups flour
1 cup blue or yellow cornmeal
2 teaspoons baking powder
1 teaspoon salt
1/2 teaspoon baking soda

Also:

Fresh berries or sliced bananas, butter and maple syrup

- In a mixing bowl, mix butter and buttermilk.
- In a separate bowl, beat the egg yolks with sugar. Then mix with buttermilk mixture.
- In a separate bowl, combine flour, cornmeal, baking powder, salt and baking soda.
- Combine the dry and liquid ingredients and mix well.
- In a separate bowl, beat the egg whites until soft peaks form.
- Fold egg whites into the batter.
- Oil and preheat a waffle iron.
- Pour approximately 1/2 cup batter onto the hot waffle iron. Remove when steaming has stopped.
- Serve with berries or sliced bananas, butter and maple syrup.

Makes 8 very large waffles or 12 seven-inch waffles

from **The Galisteo Inn**
Off Highway 41
HC 75, Box 4
Galisteo, NM 87540
505-982-1506

"We have a wonderful old waffle iron that makes huge waffles," said Innkeeper Joanna Kaufman. "We serve one waffle per guest with a dollop of sweet butter and piled high with fresh berries. Using blue cornmeal, indigenous to this area, turns the waffles an unusual but pretty color without changing the taste." Joanna, formerly a landscape architect, and Wayne Aarniokoski, formerly a landscape contractor, bought this 12-guestroom adobe estate after a vacation from California.

Other Galisteo Inn recipes:
Cranberry Smoothie Fruit Drink, page 23
Cranberry Raspberry Muffins, page 47
Galisteo Inn Cornmeal Scones, page 50
Chocolate Chip Banana Bread, page 68
Pumpkin Cheesecake, page 174

Mother's Best Ever Waffles

Ingredients:

3 eggs, separated
2 cups flour
5 teaspoons baking powder
1/2 teaspoon salt
1-3/4 cups milk
4 tablespoons vegetable oil

Also:

Maple syrup, warmed

- In a small mixing bowl, beat egg whites until stiff peaks form. Set aside.

- In a large bowl, sift together flour, baking powder and salt.

- Beat in milk and oil, then egg yolks.

- Gently fold in egg whites -- do not over-mix.

- Pour about 1/2 cup batter onto a hot, greased waffle iron. "Cook until light brown for soft waffles or browner for crisp waffles." Serve with warm syrup.

Tester's Comments: A good basic recipe, and sugarless to boot. For winter waffles, add cinnamon and/or chopped pecans to batter.

Makes about 8 waffles

from Tarlton House
211 North Pleasant Street
Hillsboro, TX 76645
817-582-7216

"This recipe was developed by my mother around 1936 when my father and his brother were drilling for oil in East Texas," said Innkeeper Jean Rhoads. Jean's children grew up loving these waffles under creamed chipped beef.

Jean and Rudy offer eight guestrooms in this three-story Queen Anne Victorian home, listed on the National Register of Historic Places. Built in 1895 by attorney Green "Duke" Tarlton, the home is a showcase for the finest craftsmanship. The front door has 123 pieces of beveled glass. The stairway is ornately carved. The seven coal fireplaces have handcarved oak mantels. The ceilings are 12 feet tall and the floors are of East Texas pine.

Jean and Rudy bought this 6,000-square-foot home after two other families attempted restoration but gave up. "We started by putting the plaster back on the walls," Jean said. The exterior hadn't been painted in 17 years. They rewired, replumbed, added air conditioning, and brought the total number of bathrooms up to 10. Their B&B opened in 1985.

Another Tarlton House recipe:
Creamed Eggs, page 169

Peachy Wheat Germ Waffles

Ingredients:

5 eggs
1 1-quart package non-fat dry milk
2 cups peach nectar
2 cups water
1-1/2 cups canola oil
1 tablespoon vanilla extract
3 cups flour
2 tablespoons sugar
4 teaspoons baking powder
1 teaspoon salt
1 teaspoon cinnamon
1 teaspoon nutmeg
1 teaspoon cloves, ground
1 cup whole wheat flour
1/2 cup wheat germ

Peach Topping:
1 peach per person, peeled and sliced
1/4 cup sugar
1/4 teaspoon cinnamon
1/4 teaspoon nutmeg
1/4 teaspoon cloves, ground
1 tablespoon cornstarch
2/3 cup cold water
1 shot peach cream liqueur per
    person, optional

🐎 Beat eggs for 1 minute.

🐎 In a separate bowl, mix dry milk, peach nectar and water. Stir in eggs, oil and vanilla.

🐎 In a separate bowl, sift 3 cups flour, sugar, baking powder, salt, cinnamon, nutmeg and cloves. Stir in whole wheat flour and wheat germ.

🐎 Stir dry ingredients into liquid ingredients, just until blended.

🐎 Pour batter into a hot, greased waffle iron. Bake until waffles are golden brown or steaming stops.

🐎 For Peach Topping: Simmer peaches and sugar in saucepan for 5 minutes. Stir in spices. In a separate bowl, stir cornstarch into cold water. Add cornstarch to peaches, and stir until bubbly and thickened. Serve over hot waffles with shot glasses of liqueur to be poured on top, if guests wish.

Makes about 16 waffles

from **B&B at Saddle Rock Ranch**
255 Rockridge Drive
Sedona, AZ 86336
602-282-7640

"Hearts are scattered through the antique-filled rooms as part of the decor, and we prepare all our waffles and muffins in special heart-shaped utensils," said Innkeeper Fran Bruno. These heart-shaped waffles often welcome guests celebrating romantic occasions. Fran, a potter, might serve them on her hand-made dishes. In addition to a flavorful-but-healthy breakfast served poolside, guests eat up the views of the red rocks. This ranch is so scenic it was used in the '40s and '50s for filming several westerns and was visited by many Hollywood stars. It was once home to Senator Barry Goldwater.

🏠*Other B&B at Saddle Rock Ranch recipes:*
Saddle Rock Ranch Jammie Cake, page 42
Grandma's Date Nut Bread, page 69

Spaghetti Squash Supreme

Ingredients:
    1 large spaghetti squash
    2 teaspoons fresh basil, chopped
    2 teaspoons fresh marjoram *or* 1 teaspoon ground marjoram
    1/4 cup butter, melted
Also:
    Parsley, basil or marjoram sprigs

- Cook squash in microwave 12-15 minutes or until flesh is soft. Cut squash in half lengthwise.
- Remove seeds and scrape the "spaghetti" from the sides of the squash into the center of the "boat."
- Sprinkle the herbs on the spaghetti. Pour the butter over it and toss to mix.
- Microwave another 30 seconds, if necessary, to serve hot.
- Garnish with sprig of fresh herb.

Tester's Comments: I'm too chicken to microwave the whole squash, fearing it'll burst, so I saw it in half first. Also, I found it easier to remove spaghetti to a large bowl to toss, then return it to the two squash-shell "boats." This makes an excellent vegetarian entree or side-dish. Use real butter, not margarine.

Makes 4-6 servings

from **Sipapu Lodge**
65 Piki Drive
P.O. Box 552
Sedona, AZ 86336
602-282-2833

"This dish is a very special surprise for most guests," said Lea Pace. "'I've never had squash for breakfast' is an often-heard remark. 'It's great!' usually follows." While the squash looks like pasta, its taste is sweeter. Lea uses leftover "spaghetti" in biscuit dough, adding it without changing the recipe.

Squash for breakfast is just one of the unusual treats guests might encounter here. Often the herbs served at breakfast are fresh from the herb garden. Guests who come to relax in scenic Sedona's Red Rock country can relax without ever leaving the inn. Co-innkeeper Vince Mollan is a massage technician who can work out guests' kinks after a day of hiking in the back country. And the back country is just down the road from this West Sedona home, as are restaurants, shopping and Oak Creek Canyon.

Other Sipapu Lodge recipes:
Fruit Frappé, page 25
Spinach Dill Sauce, page 96
Fruit Tacos, page 104
Hot, Spiced Melon, page 108
Southwest Egg and Bean Burritos, page 135

Westways Enchiladas de Zucchini

Ingredients:

5 tablespoons butter, divided
3 tablespoons vegetable oil
12 corn tortillas
1 onion, minced
1 pound lean ground beef
4 cups unpeeled zucchini, grated
3/4 cup ripe olives, chopped
1 teaspoon garlic powder, optional
Salt and pepper
2 cups Monterey Jack cheese, grated
2 10-ounce cans enchilada sauce
1-1/2 cups Cheddar cheese, grated

Also:

Sour cream

In a large frying pan, melt 3 tablespoons butter. Heat butter and oil together. Fry tortillas for about 5 seconds each side. Remove as soon as they become limp and drain on paper towels.

In a separate pan, sauté onion in remaining butter until transparent.

Add ground beef and brown thoroughly, breaking up meat as it cooks. Drain well.

Stir in zucchini, olives, garlic powder and salt and pepper to taste. Sauté 5 minutes, stirring occasionally.

Heap a rounded 1/4 cup of sautéed mixture in the center of each tortilla. Top with a heaping tablespoon of Monterey Jack cheese. Roll up and place seam-side down in a 9 x 13-inch dish.

When all tortillas are rolled, pour enchilada sauce over all. Top with Cheddar cheese. Enchiladas may be covered and refrigerated overnight at this point.

Bake uncovered in a preheated oven at 350 degrees for 15 minutes. ("If enchiladas have been refrigerated, bake for 30 minutes.") Serve with a dollop of sour cream.

Makes 12 enchiladas

from Westways Resort Inn
Off Bell Road in Northwest Phoenix
P.O. Box 41624
Phoenix, AZ 85080
602-582-3868

Southwestern fare is often on the breakfast menu of Innkeeper Darrell Trapp. The former co-owner of a New England inn with a 60-seat dining room, he knows his way around the kitchen and has an extensive recipe collection. He opened this six-guestroom inn in 1987, with private landscaped grounds.

Other Westways recipes:
Nutty Beer Bread, page 70
Keeper of the Inn Pinto Beans, page 163

Sometimes it's what goes along with the main
dish that sets a meal apart. A unique sidedish can
make an otherwise ordinary entree come alive.
Other times, there's no need for a main dish at all
-- these dishes will suffice nicely alone. Only two
of the following recipes use meat, and they can be
modified, so they all work for vegetarian menus.
And while innkeepers serve these at breakfast or
brunch, there's no reason not to use them for
lunch or dinner. Several recipes are old-fashioned
"comfort foods" that used to be family favorites.
Others are contemporary creations that add taste
and color to your meal. Whether featuring
vegetables or carbohydrates, they all are flavorful
additions.

Go-Alongs

Fiesta Baked Tomatoes

Ingredients:

6 large ripe tomatoes
5 slices bacon, diced
2 cups fresh or frozen corn
1 yellow onion, diced
1/2 red bell pepper, diced
1/2 green bell pepper, diced
1/2 to 1 teaspoon sugar
Salt and pepper
1 tablespoon flour
1/2 cup heavy cream
1/2 cup Parmesan cheese, grated
2 tablespoons butter, cut into small pieces

Cut the stems out of each tomato and scoop out the center. Sprinkle cavities with salt and turn upside down to drain.

In a non-stick skillet, fry bacon until it is almost crisp. Drain on paper towels.

Add corn, onion, red and green peppers to bacon fat. Cook, stirring often, until lightly browned. Stir in sugar, salt and pepper.

In a separate bowl, whisk the flour into the cream until smooth.

Stir the cream into the corn mixture. Cook, stirring until thickened. Stir bacon into mixture.

Place tomatoes upright in a shallow baking dish. Fill each tomato with the corn mixture. Sprinkle with Parmesan cheese. Dot with butter.

Add a few teaspoons of water to the pan. Bake in a preheated oven at 375 degrees for 15 to 20 minutes, until the tops brown and the tomato skins just start to wrinkle.

Makes 6 servings

from **Adobe Abode**
202 Chapelle Street
Santa Fe, NM 87501
505-983-3133

"This is a substantial side dish we serve with entrees such as onion pie, broccoli and cheese crepes, or any dish that needs a dash of color," said Innkeeper Pat Harbour. "We try to have a memorable Southwestern touch at every breakfast -- after all, this *is* Santa Fe -- and this recipe does the trick." Guests gather in the breakfast room and are served on one of Pat's many tablesettings, some of which are from Santa Fe potters.

Other Adobe Abode recipes:
Honeydew Compote, page 107
Santa Fe Cheese Casserole, page 132
Caramelized French Toast, page 137
Apple Skillet Cake, page 142

Herbed Broiled Tomatoes

Ingredients:

    6 ripe tomatoes, halved
    1/4 cup butter, melted

Also:

    Garlic powder
    Dried basil flakes
    Parmesan cheese

- Place tomatoes cut-side-up on a baking sheet. Brush with butter.
- Lightly sprinkle with garlic powder, then basil and Parmesan.
- Broil for 3 to 5 minutes or until the tops are golden brown and bubbly.

Makes 12 servings

from **Crystal River Inn**
326 West Hopkins Street
San Marcos, TX 78666
512-396-3739

"The tomatoes are a dynamite accompaniment to southwest egg casseroles. They're weekend staples for us," said Innkeeper Cathy Dillon. "They enhance almost any plate with their bright color and are great time-savers."

Breakfast is served in the courtyard by the fountain, on the second-floor veranda, in the dining room by the fireplace or to guestrooms. Homemade biscuits, yeast rolls and other pastries are on the weekday menu. Weekends call for a hearty brunch, complete with champagne.

Mike and Cathy opened this inn in 1984 in the 1883 home of a state legislator and judge. It was one of the few original homes on Hopkins Street, and an historic district of 19th century homes is within walking distance. The Dillons restored the home and have since done the same with the Young House across the street, opening three guestrooms there.

Guests at either house are welcome to rock on the porch swing on the veranda, sleep until noon, or be off early exploring the Hill Country. The Dillons know the area well, having fallen in love with it as Houston refugees who wanted to soak-up river life on a permanent basis. Guests often ask for help planning canoeing and innertubing on area rivers, for which all guestrooms are named.

Other Crystal River Inn recipes:
Creamy Fruit Dip, page 87
Scrambled Eggs with Chive Cream Cheese, page 133
Hot Crab Dip, page 201

Home-Fried Potatoes

Ingredients:

6 to 8 medium potatoes, washed and cubed
2 tablespoons vegetable oil
2 to 4 tablespoons paprika
2 tablespoons onion, minced
2 teaspoons garlic salt or powder

Also:

Parmesan cheese

☛ After cutting pototoes into cubes, boil for 2 to 3 minutes. Let sit in hot water for 20 minutes. Drain water off, cover and refrigerate overnight.

☛ In the morning, put oil into a frying pan and heat.

☛ Add potatoes, paprika, onion and garlic salt and mix well.

☛ Cook over low heat, turning frequently, about 30 minutes. Sprinkle with Parmesan cheese before serving.

Makes 5-6 servings

from **Bartram's White Mountain B&B**
Woodland Lake Road
Route 1, Box 1014
Lakeside, AZ 85929
602-367-1408

Innkeeper Petie Bartram keeps her ingredients few and simple, but tasty. (That's partly why she's successful in her catering business.) She has made these potatoes for years, often serving them at dinner-time.

Petie and Ray decided to open their home to B&B travelers in 1987. They were so thrilled with the Lakeside/Pinetop area that they wanted to share it. Their home is located at the end of a wooded road, with pine trees and a collie in the yard (the dog was left by former owners and "came with the house," Petie said). She and Ray recently added private patios off each of the three guestrooms, so guests can enjoy the clear mountain air.

Petie calls herself "a people person," so it's no wonder she's happily involved with B&B, catering and country crafts, as well as volunteer work. She decorated the three guestrooms and the living room, which guests are welcome to share, with her needlework and sewing, some of which is for sale. Bartram's is about 170 miles from Phoenix, and the drive through the Salt River Canyon and over the Mogollon Rim is beautiful. Petrified Forest National Park is 55 miles away, and skiing is at Sunrise Park Resort.

⌂Other Bartram's White Mountain B&B recipes:
Strawberry Stuffed French Toast, page 141
German Pancake page 148

Keeper of the Inn Pinto Beans

Ingredients:

3 cups dried pinto beans, washed and cleaned
1/2 cup vegetable oil
4 cloves garlic, chopped
1/2 teaspoon pepper
2 tablespoons chili powder
1/2 pound salt pork, diced
1 medium onion, quartered
1 tablespoon sugar

Also:

Salt

- Cover beans with water and soak, covered, in the refrigerator overnight.

- In the morning, drain off water. Place beans in a kettle and cover with fresh water.

- Mix in oil, garlic, pepper, chili powder, salt pork, onion and sugar.

- Boil for 90 minutes, skimming top occasionally. Add more water as needed to keep beans moist.

- Mash beans slightly and cook for another 30 minutes. "The beans may be served at this point, or simmered all day for fullest flavor, adding water when necessary. Add salt just before serving. Freezes well."

- To use an electric slow-cooker: After rinsing beans, place all ingredients in the slow-cooker. Cover with fresh water and cook on "low" setting 8 to 10 hours.

Makes 6 servings

from **Westways Resort Inn**
Off Bell Road in Northwest Phoenix
P.O. Box 41624
Phoenix, AZ 85080
602-582-3868

Innkeeper Darrell Trapp's zesty beans are part of his collection of Southwestern recipes. Southwestern fare is almost always on the breakfast menu at his inn. Darrell, who co-owned and operated a New England inn, opened Westways in 1987. He put years of experience in the travel industry, including consulting for resorts, to work in designing the retreat.

Guests have use of the acre of landscaped grounds, surrounded by a privacy Spanish stucco wall. A swimming pool, whirlpool, weight room and fountain are available outside. Indoors, guests may relax in the sunken living room, help themselves to refreshments, or enjoy the large-screen TV in the Arizona Leisure Room. Six large guestrooms are available in the 5,000-square-foot inn.

Other Westways recipes:
Nutty Beer Bread, page 70
Westways Enchiladas de Zucchini, page 158

Riced Potato Croquettes

Ingredients:
3 medium potatoes
Salt and pepper
3 tablespoons butter or margarine, melted
1 egg, beaten

Also:
Flour
Butter

- Bake the potatoes. Cool and peel.
- Put potatoes through a ricer. Sprinkle with salt and pepper to taste.
- Stir in melted butter and beaten egg.
- Pat mixture into 12 cone-shaped or rounded patties. Roll each croquette in flour.
- Brown on a griddle on which bacon or sausage has just been cooked, or in butter. "Needs to have a nice, golden-brown look."

Makes 4 servings

from **Davanna House**
107 East Clarksville Street
Jefferson, TX 75657
903-665-8238

"My father served these potatoes in his restaurant in a small town in the Midwest. People seemed to prefer potatoes to grits." Innkeeper Pat Tuttle got good experience in her dad's restaurant, both in cooking and learning how to deal with customers, even if her two-guestroom B&B means she's only cooking for four guests at a time.

Pat met Dave Tuttle at Purdue University in the '50s. They married and moved around the country, living for 21 years in Dallas and 17 in New Orleans, far from their native Indiana. Dave, a mechanical engineer, started carving replacement parts for furniture Pat restored at her antique shop in New Orleans. His hobby turned into more than a hobby, and now a shop with his carved figurines is part of their B&B.

Tuttles bought the restored 1860 Greek Revival home and opened their B&B in 1991. One guestroom has impressive antique walnut furniture, including an Eastlake bed, burled armoire and a secretary. The cypress-sided house has Pat's antiques throughout, plus pine plank floors, braided or oriental rugs and old-fashioned clawfoot bathtubs.

Other Davanna House recipes:
German Sautéed Apples, page 105
Layered Scrambled Eggs, page 123

Southern Cheese Grits

Ingredients:

2 eggs, beaten
2 cups grits, cooked
1 cup Cheddar cheese, grated
1/2 teaspoon garlic salt
1/2 teaspoon dry mustard
1/2 teaspoon chives, chopped
1/2 teaspoon salt
1/2 teaspoon pepper

- In a large bowl, beat eggs well.
- Mix in the rest of the ingredients, combining thoroughly.
- Pour into a greased, 1-1/2 quart casserole dish.
- Bake uncovered in preheated oven at 350 degrees for 35 to 45 minutes, or until top is golden brown and perhaps cracks a bit on top.

Tester's Comments: This is good "comfort food" that can be baked at 25 degrees higher or lower in order to bake along with other parts of the meal. Save a little grated cheese to sprinkle on top when removed from oven.

Makes 6-8 servings

from **Roseville Manor**
217 West Lafayette Street
Jefferson, TX 75657
903-665-7273

These grits often are served as a breakfast sidedish at Phillip Smith's inn. Guests feast at the dining room table, which seats 10, surrounded by oak buffets bearing Phillip's leaded cut crystal collection. The house is named after another collection, however: his Roseville pottery, made in Ohio. The pottery is displayed in the entryway and throughout the house.

Phillip bought this house in 1987, and it took two years of massive renovation before he could open five antique-filled guestrooms. In addition to redoing heating and cooling systems, adding bathrooms and completely redecorating and furnishing the house, the exterior was landscaped. Guests can relax in the courtyard hot tub or in the rocking chairs on the large front porch. Brick walkways inside a very long picket fence form a beautiful entry.

Built in 1860 as a single-story home, a second floor was added in the early 1900s so the home could serve as a boarding house. The owner for the last six decades, Jessie Kennedy, lives next door and relates anecdotes to Phillip. Phillip, a former caterer, also owns The Bakery downtown, purveyor of good meals and homebaked breads and pastries.

Anyone who has had to travel over a major holiday can understand how it could be a depressing event. But many Southwest B&Bs actually attract travelers over the holidays. These wonderful homes are decorated to the rafters with boughs and bows for Christmas. Another holiday that's popular at romantic inns is Valentine's Day, where lovers treat themselves to rooms with whirlpools or a four-poster bed. Expect special menus for Thanksgiving, Easter or St. Patrick's Day. Whatever the holiday, innkeepers rise to the occasion with fantastic fare. They've generously shared their treasured recipes, many of them long-time family favorites, so now those recipes can be a family tradition at your home, as well.

Holiday Fare

Cortés Hot Chocolate

Ingredients:

6 cups milk
3 ounces Mexican chocolate ("Cortés and Ibarra are popular; or substitute 3 ounces
    unsweetened chocolate, 1/2 cup sugar and 1 drop almond extract")
Pinch of cinnamon
Pinch of salt

Also:

6 cinnamon sticks or candy canes

- In a saucepan, bring 1/2 cup of the milk to a boil.
- Break up chocolate into small pieces. Dissolve it in the 1/2 cup boiling milk, stirring over low heat.
- Add remaining milk and slowly bring the mixture back to a boil, stirring constantly.
- Add cinnamon and salt when the mixture is close to boiling.
- Remove from heat and beat until frothy with a rotary beater or molinillo (a carved wooden beater twirled beween the palms of the hands to froth chocolate).
- Pour into six mugs and garnish with cinnamon sticks or, for Christmas, candy canes.

Makes 6 servings

from **Grant Corner Inn**
122 Grant Avenue
Santa Fe, NM 87501
505-983-6678

Innkeeper Pat Walter has what every chocolate lover would give his eye-teeth for: a relative with a chocolate company. He also has what every tropic-lover envies: a relative who lives in the Caribbean. In this case, it's Pat's Aunt Dora and Uncle Ignacio Cortés, who have the Cortés Chocolate Company in San Juan, Puerto Rico. Pat often spent his summer vacations there, and it's where he learned to love garlic and olive oil, now often used in his other kitchen creations. Pat, Louise Stewart and their daughter Bumpy "always stock up on this delicious chocolate when we're visiting Puerto Rico," Louise said.

At Christmas time, guests and breakfast patrons at the Grant Corner Inn enjoy a mug of this hot chocolate, served with a candycane, as part of breakfast. Christmas breakfast usually includes the hot chocolate, the inn's trademark frappé (with red cranberry juice), a special omelette, Parmesan potatoes and pumpkin streusel muffins. The dining room is festively decorated.

Other Grant Corner Inn recipes:
Grant Corner Inn Orange Frappé, page 26
Cheese Danish Coffeecake, page 36
Cathy's Finnish Pear Pancakes, page 146
Plum Cottage Cheese Pancakes, page 149
Sour Cream Ambrosia, page 176

Creamed Eggs

Ingredients:

20 hard-boiled eggs (Easter egg leftovers, not at room temperature for more than 2 hours)
1/2 cup margarine
1/2 cup butter
1-1/2 cups flour
3 cups milk
1 teaspoon salt
Pepper to taste

Also:

Waffles, biscuits or toast

- Peel and chop eggs. Cover and refrigerate until use.
- In a non-stick saucepan or skillet, melt margarine and butter over low heat.
- Whisk in flour, stirring constantly until bubbly.
- Remove from heat. Whisk in milk, a little at a time.
- Return to stove. Stir constantly over low heat until mixture is "thick as gravy."
- Stir in eggs, salt and pepper to taste.
- Serve hot over waffles, biscuits or toast.

Makes about 12 servings

from **Tarlton House**
211 North Pleasant Street
Hillsboro, TX 76645
817-582-7216

Innkeeper Jean Rhoads serves these creamed eggs as an Easter-time breakfast, using up those leftover Easter eggs. "You can make this up the day before," she notes. Sometimes she substitutes two jars of chipped beef instead of the eggs. (First she chops beef, boils it for 3 minutes, drains it then mixes it in.)

Breakfast is served at 9:30 a.m. in the dining room of this 1895 Queen Anne Victorian. The home was built by Green "Duke" Tarlton, an attorney who raised his family here. The three-story, 6,000-square-foot home was in need of major work when Jean and Rudy bought it in 1985 to convert to a B&B. But they knew what they were getting into. For example, "there were two-and-a-half bathrooms, but only one worked. Now we have 10," Jean said.

They also have nine guestrooms and plenty of guests who want to savor smaller-town life, 60 miles south of Dallas. Guests may relax in the parlors, music room, formal dining room or on the spacious, white-railed front porch.

Another Tarlton House recipe:
Mother's Best Ever Waffles, page 155

Impossible Coconut Pie

Ingredients:

4 eggs
1 cup sugar
4 tablespoons margarine (if making in a blender, melt margarine and cool slightly)
1/2 cup flour
2 cups milk
1 cup coconut
1 teaspoon vanilla extract
Pinch of nutmeg

- Cream eggs, sugar and margarine. (Or, in a blender, combine all ingredients and blend 30 seconds.)
- Slowly beat in flour, milk, coconut, vanilla and nutmeg. (In blender, scrape sides, blend again.)
- Pour into a greased, 10-inch glass pie plate ("Do not use an aluminum tin").
- Bake in a preheated oven at 400 degrees for 15 minutes. Then reduce heat to 350 degrees and bake for another 30 minutes. Store any leftovers in the refrigerator.

Makes 6-8 servings

from **The Marks House**
203 East Union Street
Prescott, AZ 86303
602-778-4632

This custard pie isn't "impossible" because it's so hard to make, but because the ingredients do the impossible and create a crust, explained Innkeeper Dottie Viehweg. (Or because it's impossibly easy to make in a blender!) "This was a family recipe for Thanksgiving Dinner which my mother passed on to us," Dottie said. It provided a change from traditional pumpkin or mince.

Dottie and Harold moved from Scottsdale to this B&B as an early retirement career. In 1991, their daughter, Beth Maitland Banninger, purchased the inn and convinced them to move from Scottsdale to run it. Beth, who plays Traci on "The Young and the Restless," always wanted to have a B&B, but she lives in California full-time and can't operate one herself. "Harold and I were sort of at a turning point in our lives, and our long-range goal was to retire here," Dottie said. It's a "win-win" situation for everyone.

Guests enjoy a full breakfast in the formal dining room of this 1894 Queen Anne home. They are treated to afternoon hors d'oeuvres in the parlor or on the veranda. The four upstairs guestrooms include one in the turret and another which has a 1800's bathhouse-style copper soaking tub.

Other Marks House recipes:
Zucchini Hotcakes, page 150
Buffet Salami, page 195

Irish Soda Bread

Ingredients:

4 cups flour
1/4 cup sugar
1 teaspoon salt
1 teaspoon baking powder
1 teaspoon baking soda
1 tablespoon caraway seeds, optional
1/4 cup butter or margarine
2 cups raisins
1-1/3 cups buttermilk
1 egg, slightly beaten
1 egg yolk
2 tablespoons water

- In a large bowl, combine flour, sugar, salt, baking powder, baking soda and caraway seeds.
- Cut in the butter with a pastry blender or fork. Add raisins.
- In a separate bowl, mix buttermilk and egg.
- Pour buttermilk mixture into flour mixture and blend.
- Turn dough out onto a lightly floured surface. Knead until smooth, about 25 times.
- Shape dough into a smooth ball. Place it in a well-greased round two-quart casserole dish. Cut a four-inch cross on top.
- In a small bowl, lightly beat egg yolk and water. Brush over dough.
- Bake in a preheated oven at 350 degrees for 60 to 70 minutes. To slice, cut in quarters, then eighths.

Makes 1 loaf

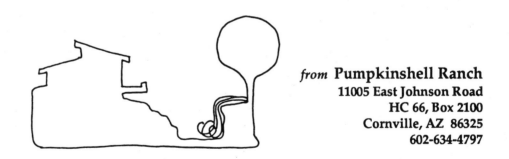

from **Pumpkinshell Ranch**
11005 East Johnson Road
HC 66, Box 2100
Cornville, AZ 86325
602-634-4797

For St. Patrick's Day, Irish soda bread will be on Kay Johnson's table. She enjoys preparing all-French, all-German or all-Irish theme meals for special events. Even on holidays, guests still may choose from among 14 breakfast entrees. Kay, a former grade school teacher, teaches international cooking, operates the B&B and has sewn the accessories for the two guestrooms.

Other Pumpkinshell Ranch recipes:
Irish Coffee, page 27
Aunt Gladys' Buttermilk Biscuits, page 44
Morning Glory Muffins, page 54
Zucchini Muffins, page 62
Hollandaise Sauce, page 90

Peach Upside-Down French Toast

Ingredients:

1/2 cup margarine
1-1/4 cup brown sugar, packed
1 tablespoon water
1 29-ounce can sliced peaches
1 loaf French bread, unsliced
6 eggs, beaten
1-1/2 cups milk
1 tablespoon vanilla extract

Peach Syrup:
    Liquid from canned peaches
    2 tablespoons cornstarch
    1/3 cup orange juice OR
    1 teaspoon lemon extract

- In a small saucepan, melt margarine. Stir in brown sugar and water.
- Cook, stirring constantly, until the mixture has thickened.
- Pour into a well-greased 10 x 15-inch or 9 x 13-inch baking dish.
- Drain peaches and reserve liquid. Place peach slices on top of cooled sugar mixture.
- Slice the French bread into 1-inch-thick slices. Place slices on top of peaches, filling in all gaps.
- Mix eggs, milk and vanilla. Pour over bread. Cover and refrigerate overnight.
- In the morning, uncover and bake in a preheated oven at 350 degrees for 40 minutes.
- Cool for 5 minutes. Then place serving tray over baking pan and invert.
- For Peach Syrup: Mix reserved peach liquid with cornstarch. Stir over low heat until thickened. Stir in orange juice or lemon extract. Serve warm.

Makes 8-12 servings

from **Durham House B&B**
921 Heights Boulevard
Houston, TX 77008
713-868-4654

For Christmas breakfast, Marguerite Swanson serves this decadent French toast topped with sliced fresh strawberries and sweetened yogurt or sour cream. "The same recipe can be made with apples in place of peaches. Use canned apples for pie, and serve French toast with maple syrup."

Breakfast usually is served in the formal dining room of this 1902 Queen Anne Victorian mansion. Marguerite and Dean have four sets of china, so the table looks different each day for the guests. Guests may choose to eat on the screened back porch, in the garden gazebo, or at a table for two in their guestroom. Five guestrooms are offered in this National Register home, which has gingerbread trim, lace curtains, a white-railed front porch with swing and is decorated with family antiques.

Another Durham House B&B recipe:
Fresh Apple Muffins, page 49

Peppertrees' Scottish Shortbread

Ingredients:

1 cup butter, softened
1 cup margarine, softened
1 cup sugar
1 teaspoon vanilla extract
4 cups flour

- Cream butter and margarine (which should be softened, but not melted).

- Mix in sugar and vanilla.

- Work in 1 cup of flour at a time, by hand. "The dough should be soft and easy to handle, but neither sticky nor dry. It may be necessary to add a little more flour to get the right consistency."

- Pat out about a 1-pound lump of dough (one-third of the batch) to 1/2-inch thick.

- Put the dough on a pie plate. Pinch the edges of the round "as you would pinch a pie crust."

- With a fork, prick the center of the round in an attractive pattern. With a knife, score 8 pie-shaped wedges.

- Repeat with the rest of dough to make three rounds.

- Bake in an oven preheated at 300 degrees for about 30 minutes, until golden brown. "If your oven does not brown evenly, you may have to move the rounds about the oven to get the desired effect."

- Let shortbread cool in the pans. Wrap well. "They will keep indefinitely in the freezer and will keep well in a cookie tin for a week."

Makes 24 servings

from **Peppertrees B&B Inn**
724 East University Boulevard
Tucson, AZ 85719
602-622-7167

Buttery shortbread is always a Christmas treat. Guests here are served this house specialty with a beverage for afternoon tea. Innkeeper Marjorie Martin quadruples this recipe to make a dozen "rounds" at a time. "Shortbread is really delicious and is not as rich in fat and sugar as many more traditional cookies. It is the use of butter that gives it the rich flavor. You cannot substitute for the butter," she warns. Nor can you get out of mixing it by hand. "Once you have mastered the technique, you will find it very simple." Marjorie also advises following the directions exactly and using plain pie plates, rather than fancy molds or stone baking dishes. Guests at Marjorie's inn, just two blocks from the University of Arizona, might enjoy this by the patio fountain, where some type of flowering plant is in bloom year 'round.

Other Peppertrees B&B Inn recipes:
Peppertrees' Coffee Coffeecake, page 41
Prickly Pear Syrup, page 95
Bananas and Strawberry Cream, page 101

Pumpkin Cheesecake

Ingredients:

3 8-ounce packages cream cheese
1 cup sugar
3 eggs
1 teaspoon vanilla extract
1 teaspoon orange extract
1 teaspoon cinnamon
1 teaspoon ginger
1 teaspoon pumpkin pie spice mix
1 tablespoon cornstarch
1-1/2 cups canned pumpkin

Crust:
1 cup nuts, finely ground
1 cup flour
1/2 cup brown sugar, packed
1/2 cup butter, melted

🖙 To make the crust: Grind nuts in a food processor. Then place in a bowl and mix in flour, brown sguar and melted butter with a fork.

🖙 Press the mixture onto the bottom and as far up the sides as possible of a 9-inch springform pan.

🖙 To make the cheesecake: With an electric mixer, beat cream cheese and sugar until light and fluffy.

🖙 Beat in the eggs.

🖙 Beat in the vanilla and orange extracts, spices, cornstarch and pumpkin, mixing well after each addition.

🖙 Pour the mixture into the prepared crust. Bake in a preheated oven at 350 degrees for at least 1 hour or "until the center of the cake barely jiggles."

Tester's Comments: Orange extract may not sound like it fits, but it bakes in nicely. Bake for full time; I had to overbake by about 15 minutes because I baked another dish at the same time, and the middle was still soft.

Makes 16 servings

from **The Galisteo Inn**
Off Highway 41
HC 75, Box 4
Galisteo, NM 87540
505-982-1506

No ordinary pumpkin pie at this inn for Thanksgiving. "This recipe was devised by one of our staff and was a big hit during the holidays," said Joanna Kaufman, co-owner. "During baking, this cake tends to crack a bit on top. As soon as I take it out of the oven, I pinch together the cracks."

🏠*Other Galisteo Inn recipes:*
Cranberry Smoothie Fruit Drink, page 23
Cranberry Raspberry Muffins, page 47
Galisteo Inn Cornmeal Scones, page 50
Chocolate Chip Banana Bread, page 68
Galisteo Inn Cornmeal Waffles, page 154

Pumpkin Cream Cheese Roll-Up

Ingredients:

3 eggs
1 cup sugar
2/3 cup cooked, canned pumpkin
1 teaspoon baking soda
1 teaspoon cinnamon
1/2 teaspoon nutmeg
3/4 cup flour

Filling:
1 8-ounce package cream cheese
4 tablespoons butter, softened
1 cup powdered sugar
1 teaspoon vanilla extract

Also:

Waxed paper and aluminum foil
Clean floursack kitchen towel (not made of terrycloth)
Powdered sugar and sieve

- In a large bowl, beat eggs and sugar. Beat in pumpkin, baking soda, cinnamon, nutmeg and flour.

- Grease a 9 x 13-inch pan or a 10 x 15-inch jelly roll pan. Line with waxed paper, then grease and lightly flour the waxed paper. Pour batter into pan.

- Bake in a preheated oven at 350 degrees for 15 minutes ("bakes fast," so test with toothpick).

- Sprinkle powdered sugar heavily through a sieve or sifter to cover a clean dish towel.

- Turn hot cake out onto the towel. Remove waxed paper. Trim off any burnt or crusty edges.

- Quickly roll hot cake up jelly roll-style with towel inside. (As you roll, you may need to add powdered sugar to any part of the towel that touches the cake.) Let cake cool at least 30 minutes.

- Meanwhile, for Filling: Beat cream cheese, butter, powdered sugar and vanilla. Set aside.

- Unroll cooled cake. Spread filling over cake. Roll up again with filling inside instead of towel.

- Wrap cake roll with waxed paper, then foil. Refrigerate or freeze. To serve, slice 3/4-inch thick.

Tester's Comments: Wonderful holiday dessert! Cool cake completely or it may stick to dish towel when unwrapped. Filling is like cream cheese frosting, so whipped cream is unnecessary Best semi-frozen.

Makes about 8 servings

from **Country Elegance B&B**
Off Page Springs Road
P.O. Box 564
Cornville, AZ 86325
602-634-4470

"This hand-me down recipe is a great favorite," said Innkeeper Rita Sydelle, a New England native who depends on pumpkin pie flavor at the holidays but likes this cake because it freezes well. Guests enjoy it on the enclosed deck.

Other Country Elegance recipes:
Zucchini Nut Bread, page 81
Date Bars á la Bernice, page 182
Grandma's Noodle Kugel, page 184

Sour Cream Ambrosia

Ingredients:

3 oranges, peeled and sectioned
1/2 pound seedless green grapes
1/2 cantaloupe, chunked
1/4 pineapple, chunked
1/2 cup moist coconut, shredded
1/4 cup pecans, chopped
1 cup sour cream
1 tablespoon honey
1/4 teaspoon vanilla extract

Also:

Pomegranate seeds

- In a medium bowl, mix fruits, coconut and pecans.
- In a separate bowl, stir sour cream, honey and vanilla.
- Pour sour cream mixture over fruit and mix well.
- Spoon into footed glass dessert dishes and garnish with pomegranate seeds.

Makes 6 servings

from **Grant Corner Inn**
122 Grant Avenue
Santa Fe, NM 87501
505-983-6678

At this Inn, Sour Cream Ambrosia is an important part of Easter Brunch, which preceeds an Easter egg hunt on the lawn. Ambrosia is served along with Eggs Benedict, hot cross buns and blueberry kolacky. Guests dine on white linen with pastel napkins, surrounded by Easter baskets and bunnies.

If you can't come for Easter, rest assured that there are bunnies at Louise Stewart's busy inn all year 'round. Ceramic ones, calico ones, stuffed ones, wooden ones, but not live ones. "I grew up in a house called 'Jack Rabbit Casa' -- my father's name was Jack -- in Arizona and watched jack rabbits and cottontails come for daily meals on the lawn. Let us say that the little furry creatures have a place in my heart," Louise explained. They also have many places in her three-story inn, situated in the heart of downtown Santa Fe. Guests can walk to shopping, located one block away, art galleries and Santa Fe's many other attractions. Louise and her family restored this home, opened in 1982, and now have 15 staff members helping operate the inn.

Other Grant Corner Inn recipes:
Grant Corner Inn Orange Frappé, page 26
Cheese Danish Coffeecake, page 36
Cathy's Finnish Pear Pancakes, page 146
Plum Cottage Cheese Pancakes, page 149
Cortés Hot Chocolate, page 168

Sweet Thick Rice

Ingredients:

1 cup white rice
2 cups boiling water
1 tablespoon butter
1/2 teaspoon salt
3 to 4 cups milk
1/4 cup sugar, or more to taste
1/3 cup butter
1 to 3 teaspoons cinnamon

🖙 In a saucepan, stir rice into boiling water. Add butter and salt.

🖙 Reduce heat to low and simmer, covered, about 20 minutes or until most of the water is absorbed.

🖙 Stir in milk. Simmer, uncovered, until rice is tender and mixture is "creamy and thick, not soupy." Stir frequently to prevent sticking and scorching. Add more milk, if needed. Sugar also may be added now, or sprinkled on top later.

🖙 Place rice in an oven-proof dish. Brown the butter lightly over medium heat. Pour butter over rice. Sprinkle with cinnamon and sugar, if sugar wasn't added earlier. Serve warm.

Makes 6 servings

from **White House B&B**
217 Mittman Circle
New Braunfels, TX 78132
512-629-9354

This dish was served at Christmas and other days, as well, by the German settlers who brought it to New Braunfels. "We have a Conservation Plaza that is a reconstructed pioneer town," said Innkeeper Beverly White. "At Christmas-time, the Conservation Society has a candlelight tour of all the buildings with samples of the food that the original colonists had in the middle 1800s." Beverly first had this dish on that Christmas candlelight tour. Now she serves it with an egg dish, fruit and various homemade breads.

Beverly and Jerry are pioneers of a sort, opening the first B&B in town in 1987. They moved to Texas, where Jerry had been in the service, specifically to open a B&B, and chose New Braunfels with its abundance of tourism draws. The town's German heritage is apparent not just at Christmas, but all year, and there's plenty of good German food in local restaurants to please visitors.

Beverly has plenty of home-cooking to please guests, too. She is a cookbook collector and often experiments with new recipes on Jerry. They join the guests outdoors on the patio for a full breakfast.

🏠 *Another White House recipe:*
Pecan and Cinnamon Clusters, page 72

"Life is uncertain. Eat dessert first," reads a popular t-shirt. Well, these innkeepers may not serve dessert *first*, but they do serve it after breakfast, the first meal of the day. Afterall, dessert for breakfast is a concept that's long overdue. A number of sensible innkeepers have become trend setters and incorporated dessert as a tradition at their B&B. Dessert for Breakfast often seems to be relatively light fare, perhaps incorporating fruit, or filled with aromatic cinnamon. Custard, cakes, cookies or kuchen, these desserts are welcome snacks or treats at other times. And speaking of fruit, feel free to use all the recipes from the Fruit chapter as Dessert for Breakfast.

Dessert for Breakfast

Apple Brown Betty

Ingredients:

4 tart apples, peeled and sliced
2 to 3 tablespoons brown sugar
1/2 teaspoon cinnamon
1/4 teaspoon cloves

Topping:
1/2 cup butter
1 cup flour
1 cup brown sugar

🐦 Butter a 9-inch pie plate. Arrange sliced apples in the bottom.

🐦 Mix brown sugar, cinnamon and cloves. Sprinkle over apples.

🐦 To make Topping: With a pastry mixer or fork, cut butter into flour and brown sugar to form fine crumbs.

🐦 Heap crumb topping evenly over sliced apples.

🐦 Bake in a preheated oven at 350 degrees for 45 minutes or until the topping is browned and apples are tender.

Tester's Comments: Cinnamon-lovers will want to double the amount. Topping is buttery and crunchy.

Makes 5 servings

from **Magnolia House**
101 East Hackberry Street
Fredericksburg, TX 78624
512-997-0306

Warm Apple Brown Betty often caps off a large breakfast served in the formal dining room of this Hill Country B&B. Innkeeper Geri Lilley serves breakfast at 8:30 a.m. from a marble-topped buffet sparkling with cut crystal. Breakfast is served on antique china with crystal and silver. The windows are adorned with lace curtains and the yellow-pine dining room floor, selected by the architect who built the home, is inset into the Berber carpet.

Each of the guestrooms here are very different. The Magnolia Suite has a fireplace of indigenous limestone. The Bluebonnet Suite also has a stone fireplace, plus a complete kitchen with an antique refrigerator. The large windows in the American Beauty Room overlook the yard and the limestone waterfall. Each room has antiques and Geri's paintings on the walls.

Magnolia House, set under the shade of five large magnolias, is a short walk from downtown Fredericksburg, settled in 1846 and listed on the National Register of Historic Places. Visitors can stop in a number of museums, take a walking tour of the historic district, feast on German foods, or enjoy an abundance of Gillespie County peaches from spring through late summer.

🏠*Other Magnolia House recipes:*
Cinnamon Nut Coffeecake, page 37
Aunt Tommy's Sausage Quiche, page 118

Chocolate Potato Drop Cakes

Ingredients:

    2 eggs, separated
    1 cup sugar
    1/3 cup vegetable oil
    2 ounces semi-sweet chocolate, grated
    1 cup mashed potatoes
    1 cup whole wheat flour
    3 teaspoons baking powder
    1/2 teaspoon salt
    1/3 cup nuts, chopped

Also:

    Fresh or frozen raspberries
    Whipped cream

- Beat the egg whites until stiff peaks form. Set aside.

- In a large bowl, mix egg yolks, sugar and oil.

- Mix in grated chocolate and mashed potatoes. Mix in flour, baking powder, salt and nuts.

- Gently fold in egg whites.

- Grease two cookie sheets. With a tablespoon, drop batter onto the cookie sheets.

- Bake in a preheated oven at 350 degrees for 7-10-minutes "or until set as a soft cookie -- do not overbake."

- Serve warm or at room temperature. Top each serving with raspberries and a dollop of whipped cream.

Makes 3-4 dozen

from **The Delforge Place**
710 Ettie Street
Fredericksburg, TX 78624
512-997-6212

"This is a small baked pancake or muffin, your choice," that is fairly bland by itself, but a sweet treat with raspberries and whipped cream, said Innkeeper Betsy Delforge. This is another of her favorite recipes from a collection discovered in a sea captain's trunk passed down through her family. Betsy and George opened their inn in 1985. They have lived in more than 40 cities over the years when George was an aeronautical engineer and Betsy developed food products for various companies. Today, they are in one place, welcoming guests to their restored Victorian home.

Other Delforge Place recipes:
Fresh Peach Soup, page 24
Belgium Torte, page 33
Mushrooms with Eggs, page 127
Cornmeal and Rice Griddle Cakes, page 147

Date Bars á la Bernice

Ingredients:

4 eggs, beaten
4 cups (2 pounds) Arizona date pieces, floured
2 cups walnuts, coarsely chopped
2 teaspoons baking soda
1 tablespoon vanilla extract

🍳 In a large bowl, beat eggs. Fold in dates and walnuts, baking soda and vanilla. Mix well.

🍳 Grease an 8 x 12-inch baking pan. Pour in the date mixture.

🍳 Bake in a preheated oven at 325 degrees for 15 minutes. Then lower temperature to 250 degrees for another 10 to 15 minutes. Cut into squares when cool.

Makes about 24 bars

from **Country Elegance B&B**
Off Page Springs Road
P.O. Box 564
Cornville, AZ 86325
602-634-4470

Rita Sydelle's friend Bernice "always comes up with a quick, easy, delicious recipe," and this one is often served as a dessert for breakfast at Rita's B&B. "There is no sugar or salt -- all natural, healthy ingredients." Rita suggests it as a snack that's easily packed for hikes into the Arizona countryside.

Exploring the area is on the agenda of all of her guests. Country Elegance is located 14 miles from the scenic red rocks and electromagnetic vortexes of Sedona, and even closer to Jerome, an historic copper mining town. Indeed, the hills of Jerome and Sedona can be seen from the deck of this home.

Rita left San Diego after 25 years for the peace and quiet of the Arizona hills. She purchased a 13-year-old home that needed her talent as an interior designer. In the process of renovation, she decided to try innkeeping, and the B&B opened in 1991.

Breakfast here is served on an enclosed deck that overlooks the garden, fruit trees, fish pond and hills. Melons from her organic garden are served in season, and melon sorbet might be served the rest of the year. Fresh eggs from "the girls," Rita's 28 "free and happy" chickens, find their way into at least one of the breakfast dishes.

🏠 *Other Country Elegance recipes:*
Zucchini Nut Bread, page 81
Pumpkin Cream Cheese Roll-Up, page 175
Grandma's Noodle Kugel, page 184

Fresh Apple Cake

Ingredients:
3 eggs
2 cups sugar
1-1/2 cups vegetable oil
1 teaspoon vanilla extract
3 cups flour
1-1/2 teaspoons baking soda
1 teaspoon salt
1 teaspoon cinnamon
1 teaspoon cloves
1 teaspoon baking powder
3 cups apples, peeled and chopped
1-1/2 cups pecans, chopped

Also:
Powdered sugar, sifted

🍂 Cream eggs and sugar. Beat in oil and vanilla and mix thoroughly.

🍂 Mix in flour, baking soda, salt, cinnamon and cloves and baking powder.

🍂 Stir in apples and nuts by hand. Batter will be fairly stiff.

🍂 Spoon batter into a greased bundt or angel-food cake pan. Bake in a preheated oven at 300 degrees for 90 minutes.

🍂 Remove from oven and cool in the pan on a rack. When cool remove from pan. Sprinkle with sifted powdered sugar.

Tester's Comments: I didn't peel the chopped apples, and no one could tell in this dark, aromatic cake.

Makes 12-16 servings

from Swan and Railway B&B Inn
Corner of Front Street and Castro Boulevard
P.O. Box 446
La Coste, TX 78039
512-762-3742

This apple cake is served as dessert to breakfast by Innkeepers Jaye and Eugene Sherrer, who opened this restored 1910 railroad hotel as a B&B in 1985. "We lived in Europe for about six years, and in traveling around over there, we loved the B&Bs," Jaye said. "They were so trusting and so homey and so relaxing. They treat you like you are so special." When they returned to the U.S., they found this hotel, bought it in 1978, and gradually restored it, commuting out from San Antonio, 25 miles to the northeast. After retirement, they moved in and opened five guestrooms. The name combines the history of the hotel and their interest in swans, which mate for life. It came from an antique sign from a European pub they discovered at an auction. Guests may use the outdoor pool, indoor whirlpool, sauna and exercise room.

Grandma's Noodle Kugel

Ingredients:

4 ounces cream cheese
4 ounces cottage cheese
3 tablespoons sour cream
4 tablespoon butter, melted
1/4 teaspoon salt
1 to 3 tablespoons sugar, to taste
1 8-ounce can crushed pineapple, drained
1 8-ounce package wide egg noodles, cooked
1 cup raisins, optional
1 teaspoon cinnamon, optional
3 eggs, well beaten

Topping:
1 cup cornflakes, crushed
3 tablespoons sugar
1 teaspoon cinnamon
4 tablespoons butter, melted

In a large bowl, beat the cream cheese and cottage cheese. Mix in sour cream, melted butter, salt and sugar. Then add the crushed pineapple.

Fold in drained, cooked noodles and optional raisins and cinnamon. Fold in beaten eggs last.

Butter an 8 x 12-inch baking dish. Place noodle mixture in dish.

For Topping: Mix crushed cornflakes, sugar and cinnamon. Sprinkle over noodles. Drizzle with melted butter.

Bake in a preheated oven at 350 degrees for 50 to 60 minutes or until a knife inserted in the center comes out clean.

Makes 6-10 servings

from **Country Elegance B&B**
Off Page Springs Road
P.O. Box 564
Cornville, AZ 86325
602-634-4470

This noodle pudding is a family favorite. "My grandmother made her own egg noodles from scratch," said Innkeeper Rita Sydelle. "As a young girl I would watch her make the dough, roll it out and then cut the noodles out quickly, using only her eyes as a guide." Rita does her grandmother proud in the kitchen of this country home. It's not unusual for Rita to make homemade bread or muffins, a gourmet entree, a side dish and a dessert for breakfast.

After buying a neglected 3,800-square-foot home 14 miles from Sedona, Rita's friends suggested she turn it into a B&B after completing renovation. Skeptical at first, she's found "all my guests have been wonderful, warm, friendly, considerate and really appreciative of being here."

🏠 *Other Country Elegance recipes:*
Zucchini Nut Bread, page 81
Pumpkin Cream Cheese Roll-Up, page 175
Date Bars á la Bernice, page 182

Holland Rusk Custard

Ingredients:

    1 package Holland Rusk toast
    1-1/2 cups sugar, divided
    1/4 cup butter, melted
    2 cups milk
    3 eggs, separated
    2 tablespoons flour
    1 tablespoon sugar

Also:

    Whipped cream, beaten with 1 tablespoon powdered sugar and 1/2 teaspoon vanilla extract

- With a rolling pin, crush all the toast between sheets of waxed paper.
- In a large bowl, mix crushed toast, 3/4 cup sugar and melted butter. Set aside.
- In a double boiler or heavy pan, mix milk, egg yolks, remaining 3/4 cup sugar and flour. Stir constantly over medium heat until the mixture thickens.
- When thick, strain through a sieve. Set aside.
- In a chilled mixing bowl, beat egg whites and 1 tablespoon sugar until stiff peaks form.
- In a 9-inch baking pan or 1-1/2 quart casserole dish, layer half of the toast mixture. Top with all of the custard, then a layer of egg whites. Top with the rest of the toast mixture.
- Bake in a preheated oven at 325 degrees for 25 minutes. Serve warm or chilled with whipped cream.

Tester's Comments: Lovely presentation with different colored layers. Whipped cream is an option on this rich dessert, and reducing the sugar in the toast portion to 1/2 cup would still be sweet enough.

Makes 6-9 servings

from **Stillwater Inn**
203 East Broadway Avenue
Jefferson, TX 75657
903-665-8415

"Holland Rusk Custard is a family recipe that I enjoyed as a child," said Innkeeper Bill Stewart. "We serve it from time to time at the inn."

Breakfast is served on the sunny sideporch, done in blue and white, where tables for two overlook the flower garden (an herb garden provides fresh herbs). Bill, a former chef at the Adolphus Hotel in Dallas, and Sharon, a gourmet cook, opened this inn and restaurant in 1984. Fresh seafood, meats and vegetables are featured on the dinner menu and an extensive wine list is offered in this 1893 Eastlake Victorian house. Stewarts' French-American cooking has earned high praise from visitors and local residents alike. Upstairs, the Stewarts offer three guestrooms with handcrafted wooden furniture and antiques, vaulted ceilings, skylights and poster beds.

Hoogie Googie Cake

Ingredients:

2 cups pitted Arizona dates, chopped
2 cups hot water
3 cups flour
1-1/2 cups sugar
2 teaspoons baking powder
1 teaspoon baking soda
2 eggs, beaten
3/4 cup vegetable oil
1 teaspoon vanilla extract
1 to 2 cups chocolate chips, divided
1 to 2 cups nuts, coarsely chopped, divided

- Place dates in a medium bowl. Pour the hot water over them and let stand.
- In a large bowl, mix flour, sugar, baking powder and baking soda.
- Beat in eggs, oil and vanilla. Mix until smooth.
- Stir in 1 cup chocolate chips and 1 cup nuts.
- Pour the dates and water into the batter and mix well.
- Pour batter into greased 9 x 13-inch baking pan. Optional: top it with another cup of chocolate chips and another cup of chopped nuts.
- Bake in a preheated oven at 350 degrees for 45 to 55 minutes or until a toothpick inserted in the center comes out clean. No frosting is needed. Serve warm or cold.

Makes 12-15 servings

from **Birch Tree Inn**
824 West Birch Avenue
Flagstaff, AZ 86001
602-774-1042

"We have no idea where the name came from for this decadently delicious cake, but the recipe came from Rodger's grandmother," who continued to cook past age 90, said Innkeeper Sandy Znetko. Rodger Pettinger is a co-innkeeper, along with Sandy's husband and Rodger's wife. The long-time friends and business partners restored this 1917 farmhouse-style home in 1989, then opened and now operate this five-guestroom B&B together. They serve this cake to guests after breakfast and before a day of skiing, hiking or a trip to the Grand Canyon or to Sedona and Oak Creek Canyon.

Other Birch Tree Inn recipes:
Spiced Peach Punch, page 30
Pineapple Stuffed French Toast, page 140
Saucy Spice Bars, page 191
Hearty Vegetable Soup, page 199
Layered Mexican Dip, page 203

Mary Ellen's Apricot Breakfast Bars

Ingredients:

3/4 cup margarine
1/2 cup sugar
2 teaspoons vanilla extract
1 egg
2-1/2 cups flour
1/2 teaspoon baking powder
1 cup nuts, chopped
2 cups apricot jam

Topping:
1 cup flour
1/2 cup sugar
6 tablespoons butter
Dash of cinnamon

✎ In a large bowl, cream margarine, adding sugar gradually.

✎ Beat in vanilla and egg, mixing well, then flour and baking powder. Stir in nuts by hand.

✎ Press dough into a greased 9 x 13-inch pan. Poke holes in the dough with a fork.

✎ Bake in a preheated oven at 400 degrees for 10 minutes.

✎ While crust is baking, make Topping: Mix flour, sugar, butter and cinnamon with a fork or pastry cutter until crumbly.

✎ Remove crust from the oven and spread jam on top. Sprinkle topping over jam. Bake another 20 minutes.

Makes 24 bars

from **Maricopa Manor**
15 West Pasadena Avenue
Phoenix, AZ 85013
602-274-6302

Innkeeper Mary Ellen Kelley created this recipe for a breakfast dessert in the inn's breakfast picnic basket, served to each guestroom in the morning. She prefers apricot preserves in the recipe, but other favorite jams will work. Mary Ellen and Paul include homemade bread, such as a mini-loaf of Arizona date bread, or muffins, fruit, a dessert, coffee and juice, butter, preserves, linens, silverware and china in the baskets. Guests can enjoy their repast out of doors, with the spring smell of orange blossoms, or in their private room.

Kelleys turned their large home and adjacent guest cottage into an urban inn after their large family grew up. In the main house, guests are treated to evening hors d'oeuvres and conversation. The two suites open to decks or the garden courtyard. Three large suites are located in the guesthouse. All guests may soak in the gazebo hot tub or enjoy the garden fountain.

🏠*Other Maricopa Manor recipes:*
Arizona Date Mini-Bread, page 65
Mary Ellen's Breakfast Cookies, page 188
Mexican Hors d'Oeuvres, page 205

Mary Ellen's Breakfast Cookies

Ingredients:

2/3 cup butter
2/3 cup sugar
1 egg
1 teaspoon vanilla extract
3/4 cup flour
1/2 teaspoon baking soda
1/2 teaspoon salt
1-1/4 cups uncooked oatmeal
1 cup Cheddar cheese, grated
1/2 cup wheat germ
6 slices of bacon, fried crisp and crumbled

- In a large bowl, beat butter, sugar, egg and vanilla.
- Beat in flour, baking soda and salt. Then stir in oatmeal, cheese, wheat germ and bacon.
- Drop cookies by a tablespoon onto greased cookie sheets.
- Bake in a preheated oven at 350 degrees for 12 to 14 minutes.

Makes about 30 cookies

from **Maricopa Manor**
15 West Pasadena Avenue
Phoenix, AZ 85013
602-274-6302

This unusual cookie recipe was passed down to Innkeeper Mary Ellen Kelley by her grandmother. Mary Ellen serves the cookies as a breakfast dessert in the breakfast picnic basket delivered to each of the five guestrooms.

Mary Ellen and Paul decided to open their large home as an urban B&B after extensive research. The Kelleys spent years owning their own business and they were ready for a new venture that included friendly personal contact. They already had the place to do it: the 1928 manor home in Phoenix, in which they raised 11 children.

The two guestrooms in the main house and three suites in the guesthouse are furnished with satins, lace and antiques. Guests gather for hors d'oeurves in the evening, before heading out for dinner. The inn's central location means guests can walk or drive just a few minutes to a variety of outstanding restaurants, shops and other Phoenix-Scottsdale attractions.

Other Maricopa Manor recipes:
Arizona Date Mini-Bread, page 65
Mary Ellen's Apricot Breakfast Bars, page 187
Mexican Hors d'Oeuvres, page 205

Peach or Pear Kuchen

Ingredients:

1/2 cup butter or margarine, softened
1/4 cup sugar
1 teaspoon vanilla extract
1 egg
1 cup flour
1/2 teaspoon baking powder
1/4 teaspoon salt
1 28-ounce can sliced peaches or pears, drained, or 3 fresh pears or peaches, peeled and sliced
3 tablespoons sugar
1/2 to 1 teaspoon cinnamon

- In a small bowl, beat butter or margarine and sugar until light and fluffy. Beat in vanilla and egg.
- Beat flour, baking powder and salt into egg mixture. Dough will be stiff.
- Grease a 9-inch springform pan. Spread dough over the bottom and 1-inch up the sides of the pan.
- Arrange peach or pear slices in spoke fashion over the dough. Sprinkle with sugar and cinnamon.
- Bake in a preheated oven at 350 degrees for 30 to 35 minutes or until edges are golden brown.
- Remove from oven and cool for 10 minutes before removing sides of pan. "Best if made fresh before serving. Tends to get mushy if made ahead."

Tester's Comments: Good with either canned or fresh peaches. Serve with nutmeg-spiked whipped cream.

Makes 8 servings

from **The White Horse Inn**
2217 Broadway Avenue
Galveston, TX 77550
800-76-B AND B (800-762-2632)

This easy kuchen "always makes the guests happy," testifies Innkeeper Robert Clark, whose friend Robin Gunther created the recipe.

Robert has a penchant for grand old homes, and he restored five in Galveston before buying this one to make over into an inn. "If you had told me five years ago I would be running an inn, I would have told you you were crazy."

But he had traveled and stayed in B&Bs, and liked the atmosphere. He opened the inn in 1988, with two guestrooms in the main house and four in the carriage house. The 1884 home was built by hardware owner J.F. Smith, who chose the finest mahogany and cypress woodwork, stained glass, brass chandeliers and ornate fretwork for his own home. The house is furnished in Victorian antiques or reproductions.

Another White Horse Inn recipe:
Baked Deviled Eggs, page 119

Raspberry Bars

Ingredients:

    1/2 cup sugar
    1 cup butter (not margarine)
    2-1/4 cups flour, sifted
    Dash of salt
    1-1/2 cups raspberry jam

- In a large bowl, cream sugar and butter.
- Mix in flour and salt.
- Press three-quarters of the mixture into an ungreased 9 x 13-inch pan.
- Spread with raspberry jam.
- Sprinkle the rest of the crumbly mixture over the jam.
- Bake in a preheated oven at 350 degrees for 40 minutes. Cut into bars and serve.

Tester's Comments: Heat jam in microwave for easier spreading -- jam may "stick" to bottom dough otherwise. Both strawberry and raspberry jam are pretty for Christmas or Valentine's Day, and kids love strawberry.

Makes 24-30 bars

from **The Oxford House**
563 North Graham Street
Stephenville, TX 76401
817-965-6885

These buttery bars are a favorite of Innkeepers Paula and Bill Oxford. They are served as a dessert bar or for afternoon teas, which the Oxfords started for fun. English High Tea is by reservation on weekday afternoons, and sometimes, for an extra flair, Victorian etiquette lessons are included.

Paula and Bill serve a full breakfast to guests in their four-guestroom inn. Some come to visit Tarleton State University, part of the Texas A&M University System and home to about 4,500 students. Guests also come to shop at a popular flea market, or take in the Historical House Museum, which has 10 buildings from the 1800s. They shouldn't leave without visiting "Moola," the Holstein statue on the downtown square, recognizing Earth County for its production of Texas dairy products.

Paula and Bill began restoring the home in 1985. Judge W.J. Oxford had the home built in 1898 for $3,000, which he paid in silver coins earned on a court case and brought home in a box on the back of his buggy. Lumber and supplies were shipped from Fort Worth, 60 miles away.

Other Oxford House recipes:
Almond Tea, page 22
Schnecken (German Cinnamon Rolls), page 77

Saucy Spice Bars

Ingredients:

1 cup raisins
1/2 cup butter-flavored shortening
1/2 cup brown sugar, packed
1/2 cup sugar
1 cup chunky applesauce
2 cups flour
1 teaspoon cinnamon
1 teaspoon baking soda
1/2 teaspoon allspice
1/4 teaspoon cloves
1 teaspoon vanilla extract
1 cup nuts, chopped

Icing:
1 cup powdered sugar
1 teaspoon butter, melted
1/4 cup milk, scalded

- Rinse raisins in hot water to keep them plump during baking. Set aside.
- Cream the shortening, brown sugar and sugar. Lightly mix in the applesauce.
- In a separate bowl, mix flour, cinnamon, baking soda, allspice and cloves.
- Beat dry ingredients into creamed mixture.
- Beat in vanilla, then stir in raisins and nuts.
- Pour into a greased jelly roll pan or a 9 x 13-inch baking pan. Bake in a preheated oven at 350 degrees for 25 to 35 minutes.
- To make icing: Scald milk. Pour into powdered sugar and butter. Drizzle icing over warm bars.

Makes 18-24 bars

from **Birch Tree Inn**
824 West Birch Avenue
Flagstaff, AZ 86001
602-774-1042

Innkeeper Ed Znetko's aunt, Hannah Wagner, was a Pennsylvania German woman who "was a marvelous baker, even into her early 80s," said Sandy Znetko, Ed's wife. These bars often are served as a breakfast dessert to guests. If guests stayed in the Wagner-Znetko Room, they stayed among Hannah Wagner's embroidered and crocheted linens. Many of the rooms here are decorated with linens made by Sandy and co-innkeeper Donna Pettinger. Everyone has his or her niche in this business: Donna has done most of the decorating, Sandy is chief cook, Rodger, Donna's husband, is the accountant, and Ed is the handyman who keeps the place running.

Other Birch Tree Inn recipes:
Spiced Peach Punch, page 30
Pineapple Stuffed French Toast, page 140
Hoogie Googie Cake, page 186
Hearty Vegetable Soup, page 199
Layered Mexican Dip, page 203

Homemade cookies with iced tea on the front porch swing. Refreshments by the fire after a day on the ski slopes. Gathering with other guests at a social hour for appetizers and conversation before dinner. All are symbols of hospitality, and savvy innkeepers know that food can help a guest feel at home. So something wonderful to eat isn't limited to breakfast. The following recipes are innkeepers' favorites, but either weren't served for breakfast or didn't fit well into another category. Innkeepers find themselves making these recipes over and over again, often by request of repeat visitors. Perhaps they will make your list of frequent favorite recipes, as well!

Other Favorites

Breakfast Appetizer Cheese Spread

Ingredients:

1 envelope unflavored gelatin
1/4 cup boiling water
12 ounces cream cheese, softened
1/2 cup butter, softened
1/2 cup sour cream
1/2 cup sugar
1/4 teaspoon lemon peel, grated

Also:

Gelatin mold
Leaf lettuce
Toasted almonds
Maraschino cherry
Crackers

- Dissolve gelatin in boiling water.

- In a mixing bowl, beat cream cheese, butter and sour cream. Then blend in sugar.

- Add dissolved gelatin and lemon peel and mix.

- Place in a one-quart gelatin mold. Refrigerate until set, about 6 hours, "preferably overnight."

- Unmold on top of clean lettuce leaves. Garnish with toasted almonds and a cherry on top. "Serve with graham crackers for sweet lovers, club crackers for those who want something a little less sweet."

Makes 12 servings

from **Yacht-O-Fun**
2216 Windsor Drive
Richardson, TX 75082
214-238-8224

If an appetizer before breakfast is a little unusual, so is this bed-and-breakfast experience. Since 1985, Diana and Buddy Greer have been hosting weekend B&B guests aboard their 51-foot cruiser on Lake Texoma, along the Texas/Oklahoma border. The Greers had an opportunity to purchase the beautiful boat and turn it into a business. In addition to B&B, they will customize other trips and host business meetings or office parties on board.

Diana, a former caterer, serves breakfast after a morning cruise. Guests boarded the evening before, cruised under the stars, slept in one of the two staterooms while the cruiser was docked, and woke up to the smell of breakfast cooking. Having only two couples and the Greers on board gives everyone plenty of room to stretch out and enjoy the cruise.

Another Yacht-O-Fun recipe:
Cantaloupe Soup, page 103

Buffet Salami

Ingredients:

5 pounds fresh lean hamburger
1/2 cup water
2-1/2 teaspoons mustard seed
2-1/2 teaspoons course black pepper
1-1/2 teaspoons garlic salt
1 teaspoon "Liquid Smoke"
5 rounded teaspoons Morton-brand "Tender-Quick" salt ("Do not use table salt")

Also:

Crackers and cheese

- Mix all ingredients well.
- Store in a tightly-covered container in the refrigerator for three days, mixing well once each day.
- On the fourth day, roll the mixture into 5 long rolls. Place on a broiler pan.
- Bake in a preheated oven at 140 degrees for 11 hours, turning each roll every 2 hours.
- Remove from the oven and cool each "salami." Wrap tightly with plastic freezer wrap and chill to serve immediately or freeze. Serve sliced with crackers and cheese.

Makes about 5 servings per roll

from **The Marks House**
203 East Union Street
Prescott, AZ 86303
602-778-4632

"We serve hors d'oeuvres each evening to our guests, and this is a favorite," said Innkeeper Dottie Viehweg. In warm weather, guests might gather on the veranda, or, in cooler weather, in the parlor of this 1894 home.

The Queen Anne Victorian is on the National Register of Historic Places. It was built by Jake and Josephine Marks. Among other endeavors, Jake had the largest liquor distributorship in Arizona Territory. That was a profitable business when Prescott was the territorial capital. The Marks' daughter and her family lived in the hillside home until the 1930s. During the Depression, to generate income, the house was divided into six apartments.

Restored in 1980, the home is again making local history as a B&B. The four-guestroom inn was purchased in 1991 by Beth Maitland Banninger, who plays Traci on "The Young and the Restless." Dottie and Harold, her parents, moved from Scottsdale to operate it. They love Prescott's history and charm, and gladly direct guests the two blocks to downtown shops and restaurants.

Other Marks House recipes:
Zucchini Hotcakes, page 150
Impossible Coconut Pie, page 170

Carrot Cake

Ingredients:

2 cups sugar
1-1/4 cups vegetable oil
4 eggs
3 cups carrots, finely shredded
1/2 cup pecans, chopped
2-1/2 cups flour
2-1/4 teaspoons baking soda
2 teaspoons cinnamon

Cream Cheese Frosting:
8 ounces cream cheese, softened
1/4 cup butter, softened
2 cups powdered sugar
2 teaspoons lemon juice
2 teaspoons vanilla extract

- For cake: In a large bowl, beat sugar and oil.
- Add eggs, one at a time, beating well after each addition.
- Stir in carrots and nuts.
- In a separate bowl, sift together flour, baking soda and cinnamon.
- Mix flour into carrot mixture.
- Turn batter into three greased and floured 9-inch round cake pans or one 9 x 13-inch baking pan.
- Bake in a preheated oven at 350 degrees for 30 to 35 minutes for round pans, longer for oblong pan, or until a toothpick or knife inserted into the center comes out clean.
- For Cream Cheese Frosting: Beat cream cheese and butter until smooth and creamy. Gradually add powdered sugar, mixing well. Stir in lemon juice and vanilla. Frost cake while frosting is at room temperature, then refrigerate it because the frosting contains dairy products.

Makes 10-12 servings

from **The Jones House**
311 Terrace Avenue
P.O. Box 887
Chama, NM 87520
505-756-2908

Guests at the Jones House who are going to spend a day aboard the Cumbres and Toltec Scenic Railroad get to enjoy this cake. "We pack a picnic basket for our guests who ride the train," said Innkeeper Sara Jayne Cole. "The menu for the basket includes this cake for a touch of something rich and sweet."

Summer and fall visitors to Chama can take the train to Osier, Colo., for lunch, then return to Chama aboard the longest and highest narrow-gauge steam railroad in the U.S. The states of New Mexico and Colorado own the railroad, which was built 1875-1883 to serve mining camps. Passengers ride over Cumbres Pass, elev. 10,015 feet, and 600-foot-deep Toltec Gorge.

Other Jones House recipes:
Hurry Up Cake, page 38
Blue Corn Waffles, page 151
Picnic Basket Quiche, page 208

Cheesy Artichoke Squares

Ingredients:

1/2 cup onion, chopped
1/2 cup water
4 eggs, beaten
1/4 cup bread crumbs
1/4 teaspoon oregano
2-3 drops hot pepper sauce
1 pound Cheddar cheese, shredded
12 ounces marinated artichoke hearts, drained and chopped

- Cook onion in water until tender, about 5 minutes. Drain.
- In a large bowl, beat eggs with bread crumbs, oregano and hot pepper sauce.
- Stir in onion, cheese and artichoke hearts.
- Spread in a greased 7-1/2 x 11-inch pan.
- Bake in a preheated oven at 350 degrees for 18 minutes. Cut in 1-inch squares and serve warm.

Tester's Comments: Let sit a few minutes before cutting, then keep size of squares small. Appetizing combination of flavors!

Makes about 30 small servings

from **Alexander's Inn**
529 East Palace Avenue
Santa Fe, NM 87501
505-986-1431

"This recipe helped launch our first annual Christmas Walk through the Santa Fe B&B community," said Manager Mary Jo Schneider. Each walker brought two canned goods for the local food shelf and got to sample treats like this, plus see inside Santa Fe's bed-and-breakfasts, decked out in their holiday best.

Food is important here. Owner Carolyn Delecluse, who opened the inn in 1988, admits to always having a penchant for cooking. "Being the oldest of five children, I naturally helped out quite a bit in the kitchen. I started baking your basic chocolate chip cookies at age 8, and was baking bread, muffins and bagels by age 13."

Now she gets help from Mary Jo, and they whip up homemade breads, muffins and granola to fortify guests about to embark on a day of exploring Santa Fe. The inn is located just down the street from the town plaza and the Palace of the Governors. Other museums and legendary restaurants are within easy walking distance.

Another Alexander's Inn recipe:
Pineapple Bran Muffins, page 57

Cornflake Macaroons

Ingredients:

3 egg whites
1-1/2 tablespoons lemon juice
Pinch of salt
1 teaspoon vanilla extract
2/3 cup powdered sugar
1/3 cup nonfat dry milk
1 cup cornflakes
2/3 cup nuts, chopped
2/3 cup coconut

- In a large bowl, beat egg whites until stiff peaks form.
- Beat in lemon juice, salt, vanilla, powdered sugar and dry milk.
- By hand, fold in cornflakes, nuts and coconut.
- Drop cookies by heaping teaspoonfuls onto greased cookie sheets.
- Bake in a preheated oven at 350 degrees for 9 to 12 minutes, or until both tops and bottoms are turning golden brown.
- Cool completely before removing from cookie sheet.

Tester's Comments: Though not a macaroon fan, I thought these were good (I used pecans). Lining cookie sheets with kitchen parchment paper or even greased aluminum foil helps bakers remove these delicate cookies without the cookies falling apart or chiseling them off. Watch them carefully so they don't under or over-bake.

Makes 2 dozen cookies

from **Copper Bell B&B**
25 North Westmoreland Avenue
Tucson, AZ 85745
602-629-9229

Guests at this lava stone inn can enjoy these macaroons with afternoon tea on the front porch, where the copper bell from a German church hangs in a place of honor. Innkeepers Gertrude Eich-Kraus and Hans Herbert Kraus brought plenty of doors, woodwork and other building materials from their native Germany when they moved to Tucson in 1989.

The innkeepers were well aware of B&B travel in Europe. When their daughter found this large house, it seemed perfect for a B&B. Gertrude cooks using old world recipes, many of which were her grandmother's. Since they are from a German town near France and Luxembourg, French and American cooking is as common here as German.

Another Copper Bell recipe:
Copper Bell's Favorite Waffles, page 152

Hearty Vegetable Soup

Ingredients:

1 pound hamburger
Salt and pepper
3 cups beef broth
1 cup water
2 15-ounce cans stewed tomatoes
1/2 cup onion, chopped
1/2 cup celery, chopped
1 10-ounce package frozen corn
2 cups zucchini, sliced
1 12-ounce package medium-width egg noodles

Also:

Parmesan cheese, grated

- In a large saucepan or kettle, brown hamburger. Break it into small pieces as it browns.
- Drain off grease. Put hamburger in a colander and rinse under hot water.
- Put hamburger back into saucepan or kettle. Season with salt and pepper as desired.
- Stir in broth, water, tomatoes, onion, celery, corn and zucchini.
- Bring soup almost to a boil. Add noodles. Simmer over low heat for 30 to 45 minutes.
- Serve with Parmesan cheese on top.

Makes 4-6 servings

from **Birch Tree Inn**
824 West Birch Avenue
Flagstaff, AZ 86001
602-774-1042

"In the winter, after a day of skiing or playing in the snow, we offer this soup with fresh-baked bread to our guests as hearty refreshments," said Innkeeper Sandy Znetko. Guests come from all over the Southwest to enjoy the snow.

This restored 1917 home with a wide-railed porch is reminiscent of the Midwest. Each of the five guestrooms have been decorated differently by Sandy and co-innkeeper Donna Pettinger. The Pella Room, for instance, celebrates their Dutch heritage in Pella, Iowa, and has a handmade tulip quilt and Dutch lace curtains. The Wicker Room is done in white wicker furniture with navy blue accents. The Wagner-Znetko Room has heirloom antique furnishings. Guests are welcome to play billiards or sit by the fireplace.

Other Birch Tree Inn recipes:
Spiced Peach Punch, page 30
Pineapple Stuffed French Toast, page 140
Hoogie Googie Cake, page 186
Saucy Spice Bars, page 191
Layered Mexican Dip, page 203

Homemade Granola

Ingredients:
1/2 cup vegetable oil
1 cup honey
6 cups uncooked oatmeal
1 cup wheat germ
1 cup coconut
1 cup almonds, sliced
1 cup pecans, chopped
1 cup sunflower seeds
1/2 cup bran cereal
1 teaspoon cinnamon
2 cups dried fruit, chopped

- In a large kettle, heat oil and honey.
- Stir in oatmeal, wheat germ, coconut, nuts, bran and cinnamon.
- Place granola on two large cookie sheets with sides. Toast in a preheated oven at 300 degrees for 20 minutes, until golden brown, stirring every 10 minutes.
- Remove from oven and cool. Place back in kettle to stir in dried fruit.
- Store in covered containers. Keeps well for three weeks.

Makes 20 servings

from **Carrington's Bluff B&B**
1900 David Street
Austin, TX 78705
512-479-0638

"Our guests always want the recipe," Innkeeper Gwen Fullbrook said about this recipe. "The important thing to remember is to stir every 10 minutes." To save time," she said, "I use the packages of dried fruit bits instead of chopping dried fruit."

A large container of this granola is always a part of Gwen's breakfast buffet. Served at a time convenient for most guests, she sets out homemade breads, fresh fruit, beverages and this granola. If the weather permits, guests enjoy it on the 35-foot-long porch that runs along the side of the house, overlooking the acre of lawn. The B&B is shadowed by an oak tree said to be 500 years old, and the tree-lined bluff provides privacy in the heart of Austin. Gwen and David opened five guestrooms here in 1989.

Other Carrington's Bluff recipes:
Pineapple Zucchini Bread, page 74
Strawberry Pecan Bread, page 79
Apple Butter, page 84
Devonshire Cream, page 88

Hot Crab Dip

Ingredients:

4 tablespoons butter, melted
1 small onion, chopped
1 8-ounce package cream cheese
1 8-ounce can white lump crabmeat

Also:

A skinny French baguette, sliced in 1/2-inch-thick slices

- In a non-stick skillet, melt butter. Sauté onion until soft.
- Cut cream cheese into pieces. With a heat-resistant spatula, blend in cream cheese. Stir until well-melted and mixed.
- Drain and rinse crabmeat. Stir it into mixture and heat until almost bubbly.
- Spread on sliced bread, or place in a bowl with bread slices surrounding it for dipping.

Tester's Comments: Very simple and very good. Add pepper or other spices to taste. Also good on crackers. Cathy Dillon also suggests mixing in bread crumbs, then stuffing it into mushroom caps to be baked or broiled.

Makes 8-10 servings

from **Crystal River Inn**
326 West Hopkins Street
San Marcos, TX 78666
512-396-3739

Innkeeper Cathy Dillon serves this as an afternoon or early evening snack to guests who are ravenous after a day "on the river." "On the river" can mean canoeing or innertubing on any of four area rivers: the San Marcos, Guadelupe, Blanco or Frio. The headwaters of the San Marcos River are right in town, a huge spring that gushes with millions of gallons of pure, crystal-clear water. A riverside walkway connects three city parks. Those who go in for the more commercial can see "Ralph the Swimming Pig" at Aquarena Springs amusement park at the headwaters.

As Houstonites, Cathy and Mike Dillon were drawn to the area, but not by Ralph. They were "river rats" themselves, and eventually decided to leave the bright lights of the big city behind. Today, they help guests plan canoe routes over the rivers they still enjoy, and after which they've named their guestrooms. Hearty breakfasts and weekend theme packages are specialties.

Other Crystal River Inn recipes:
Creamy Fruit Dip, page 87
Scrambled Eggs with Chive Cream Cheese, page 133
Herbed Broiled Tomatoes, page 161

Hot Shrimp Dip

Ingredients:

  2 8-ounce packages cream cheese, cut in small squares
  1/2 to 1 pound cooked shrimp (or crab or lobster), chopped
  1 medium onion, chopped
  1 medium tomato, chopped
  3 cloves garlic, minced
  5 mixed mild peppers (such as banana or cherry peppers), chopped
  4 mixed hot peppers (such as torrido or jalapeno), chopped

Also:

  Chips and/or crackers

- Place all ingredients in the top of a double boiler.
- Place over boiling water for about 1 hour before serving, folding ingredients together as cheese softens.
- To serve, place warm dip in a chafing dish. Serve with chips or crackers.

Makes about 15 servings

from **Long Point Inn**
On Farm Highway 390
Route 1, Box 86-A
Burton, TX 77835
409-289-3171

This recipe was handed out freely at receptions, promotion parties and public dinners at the officer's club, Fort Leavenworth, Kansas, in the mid-1960s, said Innkeeper Bill Neinast. He and Jeannine add more than the half pound of shrimp when making it as an appetizer for guests.

After Bill, an attorney, retired from the Army in 1979, Neinasts moved to this 175-acre working ranch. It was purchased by his great-grandfather, a German emigrant, soon after the Civil War. Bill is the fourth generation to raise cattle here. He and Jeannine also raised four children, and they wanted a large house for family reunions. After living in Germany, they decided on a Bavarian chalet-style, and they enlarged it in 1985. Jeannine suggested using the extra guestrooms as a B&B, and they opened two guestrooms in 1986.

Guests are served "a big Texas ranch-hand's breakfast" in the dining room, under the German crystal chandelier. Breakfast might include a fruit compote, an egg dish, cheese grits, custom-made sausage and homemade biscuits, topped with Jeannine's homemade preserves.

Another Long Point Inn recipe:
Mama Hick's Basic Cookies, page 204

Layered Mexican Dip

Ingredients:

2 to 3 ripe avocados, peeled and mashed
1 to 2 teaspoons lemon juice
1/2 cup plain yogurt
1/2 cup light sour cream
1/2 cup light mayonnaise
1/3 teaspoon red pepper
1/4 teaspoon garlic powder
1/4 teaspoon oregano
1/4 teaspoon cumin
1/2 teaspoon chili pepper
1 15-ounce can refried beans
1/2 cup tomatoes, diced
1/2 cup Cheddar cheese, grated
1/4 cup green onions, thinly sliced
1/4 ripe olives, sliced

Also:

Tortilla chips or taco-flavored crackers

- In a small bowl, mash avocados with lemon juice.
- In a separate bowl, mix yogurt, sour cream, mayonnaise and spices.
- In a shallow quiche pan or pie plate, layer the ingredients, starting with refried beans, then avocados, then yogurt mixture, then tomatoes, cheese, green onions and olives.
- Refrigerate until ready to serve. To serve, dip tortilla chips or crackers into the layered dip.

Makes 6-8 servings

from **Birch Tree Inn**
824 West Birch Avenue
Flagstaff, AZ 86001
602-774-1042

"We serve refreshments every afternoon. In the summer, our guests enjoy gathering on the porch or side deck to chat. This has become a fun addition to Southwestern fare," said Sandy Znetko. Sandy and her fellow innkeepers, husband Ed and friends Donna and Rodger Pettinger, all love to entertain. That's one of the reasons they moved to Flagstaff in 1989, restored this former fraternity house and opened a five-guestroom B&B. The place is so much like home they've been known to lend hats and coats to storm-tossed guests.

Other Birch Tree Inn recipes:
Spiced Peach Punch, page 30
Pineapple Stuffed French Toast, page 140
Hoogie Googie Cake, page 186
Saucy Spice Bars, page 191
Hearty Vegetable Soup, page 199

Mama Hick's Basic Cookies

Ingredients:

2/3 cup sugar
1/3 cup brown sugar, packed
1/2 cup shortening
1 egg, beaten
1 teaspoon vanilla extract
2 cups flour
1 teaspoon baking soda
Pinch of salt
1 cup coconut or chopped nuts

- In a mixing bowl, cream sugars and shortening.
- Beat in egg and vanilla.
- Mix in flour, baking soda and salt.
- Stir in nuts and/or coconut by hand.
- Roll heaping teaspoonfuls of dough into balls. Press down with a fork on a greased cookie sheet.
- Bake in a preheated oven at 350 degrees for 8 to 10 minutes.

Tester's Comments: Not only is the dough good, these are awfully good cookies after they're baked!

Makes about 2 dozen cookies

from **Long Point Inn**
On Farm Highway 390
Route 1, Box 86-A
Burton, TX 77835
409-289-3171

"Mama Hick is Jeannine's great-grandmother," said Innkeeper Bill Neinast, about his wife. "These cookies -- easy to make and good keepers -- were Jeannine's favorite as she was growing up. They are now some of our guests' favorite snacks." They are "basic" but tasty.

Bill and Jeannine built this copy of a Bavarian chalet on Bill's family cattle ranch after he retired from the Army in 1979. Its authenticity reminds them of the pleasant years they lived in Germany. Its size lent itself well to family gatherings. But when the grandkids weren't visiting, a lot of space was going to waste. Jeannine suggested a B&B, and they opened two guestrooms in 1986. Guests are free to meet the gentle cattle, hike to the waterfall or five stocked fish ponds, or relax in the bluebonnet country. The inn is close to Brenham, where weekday guests can tour Blue Bell Creameries.

Another Long Point Inn recipe:
Hot Shrimp Dip, page 202

Mexican Hors d'Oeuvres

Ingredients:

8 eggs
1 cup flour
2 cups milk
1 teaspoon salt
2 tablespoons butter
2 tablespoons olive oil
1 4-ounce can green chilies, chopped
4 ounces Cheddar or Monterey Jack cheese, shredded
1 4-ounce can black olives, sliced
1 tablespoon onion, chopped

- In the blender, combine eggs, flour, milk and salt and blend for 5 minutes.
- Meanwhile, in a 9 x 13-inch baking pan, heat the butter and oil until bubbly while preheating the oven to 375 degrees.
- Remove pan from oven and pour in egg mixture.
- Sprinkle chilies, cheese, olives and onion over the egg mixture.
- Bake in a preheated oven at 375 degrees for 45 minutes.

Tester's Comment: This crustless quiche is good warm, cold or at room temperature. It's even better with a dollop of plain yogurt or sour cream. Blending for 5 minutes sounds like a long time (and you can get by with less) but it goes quickly while making other preparations.

Makes 24 squares

from **Maricopa Manor**
15 West Pasadena Avenue
Phoenix, AZ 85013
602-274-6302

Mary Ellen and Paul Kelley often serve these quiche squares during an afternoon social gathering. Guests are greeted in the spacious living room of this 1928 home before heading out for dinner. The opportunity for such friendly contact with guests was one reason the Kelleys went into innkeeping.

Located in north central Phoenix, just five miles from downtown, Maricopa Manor was originally a country retreat. The oasis-like ambiance has been preserved on an acre of grounds, landscaped with a fountain, gazebo spa, patios and decks under palm and orange trees. Guests may choose from five guestrooms, two in the main house and three in an adjacent guesthouse. A homemade breakfast is delivered to their door in a picnic basket.

Other Maricopa Manor recipes:
Arizona Date Mini-Bread, page 65
Mary Ellen's Apricot Breakfast Bars, page 187
Mary Ellen's Breakfast Cookies, page 188

Miss Hattie's Pecan Cookies

Ingredients:

2-3/4 cups sugar
1 cup butter
8 egg yolks, beaten
1/2 teaspoon baking soda
1/2 cup sour cream
1 teaspoon vanilla extract
1 teaspoon lemon extract
4 cups pecans, finely chopped (or ground in food processor)
Flour to make a stiff dough (perhaps 4 cups or more)

- In a large bowl, cream sugar and butter. Mix in egg yolks.
- Stir baking soda into sour cream. Beat sour cream into egg mixture.
- Mix in vanilla and lemon extracts, pecans and "enough flour to make dough stiff enough to roll."
- If necessary, chill first. Roll out on a floured surface and cut with cookie cutters.
- Bake in a preheated oven at 350 degrees for 8 to 10 minutes or until brown. "Watch carefully!"

Tester's Comments: Miss Hattie was baking before "cholesterol" was a household word. I cut the recipe in half, used 2 whole eggs, "lite" sour cream and 1-2/3 cups flour, chilled dough, then baked in a greased 7 x 12-inch pan at 325 degrees for about 35 minutes, or until edges are brown. Made a very good bar cookie.

Makes 6-8 dozen cookies,
depending on the size of cutter

from **Raumonda**
1100 Bowie Street
P.O. Box 112
Columbus, TX 78932

These cut-out cookies were a favorite recipe of Miss Hattie Ilse, the daughter of the builders of this 1887 home. She was one of 10 children born to Ida and Henry Ilse. Henry Ilse owned a popular saloon and dance hall in town, was a rancher, sold farm equipment and served as a Confederate soldier.

The Ilse home, with a striking gingerbread-railed, two-story veranda, was purchased and restored in the late '60s by R. F. "Buddy" Rau and his parents. Natives of Columbus, the Raus took three years to complete major work both indoors and out. The 5,000-square-foot home was named Raumonda, using the letters in Raymond Rau's name. A swimming pool was added in 1977.

Buddy and his wife, Laura Ann, who own an antique shop, have furnished the home in antiques. Listed on the National Register of Historic Places, the house is all cypress, except for pine floors and woodwork, and it has its original metal roof. The Raus opened three upstairs guestrooms in 1988. Breakfast is served on the glassed-in back porch, overlooking the pool, or in the formal dining room, served by candlelight.

Pfeiffer House Favorite Cookies

Ingredients:

1 cup sugar
1/2 cup shortening
1 egg
1 tablespoon molasses
1 teaspoon vanilla extract
1 cup flour
1 teaspoon cinnamon
1 teaspoon salt
3/4 teaspoon baking soda
1 cup oatmeal
1 cup chocolate chips

- In a large bowl, cream sugar and shortening. Beat in egg.
- Add molasses and vanilla and beat well.
- Beat in flour, cinnamon, salt and baking soda.
- Mix in oatmeal. Batter will be stiff. Mix in chocolate chips by hand.
- Drop by heaping teaspoonsful onto an ungreased cookie sheet.
- Bake in a preheated oven at 350 degrees for 8 to 10 minutes. "Do not overcook. Remove from oven when they are just turning tan on top." Cool for a few minutes on cookie sheet, then remove to rack.

Tester's Comments: These got rave reviews. I prefer to substitute raisins for the chocolate chips and make cookies larger by using a tablespoonful of dough (yield 30 cookies).

Makes about 48 cookies

from **The Pfeiffer House**
1802 Main Street
Bastrop, TX 78602
512-321-2100

After wandering through town (population 5,700), guests may want to sit on the Pfeiffer House front porch and enjoy these cookies. They can munch and talk about the 125-plus Bastrop buildings on the National Register of Historic Places, the downtown soda fountain's old-fashioned milkshakes, or the isolated "lost pines of Texas" found here, away from other pine stands.

Marilyn and Charles Whites opened their 1901 home, one of those on the National Register, in 1982. It was built by J.R. Pfeiffer, a local builder, as a gift to his bride. The unusual corner porch is a Pfeiffer touch. The Whites' touches are all through the place. Long-time antique collectors, they have filled their home with antique furniture and collectibles such as advertising art and crockery. A full breakfast is served in the Victorian dining room. Early birds can help themselves to coffee upstairs near the three guestrooms.

Picnic Basket Quiche

Ingredients:

3 eggs, beaten
1-1/2 cups half and half
3/4 teaspoon salt
1/2 teaspoon white pepper
Dash cayenne pepper
1/4 cup frozen corn
1/4 cup green chilies, chopped
1-1/2 cups Swiss or Monterey Jack cheese, shredded

Also:

1 10-inch unbaked pie crust

- Beat eggs until light.
- Add half-and-half, salt, white pepper and cayenne pepper and beat again.
- Line a pie plate with a pastry crust. Sprinkle corn and chilies on the crust.
- Sprinkle shredded cheese on top of corn and chilies.
- Carefully pour egg mixture over all.
- Bake in a preheated oven at 450 degrees for 12 minutes, then reduce heat to 325 and continue baking for 20 to 25 minutes, until eggs are set. Let quiche stand a few minutes before cutting.

Makes 6-8 servings

from **The Jones House**
311 Terrace Avenue
P.O. Box 887
Chama, NM 87520
505-756-2908

This is "Picnic Basket Quiche" because Jones House guests find it in the straw picnic basket that Innkeeper Sara Jayne Cole packs for them before they board the Cumbres and Toltec Scenic Railroad, just a block from this B&B. Quiche, fresh fruit, carrot cake and mineral water, along with cloth napkins and utensils, are sent along for the train's lunch stop at Osier, Colo. "The returned basket always has a thank-you note," Sara Jayne said.

The railroad, listed as a National Historic Site because of its mining history, is one reason summer and fall guests come to Sara Jayne and Phil's four-guestroom B&B in Chama. But guests are also drawn to northern New Mexico to fish the Chama River, hike, cross-country ski or snowmobile, take in the fall colors or just get lung-fulls of clear mountain air.

Other Jones House recipes:
Hurry Up Cake, page 38
Blue Corn Waffles, page 151
Carrot Cake, page 196

Index

Contents by Inn

NEW MEXICO

Casita Chamisa, *Albuquerque*
   Basque Sheepherder's Sourdough Bread - Breads, 66

La Casa Muneca, *Carlsbad*
   Poppyseed Bread - Breads, 75
   Pineapple-Kiwi Fruit Jam - Preserves, Butters, Spreads & Sauces, 93

The Jones House, *Chama*
   Hurry Up Cake - Coffeecakes, 38
   Blue Corn Waffles - Entrees, 151
   Carrot Cake - Other Favorites, 196
   Picnic Basket Quiche - Other Favorites, 208

La Mimosa B&B, *Corrales (Albuquerque)*
   Grandmother's Spirited Berries - Fruits, 106
   Poached Pears - Fruits, 112

The Galisteo Inn, *Galisteo*
   Cranberry Smoothie Fruit Drink - Beverages, 23
   Cranberry Raspberry Muffins - Muffins, Biscuits & Scones, 47
   Galisteo Inn Cornmeal Scones - Muffins, Biscuits & Scones, 50
   Chocolate Chip Banana Nut Bread - Breads, 68
   Galisteo Inn Cornmeal Waffles - Entrees, 154
   Pumpkin Cheesecake - Holiday Fare, 174

Adobe Abode, *Santa Fe*
   Honeydew Compote - Fruits, 107
   Santa Fe Cheese Casserole - Entrees, 132
   Caramelized French Toast - Entrees, 137
   Apple Skillet Cake - Entrees, 142
   Fiesta Baked Tomatoes - Go-Alongs, 160

Alexander's Inn, *Santa Fe*
   Pineapple Bran Muffins - Muffins, Biscuits & Scones, 57
   Cheesy Artichoke Squares - Other Favorites, 197

Grant Corner Inn, *Santa Fe*
   Grant Corner Inn Orange Frappé - Beverages, 26
   Cheese Danish Coffeecake - Coffeecakes, 36
   Cathy's Finnish Pear Pancakes - Entrees, 146
   Plum Cottage Cheese Pancakes - Entrees, 149
   Cortés Hot Chocolate - Holiday Fare, 168
   Sour Cream Ambrosia - Holiday Fare, 176

Bear Mountain Guest Ranch, *Silver City*
   Bear Mountain Guest Ranch Basic Bread - Breads, 67

La Posada de Taos, *Taos*
   Homemade Salsa - Preserves, Butters, Spreads & Sauces, 91
   Cactus Quiche - Entrees, 121
   Shirred Eggs with Green Chili Sauce - Entrees, 134

216

Traveling to these B&Bs?

Contact the following state B&B associations for a listing of member inns and state travel offices for maps and publications. Also, check your bookstore's regional section for B&B guidebooks which do not charge B&Bs to be included.

Arizona:

🏠 Arizona Association of Bed & Breakfast Inns
3661 N. Campbell Ave., Box 237
Tucson, AZ 85719
602-231-6777
Send a self-addressed, stamped #10 (business) envelope for a detailed brochure describing about 30 member B&Bs.

Arizona Office of Tourism
1100 W. Washington Street
Phoenix, AZ 85007
602-542-8687

New Mexico:

🏠 New Mexico Bed & Breakfast Association
P.O. Box 2995
Santa Fe, NM 87504
Send a self-addressed, stamped #10 (business) envelope for a brochure describing about 30 member B&Bs.

New Mexico Department of Tourism
Joseph M. Montoya Building
1100 St. Francis Drive
Santa Fe, NM 87503
1-800-545-2040 from out-of-state; 505-827-0291 in New Mexico

Texas:

🏠 Historic Hotel Association of Texas
501 W. Main
Fredericksburg, TX 78624
512-997-3980
Write or call for a free brochure listing about 50 Texas B&Bs.

Texas Tourism Division
Department of Commerce
P.O. Box 12728
Austin, TX 78711
1-800-888-8839

Ordering Information

☛ **"WAKE UP & SMELL THE COFFEE - Southwest Edition"** makes a great gift for cookbook collectors, B&B lovers, armchair travelers and breakfast eaters everywhere.

Cost: $14.95 plus $2.00 postage and handling = $16.95 per book
Books are sent special fourth class rate. Please allow several weeks for delivery.
For UPS ground service delivery, please add $4.00 = $18.95 per book

If you enjoyed this book, you'll love **"WAKE UP & SMELL THE COFFEE - Upper Midwest Edition"** and **"WAKE UP & SMELL THE COFFEE - Pacific Northwest Edition."**

☛ **Upper Midwest** Edition has 180+ great breakfast, brunch and other favorite recipes from 86 inns in Wisconsin, Minnesota, Michigan, Illinois and Iowa. The format is the same as this book.

Cost: $14.95 plus $2.00 postage and handling = $16.95 per book
UPS ground service delivery, please add $4.00 = $18.95 per book

☛ **Pacific Northwest** Edition features more than 130 of innkeepers' best recipes from 58 B&Bs in Washington and Oregon. Information on each B&B is included in this edition, too.

Cost: $11.95 plus $2.00 postage and handling = $13.95 per book
UPS ground service delivery, please add $4.00 = $15.95 per book

☛ *NEW in '94!* Lake States Edition -- recipes from Michigan, Wisconsin & Minnesota B&Bs

TO ORDER BY PHONE using a credit card, call Voyageur Press in Stillwater, Minn., 1-800-888-9653 toll-free. (Shipping charges may vary from those listed above.)

TO ORDER BY MAIL, send a check to Down to Earth Publications, 1032 W. Montana, St. Paul, MN 55117. Make checks payable to Down to Earth Publications. MN residents please add 6.5% sales tax.

Mail to: Down to Earth Publications
1032 W. Montana
St. Paul, MN 55117

Please send me _____ "WAKE UP & SMELL THE COFFEE - *Southwest* Edition" at $16.95 each by 4th class mail ($18.95 each sent UPS ground service)

Please send me _____ "WAKE UP & SMELL THE COFFEE - *Pacific Northwest* Edition" at $13.95 each by 4th class mail ($15.95 each sent UPS ground service)

Please send me _____ "WAKE UP & SMELL THE COFFEE - *Upper Midwest* Edition" at $16.95 each by 4th class mail ($18.95 each sent UPS ground service)

I have enclosed $_____ for _____ book(s). Send it/them to:

Name: _____

Street: _____ Apt. No. _____

City: _____ State: _____ Zip: _____
(Please note: No P.O. Boxes for UPS delivery)

Ordering Information

🖙 **"WAKE UP & SMELL THE COFFEE - Southwest Edition"** makes a great gift for cookbook collectors, B&B lovers, armchair travelers and breakfast eaters everywhere.

> Cost: $14.95 plus $2.00 postage and handling = $16.95 per book
> Books are sent special fourth class rate. Please allow several weeks for delivery.
> For UPS ground service delivery, please add $4.00 = $18.95 per book

If you enjoyed this book, you'll love **"WAKE UP & SMELL THE COFFEE - Upper Midwest Edition"** and **"WAKE UP & SMELL THE COFFEE - Pacific Northwest Edition."**

> 🖙 **Upper Midwest** Edition has 180+ great breakfast, brunch and other favorite recipes from 86 inns in Wisconsin, Minnesota, Michigan, Illinois and Iowa. The format is the same as this book.
> Cost: $14.95 plus $2.00 postage and handling = $16.95 per book
> UPS ground service delivery, please add $4.00 = $18.95 per book

> 🖙 **Pacific Northwest** Edition features more than 130 of innkeepers' best recipes from 58 B&Bs in Washington and Oregon. Information on each B&B is included in this edition, too.
> Cost: $11.95 plus $2.00 postage and handling = $13.95 per book
> UPS ground service delivery, please add $4.00 = $15.95 per book

> 🖙 *NEW in '94!* Lake States Edition -- recipes from Michigan, Wisconsin & Minnesota B&Bs

TO ORDER BY PHONE using a credit card, call Voyageur Press in Stillwater, Minn., 1-800-888-9653 toll-free. (Shipping charges may vary from those listed above.)

TO ORDER BY MAIL, send a check to Down to Earth Publications, 1032 W. Montana, St. Paul, MN 55117. Make checks payable to Down to Earth Publications. MN residents please add 6.5% sales tax.

Mail to: Down to Earth Publications
           1032 W. Montana
           St. Paul, MN 55117

Please send me _____ "WAKE UP & SMELL THE COFFEE - *Southwest* Edition" at $16.95 each by 4th class mail ($18.95 each sent UPS ground service)

Please send me _____ "WAKE UP & SMELL THE COFFEE - *Pacific Northwest* Edition" at $13.95 each by 4th class mail ($15.95 each sent UPS ground service)

Please send me _____ "WAKE UP & SMELL THE COFFEE - *Upper Midwest* Edition" at $16.95 each by 4th class mail ($18.95 each sent UPS ground service)

I have enclosed $_____ for _____ book(s). Send it/them to:

Name: _____

Street: _____ Apt. No. _____

City: _____ State: _____ Zip: _____
      (Please note: No P.O. Boxes for UPS delivery)

About the author

Laura Zahn discovered the wonderful "Breakfast" part of "Bed & Breakfast" while traveling the backroads of Minnesota, Wisconsin and Illinois to write her "Room at the Inn/Minnesota," "Room at the Inn/Wisconsin" and "Room at the Inn/Galena Area" guidebooks to historic B&Bs and country inns.

In St. Paul, Minn., she is president of Down to Earth Publications, a writing, publishing and public relations firm specializing in travel. Her travelwriting has appeared in many U.S. newspapers and magazines. Zahn has worked in public relations in Minnesota and as a reporter and editor on newspapers in Alaska and Minnesota.

"Wake Up and Smell the Coffee - Southwest Edition" is her seventh book. In addition to the three "Room at the Inn" guides now in print and "Wake Up and Smell the Coffee - Upper Midwest Edition" and "Pacific Northwest Edition," she is co-author of "Ride Guide to the Historic Alaska Railroad."

A native of Saginaw, Michigan, she passed a written test to win the "Betty Crocker Homemaker of the Year" award in high school and says, "Now I've finally done something remotely related, besides tour the Betty Crocker kitchens." She graduated from Northern Michigan University in Marquette. She shares her St. Paul home with Jim Miller, her geologist husband; Jay Edward Miller, who visited many of these Southwest B&Bs in utero; and Kirby Puckett Zahn Miller, who was proudly adopted from the Humane Society of Ramsey County on the day the Minnesota Twins won the American League pennant in 1987.